FAD SURFING
IN THE
BOARDROOM

FAD SURFING
IN THE
BOARDROOM

Reclaiming the Courage
to Manage in the
Age of Instant Answers

Eileen C. Shapiro

CAPSTONE

The right of Eileen C. Shapiro to be identified as
author of this work has been asserted in accordance
with the Copyright, Designs and Patents Act 1988.

First published in the United Kingdom 1996 by
Capstone Publishing Limited
Oxford Centre for Innovation
Mill Street
Oxford OX2 0JX
United Kingdom
First published 1995 by
Addison-Wesley Publishing Company

This Capstone Compact edition published 1998

British Library Cataloguing in Publication Data

A CIP catalogue record for this book is available from
the British Library

ISBN 1-900961-37-7

Printed and bound in Great Britain by
T.J. International Ltd, Padstow, Cornwall

This book is printed on acid-free paper

To Ben

Thinking is the hardest work there is,
which is probably the reason why
so few engage in it.

—Henry Ford

CONTENTS

NOTE TO READERS

Please feel free to surf this book. I wrote it so that you can start anywhere you find interesting and then move to other chapters as the spirit moves you, or by following the cross-references that are built into each chapter. Lots of people have told me that they have started at the end, with "The Expanded Fad Surfer's Dictionary," and then jumped into the text. However you read it, I hope you have a great ride.

Eileen Shapiro

SURF'S UP!

The High-Stakes Thrills of Fad Surfing in the Boardroom

Fad Surfing The practice of riding the crest of the latest management panacea and then paddling out again just in time to ride the next one; always absorbing for managers and lucrative for consultants; frequently disastrous for organizations.

Welcome to the fad-surfing age, complete with a seemingly endless supply of programs and mantras for accomplishing "breakthroughs" in performance and achieving "world-class" results. To review just a few of the options: you can, if you wish, flatten your pyramid, become a horizontal organization, and eliminate hierarchy from your company. You can empower your people, open your environment, and transform your culture. You can listen to your customers, create a customer-focused organization, and commit to total customer satisfaction. You can do the "vision thing," write a mission statement, and put together a strategic plan. You can improve continuously, shift your paradigms, and become a learning organization. You can devote yourself and your company to total quality management. Or you can reengineer your corporation, with the intent, in the words of the original reengineers, of creating a "business revolution."

How to make sense of these options and put them to work for you is what this book is about. Each of them, in fact, has value and can create good results—when carefully selected as a means to achieve specific operating and performance goals and modified to meet the needs of a particular organization. Each

xiii

also can have rhetorical value, in the classic sense of the word; that is, the words used to describe the techniques can galvanize people to work differently and more effectively than before. But, precisely because they are powerful management tools, they all also hold the potential for wreaking organizational havoc and causing tremendous damage, especially when they are seen as panaceas and applied blindly across a business, without attention to where they might be useful, why, with what other techniques they are being combined, and how, if at all, they should be modified to meet the needs of the company.

The difference between these two approaches is the difference between having the courage to manage consciously and actively, and operating on autopilot. Demonstrating this courage requires the willingness to assess situations, think through the available options, decide on the tools to be used and how to adapt them as needed, and then to accept the accountability for the decisions made and the results achieved. Operating on autopilot, on the other hand, allows a manager or an organization to fall into a cookbook approach: do what other companies are doing, do it in the way the gurus say, and thereby both avoid the pressures to make independent judgments and mitigate personal accountability for deciding on a course of action.

Bill Backer, former vice chairman and chief creative officer of the advertising agency Backer Spielvogel Bates Worldwide Inc. and author of *The Care and Feeding of Ideas*, has an interesting perspective on the cookbook approach to anything: painting, writing, creativity—even cooking. Backer argues that those who follow cookbooks without understanding fundamentals will never make great chefs. Referring to the recipes of Julia Child and James Beard, Backer says, "With apologies to Julia and James, they can only teach you how to make *their* soufflé. If you want to create your own, you must first try to understand why eggs and flour rise—or don't rise—when you do certain things to them, and then begin to develop your own theories, which result in the dishes you create."

Following Backer's suggestion, in this book I have selected a group of programs and mantras that are at the core of the fad-surfing age and describe some of the implicit theories on which they are based. My premise is that if you understand the theory behind the tools and the realities of your own situation, you will then have a better chance of selecting the appropriate techniques and of knowing how to tailor them to the unique needs and opportunities facing your company.

The ancient Greeks might have agreed with this approach. Consider the story of Hercules and Linus. As a child, the great hero Hercules took lessons from Linus, his music instructor. It seems that, in the course of instructing his pupil, Linus grew cross with Hercules. No matter how long he made Hercules practice his lyre, Linus still found that Hercules didn't pay sufficient attention to his scales. In consequence, Linus hit Hercules. Hercules responded by hitting back, smacking Linus with his lyre, and killing his teacher in the process.

One wonders why Linus kept trying to make Hercules fit into the theoretic model of a young musician; even as an infant, Hercules impressed all with his athletic abilities and his acts of derring-do and his complete disregard for the finer arts. As a young boy, when he was sent to study with Linus, he already had surpassed all opponents in archery, boxing and wrestling, and had shown that his aptitudes and interests lay almost exclusively in the areas of fighting and sport. Evidently, the judges before whom Hercules had to appear held a similar point of view, since when Hercules was brought to trial for murder, they let him off. The moral I draw from this story is that trying to force real people and organizations into preset theories is not an advisable way to manage. Far preferable is to try to understand the realities and nuances of your particular situation, and then adapt the theories accordingly.

The pieces that follow are my attempt to do just that. All of them are brief, in keeping with my belief that many readers of business books are tired of long chapters. They all start with a definition meant to be humorous and, I hope, provocative, since I'm convinced that the best way to meet a fad is with tongue tucked firmly in cheek. And they each also contain a number of stories, examples, and quotations, all of which I chose solely to illustrate the points I wished to make.

Though most of these stories relate to the business press, a handful derive from the ancient world of the Greeks. Despite an aversion to the Greek myths that I have had since childhood, I was driven to take another look at them when I read yet one more treatise on management theory, which, in almost poetic terms, described the leaders of modern corporations as almost saintly creatures who put organizational interests ahead of their

xvi *Fad Surfing in the Boardroom*

own, build compelling shared visions, work effectively in teams, are able practitioners of systems thinking, and are models of integrity and sensitivity.

The Greek gods and heroes, on the other hand, were nothing like these lyrical descriptions. They were, instead, boisterous, gifted, flawed, powerful creatures; not saints at all, but rather, embodying the best and worst of the characteristics of mortal beings. Sometimes they put the interests of the universe before their own, and sometimes they didn't. Sometimes they worked effectively in teams, and sometimes they overlooked the matters of the universe as they sorted out their own shifting alliances and vendettas. Sometimes they thought through what they were trying to do and why and what the systems implications would be, and sometimes they responded to the moment, and not always wisely.

In fact, one might say, the ancient descriptions of the Greek gods and heroes are a good bit closer to how people actually *do* act than many of the modern prescriptions for how they *should* act, which is why some of the characters from these stories came to be part of this book. My sources for the myths number exactly two, both classics: Edith Hamilton's text on mythology and Robert Graves's retelling of some of the Greek myths.

Which brings us back to Hercules and Linus, and the tendency to want people and organizations to fit the theories of the day, rather than the other way around. When it comes to management fads, these tendencies aren't likely to vanish anytime soon. The reason is simple: the lures of a panacea are compelling; "guaranteed" results for managers and larger fees for consultants. It's no wonder that the proponents of any new tool grow to believe that even though all the other preceding techniques had their limits and flaws, *this* one *really is* the magic bullet.

A case in point: I first used the term "fad surfing" in a *Sloan Management Review* article I coauthored with my colleague Trina Soske and Harvard Business School professor Robert Eccles. A day after the piece appeared in print, I received a call from a senior person at a major consulting firm. He just *"loved* the article"; it was, in his view, "one hundred percent correct"— except for one mistake that he wished to bring to my attention. The mistake: the erroneous inclusion of one technique that, in his view, should not have been on the list of techniques that can be used as fads. This, of course, was the technique *his* firm currently sells and which, he assured me, really *is* the right answer. As I tried to explain to him, the point was not to identify one technique as a panacea and the rest as fads, but to push people to confront and buck the trend toward panacea-thinking—and to take responsibility for the hard work of using the available tools (and creating new ones) to craft solutions tailored to a company's unique context and needs. That is also the point of this book.

The hard truth is that there are no panaceas. What is new is the sheer number of techniques, some new and some newly repackaged versions of older methods, that are now positioned as panaceas. What is not new is the need for the courage to manage: to assess situations, set an overall course or focus, think through options, develop plans, take action, modify plans, learn and go forward. In my view, in the age of instant answers, this courage is more valuable than ever.

Eileen C. Shapiro
The Hillcrest Group, Inc.
Cambridge, Massachusetts, 1995

PART ONE

WHICH WAY IS UP?

Setting the Overall Direction

"Would you tell me, please, which way
I ought to go from here?"
"That depends a good deal on where you want to get to,"
said the Cat.
"I don't much care where—" said Alice.
"Then it doesn't matter which way you go," said the Cat.
"—so long as I get somewhere,"
Alice added as an explanation.
"Oh, you're sure to do that," said the Cat, "if you only
walk long enough."

—from Lewis Carroll's *Alice's Adventures in Wonderland*

Alice's conversation with the Cheshire Cat is often used to illustrate the importance of setting direction in the grown-up world of business and work. And though the Cheshire Cat made no judgment as to whether Alice would be better off if she knew "where she wanted to get to," many people today argue that delineating a clear direction is a prerequisite for future success. But investments in creating dazzling visions or drafting magnificent mission statements do not guarantee that a good direction will be chosen; like Alice, businesses have to make choices even though they cannot know, with complete certainty, where they will end up tomorrow as a consequence of the actions taken today.

1

And despite the many prescriptions to the contrary, setting a direction that proves to have been prudent or even insightful is a matter of both luck and skill, one that can be done in any of a number of ways depending on the people involved and their personal styles. Chapter 1, "That 'Vision Thing': Picturing the Future When Your Crystal Ball Isn't 20/20," tackles one approach—creating a "vision"—and argues that "visioning" isn't appropriate or even feasible for all situations and that even when a reasonable vision can be formulated, it will provide only a partial roadmap through the future. Chapter 2, "Mission Indecipherable: Getting to Content," looks at another way of setting direction—that of setting the boundaries for action rather than delineating a general plan—and suggests some ways to keep the resulting mission statements and related documents from becoming just more of the official background noise. And Chapter 3, "The Gambler's Guide to Setting Direction: Why a Company's Real Strategy Is in Its Book of Bets," focuses on how thinking of strategy as a gambler's book of bets can increase an organization's ability to see and seize attractive opportunities for the future.

All three chapters point out that the people responsible for imaging a future for their organizations—as well as those who, though not assigned with formal responsibility, feel compelled to do so—must find their own ways to answer the questions posed by Alice and the Cheshire Cat. Every organization ends up "somewhere"; the challenge for leaders is to increase the odds that "somewhere" is a place their organizations will be pleased "to get to."

CHAPTER 1

THAT "VISION THING"

Picturing the Future When Your Crystal Ball Isn't 20/20

Vision *What Moses experienced when he wandered for too long in the desert; coordinated and persistent hallucinations characteristic of dementia or paranoid schizophrenia.*

In the midst of his campaign for the presidency of the United States, George Bush confided to the press that he was feeling intense frustration. The source of his frustration? Not the economy, nor world affairs, but rather, as Bush put it, that "vision thing."

The situation in which Bush found himself is not unique. In companies around the globe, similar dramas are being played out as the demand for clearly articulated and compelling visions grows far faster than top management can supply them.

On the demand side are those, from the shop floor to the boardroom, who want their senior managers to provide a "vision"—a picture of the future for their organization. And not without reason; the reality of visionary management is that people truly do stretch more when they can put their actions in the context of goals that they can care about—and they truly do withhold potentially valuable contributions in the absence of such goals.

On the supply side of the market are the executives who are expected to deliver these visions. For some, communicating a compelling picture of the future is second nature; they would do so even if the management literature never spilled a drop of ink on the subject. For others, though, the pressure to articulate a vision only heightens their awareness of their ability to see only a glimpse of what the future might hold—a glimpse they worry is too vague or too incomplete to fulfill the requirements of a biblical-scale vision.

The frequent result of this asymmetric market: employees who feel deprived when asked to work hard for a company that talks of nothing more than getting by, and managers who feel resentful when pushed to articulate a future that is unknowable.

And the imbalance is getting worse, as more people, having heard the folktales of business heroes and read the formal theory of business practice, conclude that a vision is the prerequisite for the success of their organizations. This is a boon for vendors of "visioning" services. Yet the expectations about what a vision should be and how it can be generated are often deeply flawed on at least three counts: the desire for a vision to supply a 20/20 picture of the future; the presumption that a vision should provide a reasonably comprehensive blueprint for achieving this future; and the belief that a vision can be created through some broad-based participatory process.

All three of these expectations are unrealistic at best. First, visions are not, and cannot be, 20/20 pictures of the future; they are, rather, statements of *organizational ambition*, simultaneously highly specific and ill-formed, always uncertain and unclear in many respects, characterized by gaping holes and missing pieces. Second, attempting to create start-to-finish blueprints as part of the visioning process typically adds hazards to an already hazardous process; in contrast, one way to increase the odds of achieving any vision is to proceed in a stepwise fashion, revising the approach, and sometimes even the goal, as events unfold. And third, democratically based group processes do not necessarily lead to visions that will be implemented; the achievement of vision depends more on the deep, gut-level commitment of the person or people who control the critical resources of the organization than on the broadness of participation in the "visioning" process. A quartet of K's—Komatsu, Kimberly-Clark, Kodak, and King Kullen—illustrates the points.

> "The last thing IBM needs now is a vision."
>
> —Louis V. Gerstner, in 1993, shortly after becoming chairman of IBM

> "It's more fun building a bridge than putting sandbags on a levy."
>
> —Tom Whiteside, in 1993, shortly after leaving IBM to join MIPS Technologies Inc.

Forget Looking for a 20/20 Picture of the Future: It's the Ambition That Counts

Thought about from the perspective of the physics of the matter, "vision" is an odd word to apply to the task of imagining the future, since vision is a sense that works only from the present to the past. In fact, the further away we are from any object we are observing, the further back into the past we are seeing, which can be estimated by calculating the distance between us and the object and then dividing this by the speed of light, 186,000 miles per second. For relatively close objects, like the sun, the past state we see now occurred just under ten minutes ago. For objects that are farther away, such as distant galaxies viewed through a telescope, the past state we see now occurred millions or billions of years ago.

In contrast, when we talk about visions for organizations, we are obviously talking about a sense that works from the present to the future. Given that these events haven't occurred yet, why would anyone expect that a future "vision" could provide anything close to a 20/20 view of precisely where the organization is going and exactly how it will get there?

One source of distortion in the acuity of a future vision is that since the future is, by definition, uncertain, visions can seem compelling, be followed with great ardor, and still be wrong. And though the point is always obvious in hindsight, it's remarkably easy to build a grand vision on what turns out to have been an astigmatic view of the future. Roger Smith demonstrated this during his 1981–1990 chairmanship of General Motors. In this classic example, Smith clearly articulated his vision—to make GM into "the car company of the twenty-first century"—and backed it amply, putting $8 billion into acquisitions (for EDS and Hughes Aircraft) to increase the company's technological competencies, and $40 billion into plant and equipment investments (for state-of-the-art automation) to decrease the company's labor costs. Yet, with relatively little attention placed on building cars that consumers would see as better than GM's ever-improving competitors, the

"For the same amount of money, we could buy Toyota and Nissan outright."

—H. Ross Perot, speaking to GM management in 1986 (instant effect had Perot's suggestion been followed: an almost two-fold increase in GM's share of the *worldwide* market, from 22 percent to 40 percent)

company's share of its domestic market plummeted, sliding from about 46 percent to less than 35 percent during Smith's tenure at the helm. And Smith is hardly alone; from General Electric's foray into the "factory of the future" to Sears's diversification into financial services, the road to failure has been paved with compelling but flawed visions.

And even when the vision is directionally correct, it is almost always still characterized by gaping holes and monstrous omissions. Recognizing that even prescient visions do not provide a 20/20 picture of the future, in 1986 C. K. Prahalad and Yves L. Doz, professors at the University of Michigan and INSEAD respectively, proposed an alternative concept, "strategic intent," which they defined as the process of "aiming for goals for which one cannot plan." But whether the term used is "vision" or "strategic intent," the critical point is that such statements express the *ambition* of an organization, an ambition that must be clear in overall thrust but that inevitably will be unclear in a host of details.

The classic example of vision as ambition is the goal set in the 1960s by Yashinari Kawai and his son, Ryoichi, for the earthmoving equipment company Komatsu. Transliterated into English, the Komatsu vision was short and simple: "Maru-C" or, roughly, "encircle Caterpillar." At the time the Kawais set about turning this vision into reality, it would have been hard to imagine a more preposterous goal. Caterpillar Inc. was the world leader, with sales of $1.4 billion and more than 50 percent of the worldwide earthmoving equipment market. The company was also universally known for the superior technology of its products and its production facilities, and for the unparalleled quality of both its equipment and its after-sales service. Komatsu, on the other hand, had sales of only $168 million, no presence outside Japan, a limited product line, and little technical know-how. In addition, the company's reputation for the quality of its machines and service was dreadful—"only half that of the international standards," as one senior Komatsu executive later put it. Even more worrisome, in 1963, Japan's Ministry of International Trade and Industry (MITI), convinced that neither Komatsu or Japan would build a long-run competitive advantage in construction equipment, authorized a joint venture between Mitsubishi and Caterpillar. Given the enormity of the challenge, there was no way the Kawais could have provided a 20/20 view of what they meant by Maru-C. Yet by 1984, just over twenty years later, Komatsu held 25 percent of the world market for earthmoving equipment, with sales of ¥713 billion (about $3 billion) and profits of ¥23 billion (about $95 million), to Cat's 43 percent of the market, with sales of $6.6 billion and a bottom-line loss of $428 million. Cat has recovered strongly since then, but Komatsu remains a powerful competitor, now a giant in its own right, having achieved what most people would have regarded as impossible when the Kawais first articulated their organizational ambition.

"Nobody in his right mind tries to cross a broad ditch in two steps."

—Karl von Clausewitz (1780–1831)

Or consider the vision set by Kimberly-Clark in 1920, then a Midwestern manufacturer of printing papers, to create and dominate a market for a new disposable paper consumer product it had introduced the year before. The original ambition was simply that the new product be successful enough to fill the company's idle Cellucotton absorbent wadding capacity, which K-C had developed in 1914 as a substitute for cotton. K-C needed a new product because, though Cellucotton sales were brisk during World War I—a conflict in which, as John R. Kimberly later recalled, one of every two soldiers was either wounded or killed—they fell precipitously after the armistice, thus leading to the unused capacity. The obstacles to K-C's 1920 vision of filling this capacity with its new disposable consumer product were huge, however, for three reasons. First, the company had never participated in a consumer products market. Further, in 1920, disposable paper goods represented, for the most part, a new product category; disposable paper plates, cups, towels, and diapers did not exist. And finally, was the product itself: Kotex feminine protection, the first product of its kind, inspired by reports, as later described by John Kimberly, "that during World War I some nurses had packed Cellucotton in gauze and used the combination as sanitary napkins." It was, Kimberly subsequently noted, "a product that many people wouldn't stock, wouldn't sell, and wouldn't even talk about." But even though in 1920 K-C's executives could not provide a 20/20 picture of their ambition or how they would fulfill it, today K-C

"If at first the idea is not absurd, then there is no hope for it."

—Albert Einstein (1879–1955)

holds over 30 percent of the almost $1 billion U.S. sanitary nap-kin market—and, with $7 billion in sales, the company is indeed a leader in the U.S. industry for disposable paper consumer goods.

And finally, consider the vision set in 1870 that led to the development of the Eastman Kodak Company: the ambition of putting photography into the reach of the common person, by creating cameras that were affordable, lightweight, and easy to use. In the 1870s, when George Eastman first formulated his vision, photography, in his words, was "an elaborate and pains-taking ordeal" that required a wagonload of heavy and hard-to-use equipment including "a camera about the size of a soap box [about the size of an orange crate today], a tripod heavy and strong enough to support a bungalow, a dark tent, a nitrate bath, and a container for water"—all necessary because at that time photographers had to develop and finish their negatives right where they took their photographs. By 1888, following more than a decade of work, Eastman had created a camera system, which he later dubbed the "Kodak," that met his goal. The essence of simplicity, the camera had a string to set the shutter, a button to release the shutter, and a lever to advance the film, while the film could be sent back to Kodak for processing. When he started, Eastman could not have provided a 20/20 picture of the future he envisioned for his company. But, as at Komatsu and Kimberly-Clark, success at Kodak began with a compelling ambition that was clear in its overall thrust—and unclear in many of its details.

In retrospect, tales of setting out to encircle larger competi-tors, invent new classes of products, and democratize complex technologies for mass markets seem like the stuff of which dreams are made, the kind of fully articulated visions that many insiders wish their own executive teams would provide. But in fact, these visions, which now seem so clear and clean, were at the time grand stretches, precise and clear in some ways and hopelessly vague and unsubstantiatable in others—an impor-tant reminder that while a vision can crystallize the ambition of an organization, it cannot transmit a 20/20 picture from the future of what will be and how it will be achieved.

**Forget the Quest for a Start-to-Finish Blueprint:
It's the Stepwise Approach That Increases the
Odds for Success**

Ambitions that are larger than an organization's ability to plan
may seem an invitation to chaos. Yet as the case studies done by
James Brian Quinn, professor at Dartmouth's Amos Tuck School,
have illustrated, the real strategies, even of the biggest and most
sophisticated organizations, tend to "evolve" through a
process he calls "logical incrementalism." Quinn's work
suggests that any company that tries to adhere to a
start-to-finish blueprint, with little deviation, reduces
the odds for achieving its long-term goals if, as often
happens, the future develops differently from what was
anticipated. An alternative is to craft the implementation of the vision step by step, reassessing the key
assumptions on which the vision was based as events
unfold. As followed by companies such as Komatsu and
Kimberly-Clark, such stepwise approaches can be far
more successful than relying on start-to-finish plans.

"If you have built
castles in the air,
your work need
not be lost; that
is where they
should be. Now
put the founda-
tions under
them."

—Henry David
Thoreau (1817–
1862)

For the Kawais at Komatsu, for example, a key
assumption was that the Mitsubishi-Cat joint venture
jeopardized the company's very existence. Komatsu
therefore immediately sought regulatory relief from
MITI, in the form of a request to overturn the
Mitsubishi-Cat joint venture; in response, MITI delayed the
implementation of its decision for two years, until 1965. Two
other key assumptions held by the Kawais were that, with the
Mitsubishi-Cat venture going forward, albeit with a delay,
Komatsu's future success in the earthmoving equipment industry would require far more advanced technology and far better
product quality than the company had at the time. Accordingly,
for the next twenty years, Komatsu's strategy focused on
strengthening the company in these two areas, one step at a time.

To make the needed improvements in its technology position, the company quickly built on its two-year reprieve to enter
into technology agreements with International Harvester,
Bucyrus-Erie, and Cummins Engine. In addition, to hedge its
dependence on these foreign technology suppliers, in 1966

Komatsu also established its own R & D laboratory. By 1982, the company had found ways to terminate both the IH and Bucyrus-Erie licensing agreements. (As one senior Komatsu executive later remarked, "Komatsu had digested its licensed technology and had established its own technology. Therefore, we just got out of the various licensing agreements.")

To make the needed improvements in its quality position, Komatsu again took advantage of its two-year reprieve and, building on the Total Quality Control effort it had begun several years earlier, initiated "Project A"—a full-court press aimed at improving the quality of Komatsu's bread-and-butter products: small- and medium-sized bulldozers. The first Project A 'dozers appeared in 1966 with twice the durability of their predecessors and, despite a longer warranty period, a 67 percent decrease in warranty claims. The company then initiated the second phase of Project A: reducing the costs of the 'dozers. In 1972 came "Project B," which focused on improving the quality and then reducing the costs of Komatsu's main export, large bulldozers. And in 1976, as worldwide demand for construction equipment began to slow, came the "V-10 campaign" with the goals of reducing costs by 10 percent while maintaining or improving quality, reducing the number of parts by at least 20 percent, and rationalizing the company's manufacturing capacity. The beauty of Komatsu's incremental approach was not only that each step put the firm in a better competitive position than before, but also that each would have been worthwhile even if the firm had never come close to its overall goal of Maru-C.

At Kimberly-Clark, the core belief about the future was that disposable paper goods could replace nondisposable goods and that the company, with its paper technology and some perseverance and experimentation, could create and learn to market these new consumer products. Having started its campaign to create this new market with its invention and introduction of Kotex, K-C's next step focused on overcoming what Kimberly called the "taboos [against] the open discussion of feminine hygiene": 22 free packages to dealers for every 144 packages ordered, free samples to consumers, free samples to nurses, advertising campaigns, plain-paper packaging for retail counters, and massive educational campaigns. (The company also hedged its bets by creating, as John Kimberly later explained, a "separate company to promote and sell the new product without

involving the established company [Kimberly-Clark] name."
The subsidiary regained the K-C name in 1950.)

Buoyed by its success, in 1924 K-C took the next incremental step, and introduced its second disposable paper consumer product—a "sanitary cold cream remover"—based on another K-C wartime technology, this one a process for making cellulose into a very thin and soft paper fabric suitable for gas mask filters. The product, of course, was Kleenex. The company worked to make the tissues softer and stronger, and sales progressed modestly until K-C executives, increasingly hearing that women were using Kleenex as a hanky and not as a cold cream remover, commissioned some consumer research in 1930. The research found that 61 percent of the respondents thought of Kleenex as a handkerchief, 39 percent as a cleansing towel. Inspired to change its advertising, K-C doubled its Kleenex sales over the next year, providing the cash flow to invest in new equipment for its disposal paper products businesses, and the impetus for a revised, broader ambition: to "change basic living habits for an entire nation by opening a whole new field of disposable paper products."

That the great visionaries of business follow a stepwise approach might not surprise great visionaries of another sort: chess players. A 1966 study that looked at the time taken by chess players to make a second move after their opponents had made theirs showed significant differences based on how expert the players were, with Class C players taking only a few seconds, Experts taking seven minutes, Masters taking ten minutes, and Grandmasters taking twenty minutes. The reason: the opponent's move provides an opportunity to reconsider the options on the board, an opportunity that the better players capitalized on fully. Similarly, organizations with great ambitions and overall schemes for achieving them still need to delineate the building blocks, plan the order in which they will be implemented, focus on the handful of top priorities, and then be willing to revise their bets according to the new set of circumstances.

As executed by companies like Komatsu and Kimberly-Clark, such stepwise approaches have three advantages. They mitigate the need for the "visionary" to have clairvoyant

"Dreaming is zero-value. I mean anyone can dream. . . . Vision is free. And it's therefore not a competitive advantage any way, shape or form. . . . The big thing I do is I write down in a fairly crisp fashion what I believe the company should do. . . . I let people know the basic framework we're in and then I review projects."

—Bill Gates, founder and chairman, Microsoft Corporation

skills, since the approach for achieving the organizational ambitions is a work in progress. They increase the odds for an improved competitive position, even if the overall ambition is never met. And finally, they allow the company (or company unit) to spot and capitalize on opportunities or threats that it could not have foreseen at the beginning of the process.

Forget the Broad-Based, Democratic Visioning Processes: It's Those Who Control the Resources Who Are the Gatekeepers to the Dream

Dreams and visions can originate anywhere in an organization. But if they require major amounts of any corporate resource that is in short supply—capital, R & D time, use of production capacity, or advertising dollars, for example—or if they require changes that go far beyond the implicit rules of "how we do business around here," they will require the buy-in of the unit head, CEO, or board, or anyone else with de facto power over the allocation of assets or the revision of rules. No matter what CEOs say about "flattening the organization" or about broad participation in the "visioning" process, whoever controls the resources is gatekeeper to the dream. (For more on flattening the organization, see "The Flat-Org Theory of Modern Management," pp. 39–50.)

Consider the saga of King Kullen. In 1930, in the midst of the Great Depression, the average grocery store was 500–600 square feet, had sales of about $500–800 per week, was located in the town center, and incurred high labor costs since few of the items were available on a self-service basis. Michael Cullen, age forty-six and the manager of the Herrin, Illinois, branch of the Kroger Grocery & Baking Company, was sure that these were the characteristics of an industry that would drive itself into obsolescence. Cullen therefore wrote to the vice president of Kroger, then a chain of small stores, with a better idea: transforming Kroger into a chain of supermarkets, starting with a trial of five stores, to be called, in his plan, the Cullen Stores. Here are just a few of the other details he described:

- average store size: 5,800 square feet (40' by 130'–160' deep)
- location: three blocks from the "high-rent district," with plenty of parking
- percent self-service: 80 percent

- expected revenues per week: $8,500 in groceries, $1,500 in fruit and vegetables, $2,500 in meat

- expected gross profit margin, based on detailed pro formas of operating expenses: 2.5 percent for fruit and groceries, 3 percent for meat

- pricing strategy: 300 items at cost, 200 items at 5 percent above cost, 300 items at 15 percent above cost, and 300 items at 20 percent above cost

- advertising strategy: two-page newspaper ads, announcing the availability of "300 items at cost and another 200 items at practically cost"

Today, Cullen's letter is remarkable for its comprehensiveness, audacity, and accuracy. Yet, the vice president not only turned down the idea, he wouldn't even see Cullen to discuss it further. Cullen went on to establish King Kullen, a Long Island, New York, chain that boasted fifteen supermarkets in 1935; Cullen died in 1936, before he could start implementing his ideas for national expansion. Meanwhile, after Cullen left, Kroger reconsidered the ideas that Cullen had proposed and, by 1935, had fifty supermarkets, six with parking lots.

Visions are implemented when the people who control the resources believe, deep in their guts, that the ambitions being described correspond well to how their industries will evolve, or could evolve if they were to take a certain set of initiatives. If they don't like the person who proposes a new vision, need more data before they can develop gut-level commitment to the new idea, or have a different view about key future trends in their industry than that implicit in the proposed change in direction, they will be unlikely to dedicate the resources required for its implementation. Consequently, in the absence of data that fundamentally alter how these people view the future, visioning sessions will create lovely flip charts but little change in direction. For visions grow out of mindsets and passions, not mechanics and process, and any vision that does not capture the mindsets and passions of those who control the resources required for its implementation stands little chance for success.

Visions really can make a difference. In changing times, the future vitality of an organization often depends on fundamental shifts in the beliefs and behaviors of many people. But these shifts typically require giving up familiar ways of doing business, time-honored traditions, or cherished products. Visions are one way leaders map out these required changes and induce others to buy into them. Yet, without the commitment of those who control the resources, "visioning" becomes just another activity that marks the box on some "management excellence" checklist—but doesn't actually change what the organization is doing in a significant way.

Nor is there a standardized format for successful visions. Not all visions should be as grand as Komatsu's. Not every industry is ripe for revolution, and not every executive is cut out to be a pioneer. In contrast, many companies would do well to aim for providing products their customers want to buy and environments in which their employees want to work. Similarly, not all visions need be as detailed as King Kullen's; though many visions celebrated today look as if they were unveiled with complete start-to-finish blueprints, most in fact are what we might call "post-strategic rationalizations," fully articulated only after the journey is complete. Business, like any other human endeavor, develops its own mythology for honoring its heroes.

For most organizations, the best option is for those who control the resources to understand their own assumptions about future industry dynamics, invite others in the organization to provide their viewpoints (and contribute evidence that is contrary to the prevailing points of view), and then, having considered these varying perspectives, articulate an ambition and build and modify it incrementally. Whether the resulting vision is grand or modest, an approach of this kind allows insiders to be rooted in reality while focused on the stars—a useful approach for navigating through a future that no one, not even visionary leaders, can know fully.

"The last little secret of vision is that ultimately it's in the eye of the beholder, and almost always after the fact. . . . [W]e rarely recognize a leader as having vision until it has been proven true."

—Walter Kiechel III, editor, *Fortune*

"He started to sing as he tackled the thing / That couldn't be done, and he did it."

—from "It Couldn't Be Done," by Edgar Albert Guest (1881–1959)

CHAPTER 2

MISSION INDECIPHERABLE
Getting to Content

Mission Statement 1: A short, specific statement of purpose, intended to serve as a loose musical score that motivates everyone to play the same tune without strict supervision; 2: Frequently, an assertion of undying commitment to some amalgam of "total quality," "low-cost producer," "empowered workforce," "excellence," "continuous improvement," and other bizbuz shibboleths that, although written for a specific organization, is equally applicable to an aircraft manufacturer, a software development firm, a community hospital, a department store chain, or the local dry cleaner; 3: In some companies, a talisman, hung in public spaces, to ward off evil spirits.

"Mission statements" are often used as a way to communicate a company's vision of itself and its future. They may include declarations of the way the company conducts its business, the values by which it operates, the future to which it aspires, and/or the strategy by which it means to achieve this future. Those who believe that writing a mission statement is essential to achieving such visions, however, may wish to consider the case of F. Kenneth Iverson, and the company of which he is the CEO, Nucor Corporation.

There's no question that Iverson is one of the classic visionaries of American business. His company, Nucor, has stood every assumption about steel making on its head, from the raw materials (scrap replacing iron ore) and technologies used (electric arc furnaces replacing the sinter mills, coke ovens, blast furnaces,

15

and basic oxygen furnaces of the big integrated steel companies)
to the employee-relations and compensation policies followed
(nonunion with an aggressive gain-sharing program). When he
took over Nucor in 1965, the big integrated steel companies
scoffed at the $22 million minimill which, that year, was on its
way to losing over $2 million. Almost thirty years later, in 1993,
Nucor had passed integrated rival Wheeling-Pittsburgh in sales
($2.2 billion versus $1.0 billion), exceeded Bethlehem Steel and
Inland Steel Industries in profits ($124 million versus losses of
$266 million and $38 million), and boasted a market value 33 percent greater than that of Armco, Wheeling-Pitt, Bethlehem, and
Inland *combined* ($5181 million versus the combined total of
$4482 million, as of March 1994). Adding insult to injury, at a
time of industry contraction, Nucor was growing, continuing its
march into flat rolled sheet, a product category once thought
immune to the onslaught of the minimills.

Not surprisingly, Nucor and Iverson have been the subject
of many articles. And not surprisingly, Iverson occasionally
receives calls requesting additional information. Here's Iverson's
account of one of these, from a speech he gave to The Planning
Forum in 1993:

> Nucor is a case study for a number of business schools. . . . [One
> student called] and he said: "Well, could we have a copy of your
> mission statement?" I said "No." And he says, "Why?" And I
> said, "We don't have any mission statement." And if you look at
> most of the mission statements by corporations, they're a bunch
> of nonsense, they're some pleasant-sounding flowery words that
> most employees don't read . . . and they really bear hardly any
> relation to what the company is doing or how it is operated.

Iverson is right. Companies with great visions and values, as
Nucor has, do not *require* mission statements to turn their ambitions into reality, as long as they have other ways for communicating with their constituencies, as Nucor also has. Conversely,
mission statements, no matter how elegantly written nor how
widely distributed, do not *create* visions or values that otherwise
have no foundation in the company.

Nucor notwithstanding, however, more and more organizations have such statements, including over half of big companies in 1994, a doubling from five years before, according to the
count by one major consulting firm. Given the growing invest-

ment in mission statements, what can companies do to ensure that theirs will not be "a bunch of nonsense"— those "pleasant-sounding" words that "bear hardly any relation to what the company is doing or how it is operating"?

Mission statements are communication devices. While helpful for telling customers, regulators, and suppliers about the company, their real usefulness is in setting the boundaries for, and providing meaning to, the collective efforts of the people who work inside or with the company. These boundaries create what I call the "organizational frame," the organization's overall framework for action. Activities that fit inside the frame are acceptable; those outside it are not. Levi Strauss & Co.'s mission statement, for example, states that the company's product is "branded casual apparel"—clearly labeling brand-name jeans as within the Levi Strauss frame, and haute couture, though certainly an honorable (if expensive) business, as outside it.

But while mission statements can be effective in creating organizational frames, they often are not. For companies that choose to use them and want to make sure that they're helpful, the "three-C audit"—which checks *content, congruence,* and *credibility*—is a good place to start.

Content—or, Too Many Clefs Wreck the Tune

A CEO I once met at a meeting asked me what I thought of mission statements. In response, I asked him whether his organization had one and if so, what it was. After a few moments of mumbling, he excused himself and, rummaging through his briefcase, found a copy to read to me. If he had to look at the paper to remember what it said, what do you think the odds were that the other people in his organization had internalized the message and could use it to provide context for their own actions?

A generic mission statement:

"Our mission is to be the best-managed company in the world in the [fill-in-the-blank] industry through our commitment to total customer satisfaction delivered by our totally empowered employees who work in the new team paradigm to continuously improve our position of unequaled quality and lowest costs, and in so doing, produce superior returns for our shareholders."

Mission statements from two newspapers:

"All the news that's fit to print" —motto of *The New York Times*

"The worst newspaper in the world" —motto of *The Marshall Islands Journal*

This case of the forgettable mission statement is not unusual; many corporate statements of purpose obscure rather than clarify the organizational frame either because they include such generic words that little real meaning is conveyed, or because they use so many words that the meaning gets lost in the verbiage. Consider the first of these two problems—the use of one-size-fits-all, generic "foof-ball" phrases. The apparent preference for vacuous, empty words is so pervasive that one guidebook on writing mission statements even suggests that companies use sentences like: "We are committed to providing unequaled quality." Judging from the mission statements I see, quite a few companies have followed similar instructions, resulting in fervent commitments to "creating value" and "being the best," without defining the goals beyond these inter-galactic statements or setting any boundaries for how they will be achieved. In contrast, listen to the words in Ben & Jerry's mission statement: "To make, distribute and sell the finest quality all-natural ice cream and related products in a wide variety of innovative flavors made from Vermont dairy products." Or this one for McDonald's: "To satisfy the world's appetite for good food, well served, at a price people can afford." "Unequaled quality" is just empty calories compared with these two.

The second problem, too many words, can also obscure the message. Some companies seem to think of their mission statements as expanding suitcases: they just keep cramming stuff in until, once packed, these intellectual bags are too heavy to lift. The result: mission statements with so many words, all carefully negotiated and crafted by a committee, that few people can cut through all the ink to figure out the main message. Such mission statements often do provide strength and perspective to some portion of the organization (and almost always to the people who drafted the statement). For most, however, without some sort of succinct summary, the document becomes just part of the background buzz—more blah-blah-blah from the executive suite.

> "Too many notes."
>
> —one (alleged) commentary on Mozart's music

Mission statements that pass the "content" check use words that convey real meanings to the people inside the organization, delivering a central message or set of messages. The Ritz-Carlton hotel chain does this by telling its employees that they are "ladies and gentlemen, serving ladies and gentlemen." When

Sigi Brauer was general manager of the Boston Ritz-Carlton, he would explain to new members of the Ritz staff that the idea of "serving ladies and gentlemen" means a Ritz employee says "May I help you?" rather than "Whaddaya want?" and that the idea of "*ladies and gentlemen* serving ladies and gentlemen" means that a Ritz employee is not a servant, but a valued staff member. Or consider the mission that drove the development of the Macintosh computer: "To create a low-cost portable computer so useful that its owner misses it when it's not around." For both companies, the words create frames that are specific and compelling.

A useful experiment to test the content of your mission statement is to ask people at all levels what they would say if asked to convey its main messages to a new employee. If they can provide a thoughtful rendering, even if the words aren't the same as those in the formal statement and even if the ideas are not quite in the same order, you have a mission statement that passes the content test. If they can't, you know that you either have words that convey little meaning, or too many words, or both.

A powerful mission statement:

"We try to remember that medicine is for the patient. We try to never forget that medicine is for the people. It is not for the profits. The profits follow, and if we have remembered that, they have never failed to appear. The better we have remembered it, the larger they have been."

—George W. Merck, president of Merck & Co., 1932–1957

Congruence—or, The Frame Is Mightier than the Sword

Mission statements are not infinitely flexible. Competitors change. Regulators change. Customers change. At some point these changes are so great that what a company says to itself—in its strategies, in its mission statements, in its basic mindset—has to change as well. In these cases, the old mission statements aren't helpful guides to behavior because they are no longer congruent with the likely—or even possible—requirements for future success.

Nonetheless, many companies come to regard their mission statements as corporate immutables. In part, this is because changing the frame represents a major shift in strategy or orientation, a step not to be taken lightly—and, in part because, in some organizations, the process for drafting such statements was so tedious and expensive that few people want to go through it

Another power-
ful mission
statement:

"Establish life-
time relationships
with the patients
and other cus-
tomers . . . by
play[ing] the role
of provider, refer-
rer and advocate;
ensuring that cus-
tomers receive
the highest
quality service,
whether that ser-
vice is provided
by the Commu-
nity Medical Cen-
ter or another
community
agent, [i]n this
way . . . act[ing]
as an important
hub in the health
and happiness of
the community."

—Community
Medical Center,
Toms River, New
Jersey, 1989

again. The more permanence assigned to formal pronouncements of mission and purpose, however, the
greater the implicit taboo against any proposed alter-
ations. Then when the mission statement should be
changed, the taboo effectively keeps the organization
tethered to outdated or simply incorrect conceptions of
what it takes to win in the marketplace.

Consider the dilemma of the executives of a major
bank that, based on growing market research data,
determined that its customers did not want one-stop
shopping for all their financial needs, a direct contradic-
tion of part of the guidelines set out in their company's
mission statement. None of the executives was willing
to address the issue directly; too risky. Instead, the data
were ignored, foreclosing several strategic options that
fit the bank's strengths and capabilities. The mission
statement, rather than facilitating the right behaviors,
blocked them.

A more extreme example comes from a large electronics company, whose senior executives concluded
that the company's only hope for the future lay more in
software and services than in hunks of iron and miles of
wire. The chairman agreed with this analysis, until
someone mentioned that the mission statement should
be modified to reflect this change in direction. "Oh no,"
replied the chairman in abject horror, "it took us two
years to agree on this mission statement. We can't
change it now." The result of staying the course was just
as the analysis predicted: continued deterioration of
margins and massive layoffs.

When mission statements remain fixed despite new
information, as in the first example, or changing markets, as in the second, the odds go up that their beautiful
words, faithfully reproduced in annual reports and on
glitzy posters, will at best be irrelevant, and at worst, injurious. If
your company has a mission statement, or is planning to write or
rewrite one, it's worth checking the "congruence C" of the three-
C audit, to determine whether the frame it communicates fits
with the actions required for the organization's success in the
future—as opposed to what worked in the past or what the writers wish the requirements to be for the future.

Credibility—or, The Aerodynamics of Flying Pigs

Many mission statements are unintentionally hilarious. We've all seen them, companies that rhapsodize about customer service when customers are routinely disdained and disregarded, enthuse about employee empowerment when employees are treated with even less respect than the customers, or declaim about becoming "the best managed" or "the number one" company in their industries while steadily losing market share. In each case, thoughtful insiders might assess the date of achieving these goals as about the same as "when pigs fly."

" 'Visioning' Missions Becomes Its Own Mission"

—headline in *The Wall Street Journal*

Managers in these companies sometimes justify such patently absurd mission statements as "calls to arms"—rhetorical devices for changing the culture and direction of their organizations. But research by Andrew Campbell, a director of the Ashridge Strategic Centre in London, and Laura Nash, a researcher at Boston University, shows that one effective use of mission statements is as *reinforcing* devices for actions that are *already* in progress. How much progress is a matter of judgment. At one extreme is Komatsu. Though its goal of "Maru-C"—or: encircle Caterpillar—was audacious, the company's actions to improve the quality of its small- and medium-sized bulldozers provided a way for all to see that at least the first steps were being taken. (For more on Komatsu and its ambition of Maru-C, see "That Vision Thing," pp. 3–14.) At the other extreme is British Airways. Colin Marshall, BA's chairman, started the company on its turnaround path in 1983—and promulgated the mission statement about BA's commitment to customer satisfaction in 1986, once the company had racked up a several-year track record of improvements on this dimension.

In the cases of both Komatsu and British Airways, the slogans amplified work in progress, and corresponded with the real rewards provided within the organizations. In the absence of such foundations, mission statements that describe bold goals are apt to backfire. Some employees grow increasingly frustrated as they earnestly try to decrease the large gap between the espoused and the actual. Others, perceiving the wide gap as hypocrisy, become increasingly cynical and, feeling that their

The ultimate mission statement:

"We hold these Truths to be self-evident, that all Men are created equal, that they are endowed by their Creator with certain unalienable Rights, that among these are Life, Liberty, and the Pursuit of Happiness—That to secure these Rights, Governments are instituted among Men. . . . We . . . solemnly Publish and Declare, That these United Colonies are, and of Right ought to be, Free and Independent States. . . . And for the support of this Declaration, with a firm Reliance on the Protection of divine Providence, we mutually pledge to each other our Lives, our Fortunes, and our sacred Honour."

—Thomas Jefferson, *The Declaration of Independence,* 1776

employers are operating in "bad faith," also become contemptuous of their leaders. In my observation, however, most exhibit "split-brain syndrome": they recite and discuss the mission statement with the "mission-statement" side of their brains and make their workday decisions with the "internal-game" side of their brains—and rarely if ever recognize the gulf between the standards they espouse and the actions they take. "War stories" of heroic attempts to keep the mission statement alive can intensify the split-brain syndrome, by obscuring the far larger number of incidents in which the mission statement was ignored or violated. ("Decoding the Corporate Culture," pp. 51–64, delves further into how the real rules of an organization are remarkably impervious to both enthusiastic exhortations and official procedures.)

Mission statements by themselves don't change behavior, and they certainly don't change behavior for organizations whose internal game and rewards continue to support the status quo. Companies that advertise lofty goals in their mission statements would do well to conduct periodic anonymous surveys of their employees and customers to measure real progress against the standards implied by their formal proclamations. If the respondents tell you that the goals are great but do not reflect how business is really done in your organization, that will indicate how you have fared against the "credibility C" in the three-C audit—and alert you to the risk that your mission statement is seen as just so many words, piously mouthed while routinely ignored, thereby contributing to the cynicism of the workforce that it is supposed to motivate.

------------◾------------

At a training program on mission statements, the trainer presented the group with the shortest mission statement ever, from the Lexus car company: "BEAT BENZ." Having revealed this nugget, he asked what the participants in the class thought. One intrepid soul raised his hand and said "It's great. It's short, to the point, and motivating." "*NO!*" thundered the trainer, "it's *NEGATIVE! Very* bad!" (Evidently this trainer had not been out on the roads very much. If he had, he would have seen the bite Lexus had taken out of the Mercedes market by providing many of the benefits of a Benz at a lower price.)

A mission statement is not a talisman. It has no power beyond its ability to serve as a public statement of the desired "organizational frame" and thereby to reinforce a set of desired behaviors. But when the messages don't pass the three-C audit of content, congruence, and credibility, the mission statement becomes a parody of its original purpose, chock full of fine-sounding, generic words that are disconnected from the real strategy of the firm. Which describes your mission statement: a living frame of reference, or yet another business cliché, one that is more likely to impede progress than to speed it?

CHAPTER 3

A GAMBLER'S GUIDE TO SETTING DIRECTION

Why a Company's Real Strategy Is in Its Book of Bets

Strategic Plan 1: A set of analyses, packaged in accordance with corporate requirements, that is undertaken in order to justify a campaign already under way or a budget about to be submitted; 2: (alt.) A set of analyses, packaged in accordance with corporate requirements, that nonetheless bears little or no resemblance to the real strategy being followed (but that, once printed and bound, can, in a pinch, be used as a doorstop or a bookend).

Corporations harbor legions of gamblers. Some of these gamblers dress in wingtips and pinstripes, some in silks and pearls, and some in jeans and work boots, but all of them make a practice of betting on behalf of their employers. The chits they ante up are corporate chits, ranging from how they deploy the human assets within the company to how they deploy the corporate funds available to the organization. The bets they place are corporate bets, determining which industries and markets will be attractive for their companies and focusing on what it will take for their companies to win within these arenas. And, aggregated over time, this book of bets and the actions that it produces, represent the real direction followed by any organization.

In short, every company has a strategic direction, because every company has a book of bets. What every company does not necessarily have, however, is a *good* strategic direction. Not all beliefs are created equal, and when corporate gamblers bet on the basis of flawed assumptions, their odds of achieving the outcome they seek plummet.

And though many companies invest in elaborate planning processes in hopes that a written plan will lead to a stronger and more informed book of bets, there are plenty of companies that, having produced their plans in compliance with copious corporate requirements, still bumble along with performances that are mediocre at best. And, conversely, there are still plenty of other companies that, having no written plans, still have great track records of placing bets with attractive odds; as one example, when Harvard Business School professor Amar Bhide interviewed the founders of 100 companies on the *Inc. 500* list of the fastest-growing companies in the United States, he found that fully two-thirds had started their companies with either only back-of-the-envelope type business plans or with no business plans at all.

One explanation for this phenomenon has to do with the nature of the bets companies must place when they see or wish to create a new direction. In the perfect world of plans, a blueprint can be laid out, with timetables and responsibilities. In the messy world of bets, circumstances shift unexpectedly and odds change—not an environment in which inviolable plans and rigid schedules will necessarily be very helpful. Two observations about how skilled gamblers adjust their book of bets may help in the discussion of the direction setting process. First, good gamblers are receptive to attractive bets that are unplanned and unpredictable, and therefore seldom let the strictures of a strategic plan stand in the way of capitalizing on a serendipitous strategic event. Second, good gamblers apply disciplined and focused analysis to assess and improve the odds on the most important bets in a company's portfolio. In combination, these two traits can boost the odds of success on a corporate book of bets. The case study of the Fremont Canning Company, which follows shortly, takes a closer look at how thinking about the set of choices of where and how to compete as a book of bets can make dramatic differences in a company's ability to chart and change its direction, profitably.

> "No single subject has so dominated the attention of managers, consultants and management theorists as the subject of corporate strategy. . . . [What is] puzzling is the fact that the consultants and theorists cannot even agree on the most basic of all questions: what, precisely, is a corporate strategy?"
>
> —*The Economist*

1. Good Gamblers Know That They Can Pull Aces from the Sky (Unless the Strategic Plan Keeps Them from Seeing or Acting on the Aces That Appear)

Serendipity and corporate plans typically do not mix well. Serendipity is messy and disruptive, arriving unannounced and according to its own schedule. Plans, on the other hand, are orderly and detailed, filled with precise goals and clear timetables. When people, as part of following a plan, ignore a serendipitous opportunity because its appearance doesn't fit into the sequence or direction already agreed upon, Serendipity responds as any uninvited guest should and just leaves quietly and goes to call on someone else who might be more attentive. Good gamblers know these things about the role of chance in managing a book of bets. And, based on this understanding, they make special efforts to be receptive enough to see what isn't in the plans and flexible enough to design and place side bets on the fly. The timing isn't always convenient and the bets don't always pan out, but that's the price of trying to combine the discontinuity of a serendipitous opportunity with the discipline of a strategic plan.

When Serendipity Comes a Calling: The Story of Daniel and Dorothy

Consider the story of Daniel and Dorothy, a young couple living in Fremont, Michigan (population: 2,000), who, one summer's night, were planning an evening out. The year was 1927. Daniel, then a twenty-nine-year-old World War I vet, was an employee of the Fremont Canning Company, a modest-sized fruit and vegetable packer owned by his father, Frank. On this particular evening, Daniel, set for the evening ahead, was waiting for Dorothy to finish dressing. Dorothy, however, hadn't even started to get ready. Instead she was in the kitchen, straining peas for the younger of their two daughters, seven-month-old Sally. That Dorothy was straining peas was itself a noteworthy event since, in 1927, the dominant theory of

"People in our firm frequently ask me to discuss Goldman Sachs' strategic vision.... I won't try to outline a detailed long-range blueprint for the firm. That's really not the way I or others on the Management Committee approach the strategic planning process. We spend a lot of time deciding on specific initiatives we may want to undertake and the general direction in which we're headed; however, along the way, we try to maintain our flexibility and nimbleness in adapting to a volatile world."

—Letter from the Chairman, *1993 Goldman Sachs Annual Report*

nutrition was that infants be fed a liquid diet for almost all of their first year.

Given the situation at hand, Daniel encouraged Dorothy to hurry and Dorothy in turn suggested that, if Daniel wished to expedite the proceedings, he should take over the pea-straining task. The result, as related by Daniel years later: "While [Dorothy] dressed, I launched the battle of the strainer. Rolling my sleeves high, I armed myself with a serving spoon and went about the business of demonstrating man's superiority over woman. I pushed and squashed valiantly, and the peas soon were everywhere but in the strainer."

Dorothy was delighted with the mess that greeted her when, having dressed for dinner, she came back into the kitchen. Looking at the pea-spattered floor and sink, she turned to her husband with a question she had wanted to ask for some time. "Why," she inquired, "can't we end all of this nonsense? You can purée tomatoes at the plant. Why not vegetables for Sally?" Daniel, on the other hand, was incredulous. Convinced that the problem must have been that his wife had the wrong tools at hand, he spent the next day first at the Fremont hardware store, where he purchased a strainer, and then at his office, where, armed with strainer, fork and soup ladle, he started the process anew—and obtained the same unsatisfactory results as he had the night before. Now converted to Dorothy's point of view, Daniel sought out his father to see if Fremont Canning might want to investigate the idea of "modestly-priced, commercially-prepared foods for babies." As Daniel recalled years afterwards: "It wouldn't be quite true to say that Dad jumped . . . with joy at this suggestion. On the other hand, he said he couldn't think of any good reason why mothers wouldn't like the idea and suggested that I go ahead with the project."

And with that, Dorothy, Daniel and Frank Gerber were on their way to transforming the Fremont Canning Company into the Gerber Products Company. By the time the company changed its name and dropped its adult food lines in the early 1940s, it had already become the preeminent baby food manufacturer and marketer in North America. Two decades later, when Daniel Gerber recounted the company's story in his 1964 memoir, "Babies Are Our Business" (in Furst and Sherman's *Business Decisions That Changed Our Lives*), the Gerber brand had virtually become the generic name for baby food, a position the company still held in 1994 when it was acquired by the Swiss conglomerate Sandoz for almost $4 billion.

Wooing Serendipity: From Chemical Spills to Kayak Spills

Some might say that Daniel and Dorothy were just lucky, but I don't think that's correct. Though the Fremont Canning Company was following a strategic direction, the Gerbers were sufficiently open to a visit from Serendipity that they were willing to place initial side bets to see whether Dorothy's idea was a deuce or an ace. Nor were the Gerbers a rare instance of a company able to incorporate chance opportunities into its strategy. In Professor Bhide's study, for example, the founders of 20 percent of the leading entrepreneurial companies he studied told him that they had discovered the ideas on which they based their successful firms "serendipitously."

Companies can increase their odds of pulling aces from the air. Some companies, like 3M and DuPont, make a practice of allowing their researchers to explore the paths provided by chance inventions. 3M's Scotchgard, for example, came into being when a researcher accidentally spilled some experimental brew on a sneaker, noticed that the area of the spill seemed resistant to stains, and saw the potential for a new product. Similarly, DuPont's Teflon was born on April 6, 1938, when a young scientist named Roy J. Plunkett investigated the residua of a failed experiment aimed at creating a nontoxic refrigerant and found, instead of the gaseous tetrafluoroethylene he expected, a white waxy powder, one that was very slippery, resistant to acids, bases, heat, and solvents—thereby creating the base for a billion-dollar-per-year business for DuPont. At both 3M and DuPont, the scientists knew from past experience that they were allowed to welcome Serendipity into their labs, and therefore felt authorized to place side bets aimed at exploring unexpected

---

How the famous "dance of death" scene was filmed as part of Ingmar Bergman's *The Seventh Seal:*

"We had packed up for the day because of an approaching storm. Suddenly, I caught sight of a strange cloud. Gunnar Fischer hastily set the camera back into place. Several of the actors had already returned to where we were staying, so a few grips and a couple of tourists danced in their place, having no idea what it was all about. The image that later became famous... was improvised in only a few minutes."

—from Ingmar Bergman's *Images: My Life in Film*

ideas, even if these potential products were not specified in their unit's strategic plans.

Kodak takes a similar approach on the marketing side of its business with its policy of giving employees free cameras and film on Fridays with the requirement that the camera be returned and the film dropped off for processing at the company's facility on the following Monday. As Harvard Business School professors Steven Wheelwright and Kim Clark tell the story, Kodak developed the Weekender, the waterproof version of its Fun-Saver disposable camera, after a Kodak employee, having capsized his kayak, returned his borrowed test FunSaver camera inside a plastic bag filled with the water it had fallen into. As a Kodak employee, he knew that film, once wet, would not be damaged as long as it was kept wet until developed, thus sparking the idea for a product that became a strong contributor to the 60 million Funsavers sold annually as of mid-1994. Kodak's practice of testing its experimental products with its own employees not only provides the company with instant feedback on its experimental films and cameras, but also increases the odds of Serendipity making a profitable visit.

But whether Serendipity arrives unannounced or is wooed, such chance opportunities pose the challenge of how corporate gamblers can keep strategic plans from becoming strategic straitjackets. The world hardly ever evolves exactly as described in a strategic plan, and even more rarely adheres to the schedules specified therein. Those who refuse to see and evaluate these unexpected shifts and variations may hold to their plans, but only at the cost of neglecting changes in direction that may have put their organization on a more advantageous (and profitable) course.

2. Good Gamblers Know That to Play the Odds Successfully They Need to Assess the Odds Astutely (Unless the Strategic Plan Obscures Their Ability to See the Real Odds on the Bets They Carry)

Planning exercises provide a great opportunity for participants in a business to take a time-out and check key assumptions. The corporate guidelines for the analytic portions of such plans usually require volumes of data; typically including sections on market size and trends, industry structure, competitor profiles, customer dynamics, product economics, and the ubiquitous SWOT analysis (strengths, weaknesses, opportunities, and threats). The problem is not so much that the plans don't require the right data as that they can overwhelm the bettors with data. In the rush to complete a MECE plan, one that contains analyses that are "mutually exclusive and comprehensively exhaustive," the goal of placing informed bets with attractive odds can get lost. In consequence, such plans can be completed in accordance with corporate guidelines without ever forcing a careful assessment of the most important bets facing the business, and therefore without forcing a careful assessment of the possible actions for improving the overall book of bets.

> "None of us really under- stands what's going on with all these numbers."
>
> —David A. Stock- man, as chief of the Office of Manage- ment and Budget under President Ronald Reagan

One approach for keeping the focus of the planning process on the most important bets is to apply what I call the "good deal at a profit over time" standard. This standard is based on the simple concept that continued success in the marketplace requires a company to give some group of customers what they see as a good deal relative to the alternatives while still making a profit for itself, and continuing to find ways to do so as circumstances change. Again, the Gerbers' experience in using a new product to change the direction of their company provides a useful example. Although the Gerbers didn't have a business-school-approved strategic plan, they did know how to seize the bets that would allow them to adjust their strategic direction. And although they certainly didn't explain what they were doing in the terms of the "good deal at a profit over time" standard, they did work assiduously to improve the odds on their baby food bets by applying the principles of this standard, and thereby changed the direction of their firm.

A Good Deal at a Profit over Time: Top Quality Baby Foods at Sensible Prices ... and Reasonable Costs

Consider the "good deal at a profit" part of the standard. The Gerbers' initial proposition was that "modestly-priced, commer- cially-prepared foods for babies" was the kind of deal that could create a market. Their initial gamble was a very small side bet to test the feasibility of the idea: they produced small batches of baby food as "experiments" with Mrs. Gerber and baby Sally as the first testers. Soon the company's workers and townspeople began to request the new food for their own children. And as soon as that happened, and before venturing beyond the local Fremont market, the Gerbers set to work on the *cost* part of the equation. Or as Daniel Gerber later told the tale: "Many questions arose. . . . Would the medical profession recommend commercially prepared baby foods? Would a grocer, who had never been asked for baby foods, agree to stock them? Would a cautious mother, who knew nothing about our company, buy this strange product? While seeking answers to these questions, many months were spent improving processing techniques and determining how the product could be refined and produced at a reasonable cost."

Moving into 1928, the Fremont Canning Company made larger bets in the baby food business, using its spare capacity to create an initial line of baby food, while still keeping an unwavering focus on providing the good deal and doing so at a profit. "We were moving into uncharted waters and, to learn something of the new market, we conducted a national survey to determine the buying habits of young mothers. . . . The survey told us that mothers would be receptive to the idea of prepared baby foods, providing they were reasonably priced and could be purchased in grocery stores along with regular family staples. . . . Right then and there Gerber established its policy of producing top-quality baby foods at sensible prices."

Based on these findings, the Gerbers launched their new baby food line in late summer 1928. The retail prices for their four strained foods (carrots, peas, spinach, and prunes) were fifteen cents per 4.5-ounce can. They set these prices in the context of the two alternatives they saw to their new product: 1) regular unstrained peas (like the ones that Dorothy and Daniel had strained only with great difficulty), which were available at grocery stores nationwide at ten cents per 18-ounce can, and 2) strained baby foods (like the ones that Fremont Canning was now introducing), which were just beginning to appear in some drug stores on the East Coast and which were priced at thirty-five cents per serving.

In short, the Gerber version of the "good deal at a profit over time" standard was "top quality baby foods at sensible prices and reasonable costs," and they used this standard to make sure that the bets they were placing had attractive odds. To do this, they managed three elements—the benefits their product provided, the prices they would charge, and the costs of providing these benefits—as part of one simultaneous equation. One way to visualize this simultaneous equation is shown in Figure 1. Though the Gerbers' approach may seem obvious, just think about how many companies today prepare elaborate business plans—and then stumble when they find that they cannot both provide a deal that their target customers see as worth buying and keep their costs low enough to provide a profit that they see as worthy of their efforts.

A Good Deal at a Profit over Time: Continuous Change Versus Discontinuous Change

The Gerbers were equally tenacious in thinking through the "over time" part of the standard. Their questions weren't about whether there would be changes that would affect their businesses; they knew then, as we know now, that change is inevitable. Rather their questions were about the shape and rate of change that they would likely confront. More specifically, they understood that they needed to assess whether the introduction of solid foods at the baby's fifth month, then seen as "revolutionary thinking," would take hold gradually and slowly or be welcomed, suddenly and quickly, by millions of moms and their pediatricians.

To assist in making this critical assessment, the Gerbers sought out the experts: "When in the late summer of 1928 I showed the line, ready for the market, to our pediatrician in Grand Rapids, he told me that in spite of my enthusiasm, I was still underestimating the real potentials. . . . More [Gerber] family conferences were followed by countless consultations with nutritionists and home economists . . . [who] were even more enthusiastic than we were with the great possibility that lay ahead." Combining the opinions of the experts with their own gut intuitions, the Gerbers were then willing to bet that "this revolutionary thinking" would disrupt the trend line of prepared baby food sales—which at that point were growing slowly from a small base—and thereby create a large opportunity for their company.

"The real challenge in crafting strategy lies in detecting the subtle discontinuities that may undermine a business in the future. And for that there is no technique, no program, just a sharp mind in touch with the situation."

—Professor Henry Mintzberg, McGill University, in his classic *Harvard Business Review* article, "Crafting Strategy"

Figure 1: A Way to Visualize the "Good Deal at a Profit" Portion of the "Good Deal at a Profit over Time" Standard

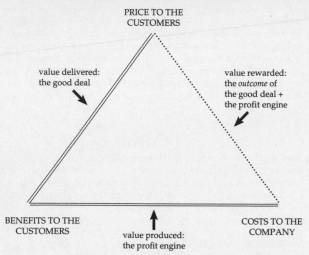

PRICE TO THE
CUSTOMERS

value delivered:
the good deal

value rewarded:
the *outcome* of
the good deal +
the profit engine

BENEFITS TO THE
CUSTOMERS

value produced:
the profit engine

COSTS TO THE
COMPANY

Value delivered: The bundle of benefits and price we have to deliver in order for our target customers to choose the deal we offer over the competing bundles of benefits and prices available in the marketplace; our good deal.

Value produced: The costs we must have to deliver this bundle of benefits, given the volumes we think we can achieve and the cost structure of the alternative products; our profit engine.

The Gerbers bet on discontinuous change and a year later, when the stock market crashed in 1929, they placed even larger bets in the baby food business. "Baby foods had been considered a good supplement to our regular business. As the nation entered the Depression, baby foods began to carry the load. The Fremont Canning Company faced a major decision—whether to ride with the times, or to expand its sales and advertising efforts. We gambled again, and baby food sales continued to climb." As the Depression deepened, the company invested even more, building research laboratories, hiring high-level professionals, and instituting an aggressive market research program of nationwide panels. By 1943, the hedging strategy of producing both baby food and adult foods had pressed the company's capacity to the limit. With the phenomenal success of its baby foods, the newly renamed Gerber Products Company voted to discontinue its adult food products, putting it in perfect position for its soon-to-be-famous tag line, "babies are our only business."

Companies publish summaries of their bets about the shape and rate of change all the time, in the form of budgets. But unlike the Gerbers, they don't always spend the time to identify the underlying trends and then be explicit about whether and why these changes are expected to be gradual or discontinuous. Some, like Apple with its introduction of the Newton, assume that the hoped-for discontinuity is just around the corner. Others, like the weather-girl Daisy Fay Harper, the narrator of Fanny Flagg's novel *Daisy Fay and the Miracle Man,* extrapolate the current trendline into the future. As Daisy Fay put it, "the job [of forecasting the weather] is easy. All I do is move the five o'clock weather girl's weather a few inches to the right. When it all winds up on the East Coast, I start it back in California." Both can be dangerous. The initial launch of the Newton MessagePad as a consumer product was a fizzle relative to its advance hype. And Daisy Fay was fired right after her boss called her into his office and "said there had been the biggest floods in the Midwest in twenty-five years and asked what the hell all my weather was doing in California where they were having a drought."

> "In the late nineteenth century, statisticians were predicting that by 1940, New York City would be six feet deep in horse manure, from the projected increase in horse carriages."
>
> —Maryann Keller, *Rude Awakening*

Seeing Patterns in the Data: It's the Odds That Count

A risk in today's planning processes is becoming so immersed in the data that the task of assessing the direction set by the company's book of bets becomes obscured. The "good deal at a profit over time" standard provides one way to get a start in identifying these bets and then in deciding which bets make sense and how to improve their odds.

Under the guidance of the Gerbers' version of this standard, Fremont Canning Company was able to take a number of actions that today are espoused as fundamentals of "new" management theory but the Gerbers saw as just part of a prudent approach to assessing and placing bets that could change the company's direction. In consequence, the Gerbers didn't need Total Quality Management (TQM) specialists to exhort them to "hear the voice of the customer"; they already knew that they needed to learn more about what moms could or did want, and did so even though national surveys were a relatively new technique in the 1920s. Nor did the Gerbers need the Japanese to prompt them to "design to cost"; within the first year of their initial experiment with baby foods, they understood that they had to find ways to lower their costs without compromising on nutrition or taste so they could reach the goal of "top quality baby foods at sensible prices." And they didn't need "futurists" to tell them about "discontinuous change"; they could see for themselves that they needed to assess the trajectories of the trends that would determine the potential market for their new product. With master gamblers like the Gerbers in mind, it appears that many of the techniques for setting direction touted as "new" today aren't so new after all.

"The art of prophecy is very difficult— especially with respect to the future."

—Mark Twain
(1835–1910)

Marrying the discipline of applying strategic analysis with a receptivity to unplanned strategic opportunities may seem like a shotgun wedding of sorts. But as the Gerbers demonstrate, it's a marriage that can be extremely profitable, and holds far better odds for success than either rigidly adhering to plans on the one hand, or sitting around waiting for Serendipity on the other. Almost three-quarters of a century after Dorothy made her suggestion to her husband Daniel, the Gerbers still stand as great examples of how taking a gambler's perspective on setting strategic direction can increase the odds for hitting a jackpot—or at least of betting right in enough cases to make the game worth playing.

PART TWO

LIFE IN THE UPSIDE-DOWN PYRAMID

Facilitating Collective Action

"The whole history of civilization is strewn with creeds and institutions which were invaluable at first and deadly afterwards."

—Walter Bagehot (1826–1877)

Some people say that the way to make organizations more effective is to stand the org chart on its head and obliterate hierarchy. Others call for massive programs aimed at cultural transformation. And still others insist that declaring their organizations to be open and conducive to the free flow of information allows high levels of continuous improvement, organizational learning, and employee loyalty.

The problem is that *organizations* are more effective only when mechanisms are in place that make it easier for all the *individual participants* to contribute to a larger set of goals. Yet the application of glib solutions for "reinventing the organization" can have the exact opposite effect, making it harder for individuals to do the right things well. Then everyone rails about the intractability of organizational problems, when in fact it is the medicine, inappropriately applied, that has exacerbated the underlying diseases—or caused new ones.

As the following three chapters argue, organizations can be made more conducive to productive action, but it takes more than simply redrawing the org charts, instituting formulaic programs, or making grand proclamations about the free flow of information. Chapter 4, "The Flat-Org Theory of Modern Management: Organizing for People Instead of for Theories," looks at why hierarchy is inevitable and how to manage it so that it is useful. Chapter 5, "Decoding the Corporate Culture: Time to Say Good-bye to the Excuse for All Seasons," focuses on one of the most direct, but often least used, ways of changing a corporate culture: changing the internal game. And Chapter 6, "Open Environments and Other Organizational Fantasies: Who Knows Where the Information Goes?" explores ideas for keeping information flowing in ways that will aid the achievement of organizational goals.

All three chapters focus on different aspects of the same point: Organizations will not change through cosmetic actions alone; slogans, pep rallies, and symbolic gestures are rarely sufficient. Nor are most organizations so ossified that managers no longer have either the power or the tools to effect a transformation. Rather, keeping an organization vital is a matter of continuous action and review, and the endless tinkering of an enormously complex ecosystem: the collection of many human beings, each with his or her own unique set of preferences and ways of viewing the world, gathered together to pursue goals that can be realized only by collective action.

CHAPTER 4

THE FLAT-ORG THEORY OF MODERN MANAGEMENT

Organizing for People Instead of for Theories

Flat Organization 1: *The process of reducing the number of levels that make up an organization's structure in order to increase its ability to respond quickly and effectively to changes in customer needs and competitive dynamics; 2: A set of actions, once known as "decentralization," that historically has in turn precipitated an equal and opposite set of reactions—namely re-centralization; 3: An organizational concept that aims to abolish all hierarchy and thereby produces new organizations with slower decision-making and greater focus on internal politicking than ever before.*

In the theology of fad surfing there are many angels—and at least one devil: hierarchy. Universally reviled, hierarchy is branded as the curse of organizations, enemy of employee empowerment, and obstacle to timely action. Among the horrors of which hierarchy stands accused are the following:

- command-and-control management styles that allow employees little leeway to exercise their own judgment or suggest new ways of approaching problems
- one-over-one communications, in which employees can talk only to their direct supervisors

- wholesale disregard for the ideas, input, and involvement of employees

- excessive number of layers in the organization, leading to inappropriately small purviews for each employee and ultimately to slow, inefficient business processes

- excessive bureaucracy and bureaucratic procedures in the organization, which also waste time and money

- complex job and pay-grade systems that keep employees in rigid job categories and more focused on the internal game of progressing through the system than on serving their customers well

- only one person or a very small group of people making all the decisions, vastly underutilizing the organization's knowledge and judgment base

- huge pay disparities that result in compensation packages for top managers that are a hundred times or more than those for the lowest level employees

And if hierarchy is the evil force behind these ills, then the solution must surely require an organizational exorcism. Accordingly, many theorists and managers have set out to obliterate hierarchy, changing reporting relationships and titles. In the resulting "post-hierarchical organization," the traditional org charts have been smashed; the pyramid is now "flattened," "turned upside down," or recast in new, "lateral" shapes as a "wagon wheel" or a "shamrock" or even "the horizontal organization." The traditional power relationships have been gutted; one cannot talk about "subordinates" and "superiors" or about people being "lower" or "higher" in the structure, but rather must refer to "associates" or "colleagues," or to "sponsors" or "advisers." And the traditional work units have been overhauled as well; the new work unit is the team, including, but not limited to: "project teams," "cross-functional teams," "self-directed work teams," "self-managing teams," "autonomous work groups," "semiautonomous work groups," "self-regulating groups," and "self-designing groups."

In the rush to rid organizations of hierarchy, people often neglect to consider whether hierarchy, in and of itself, is the real problem. I, for one, believe that it is not. As a nonadherent of the theory that hierarchy can or should be obliterated, here are my three counterpremises:

1. The goal of creating a nonhierarchical organization is nonsensical because there is no such thing as a nonhierarchical organization.

2. Though the problems described at the beginning of this chapter are real, they are due to *inappropriate* and *badly managed* hierarchy, not to hierarchy per se.

3. Solutions aimed at obliterating hierarchy create debilitating and destructive results for an organization, including "The Molasses Syndrome" and "Animal Farm-itis."

My conclusion, based on these counterpremises, is that managers need to change their goal, from banishing hierarchy, to designing hierarchies that work *for* their organizations.

No Such Thing as the "Nonhierarchical" Organization: The Case of the Nonhierarchical Meritocracy

The worldwide consulting firm of McKinsey & Co., Inc. is often given as a classic example of a nonhierarchical organization, or a "nonhierarchical meritocracy" to use the phrase coined by one of the firm's founders, Marvin Bower. When I worked at McKinsey, I accepted this phrase as gospel, as did many of my colleagues. Schooled in the firm's history, we all knew that as early as 1939, Bower and his fellow partners had identified the avoidance of a hierarchical structure as a key goal for the "professional services firm" they were creating, one that in their vision would encourage flexibility of roles and openness of discussion.

In most corporate cultures, people learn to repeat the corporate dogma while following the real rules, and seldom consciously recognize any gap between the two. (For more on the espoused rules and the real rules of

"We have tried to avoid a hierarchical structure, and have not stressed positions or titles either inside or outside the firm. In all successful professional groups, regard for the individual is based not on title but on competence, stature, and leadership."

—Marvin Bower

any organization, see "Decoding the Corporate Culture," pp. 51–64.) For this reason, I probably wouldn't have thought explicitly about the McKinsey credo of the "nonhierarchical meritocracy" had it not been for a trivial happenstance that occurred when, as part of preparing a presentation on the firm to a group of visiting dignitaries, I sent some handwritten slides to the Visual Arts Department that included this sentence:

McKinsey is a nonhierarchical meritocracy.

This is what I got back, in the typeset version of my slide pack:

McKinsey is a hierarchical mentocracy.

As typographical errors go, this one, whether by intent or by accident, was uncannily accurate. Though there's no such word in English as "mentocracy," one could imagine coining such a term to describe an organization that uses the mental and intellectual abilities of its members as a key criterion for advancement—an apt description of what I had observed at McKinsey. And though Bower had worked hard to have a flat organization at McKinsey, the firm's hierarchy in practice had many more layers than Bower's prescription would have indicated.

Consider the first six or so years of a consultant's life at McKinsey. In Bower's reckoning, there was really only *one* level of hierarchy during this six-year period, the associate, who might, as appropriate, from time to time take on the role of engagement manager. But within the real hierarchy, as it had developed by the time I was there, there were at least *three* gradations of nonpartners that those within the associate ranks recognized—associate, engagement manager (EM), and senior engagement manager (SEM). And, depending on who was doing the reckoning and the size of the engagement team, there could even be up to *six* levels: junior associate, associate, senior associate, junior engagement manager (JEM), engagement manager (EM), and senior engagement manager (SEM), each with progressively more scope and control—and each with progressively higher billing rates.

The shadow hierarchy within the associate ranks was reinforced by the powers ceded to the EM role: in most cases, managers organized the study efforts, effectively exercising line authority over those more junior to them by managing how the assignment was to be divided up and determining who would do what tasks. The managers also typically drafted the performance evaluations on the professionals more junior to them. These evaluations, done on a study-by-study basis, were perceived by nonpartners to be the currency within the firm, the basis on which their compensation and progression toward partnership were determined. Though the partner who served as the engagement director (ED) on the team reviewed these evaluations, the final versions submitted typically were, and were known to be, pretty close to the drafts prepared by the EM or SEM.

Bower was acutely aware of this real hierarchy and, because he believed that it had more levels than he regarded as optimal, he tried to convince the participants in this hierarchy to trim it back. Though his term as managing director had ended in 1967, he used his continuing "of-counsel" association with the firm as a kind of bully pulpit. Accordingly, Bower preached that the managers were coordinators who exerted no line authority. He implored the partners to go back to writing the evaluations of all the associates on the team—from the fresh-outs, who had just graduated from business school, to the SEMs, who were on the cusp of being elected to the partnership. And he urged the associates to see the various EM designations as merely temporary roles. But for the most part, the hierarchy within the associate ranks remained unchanged, and many associates therefore saw promotion through the levels as a way to measure their own—and their colleagues'—progressions to partner. Once made an EM, few would willingly revert back to the role of a non-EM or to work for another EM; to do so, it was thought, would be to move downward on the ladder. Just as importantly, each step upward corresponded to both increasing skill as a consultant as well as to jobs that were more satisfying because they allowed more control over the work and how it was to be done.

"Work is of two kinds: first, altering the position of matter at or near the earth's surface relative to other such matter; second, telling other people to do so. The first kind is unpleasant and ill-paid; the second is pleasant and highly paid."

—Betrand Russell, philosopher (1872–1970)

From an internal point of view, then, McKinsey did have a hierarchy within its associate ranks; associates in the firm recognized its existence and Bower did as well. Did this hierarchy mean that McKinsey was a bloated, constipated organization unable to move agilely versus its competitors? Of course not. It didn't even mean that McKinsey had an *unhealthy* hierarchy. It simply meant that this firm had a hierarchy, just like every other organization that I've ever seen. The reality is, hierarchies evolve whether managers or theorists want them or not; they are inevitable, integral to all organizations. The question is whether the hierarchy that develops is one that facilitates the organization's achievement of its goals or one that impedes effective action.

It's Accountability and Authority That Matter: Why Hierarchy Is Not the Root of All Evil

Imagine a bank with many vice presidents, all very young, all with very small kingdoms, and all with their own multilevel hierarchical staffs reporting to them. Now imagine that these vice presidents report to senior vice presidents, who in turn report to executive vice presidents, who in turn report to local bank presidents, who in turn report to the president of the bank holding company. Is this bank an example of the evils of hierarchy?

Many people would immediately say that it is. But now imagine that this is a bank in the United States just after World War II. As Peter Drucker pointed out in an interview with *Industry Week:* "Certainly after World War II—I don't think you can imagine . . . how denuded we were of people . . . As the business economy began to expand right after the war, you needed people and you had none . . . [For example, before the war] it traditionally took 30 years to become a vice president at a bank . . . Then suddenly, because of manpower shortages, you had 26-year old vice presidents. You had to! And we made the jobs very small."

Assessing the utility of a hierarchy is not a matter of ideology ("hierarchy is bad") or a matter of rules of thumb ("hierarchy is okay as long as there are no more than four levels between the CEO and the shop floor"). Rather, the goodness or badness of a hierarchy is related to how appropriate it is to its environment and how well managed it is. And, since we have to live with hierarchy, we need to take a look at what a hierarchy entails. The definition of hierarchy I use, based on the work of psychoanalyst Elliott Jaques, author of fifteen books on organizational design, goes like this: "Hierarchy is the system of accountability and authority by which an organization manages the production of its products and services." According to this definition, if one wishes to assess how healthy any hierarchy truly is, then the first place to look is not at the org charts, which frequently do not reflect how work gets done, but at how and where accountability and authority are distributed through the organization.

Jaques' descriptions of "accountability" and "authority" are essential to mapping out and modifying any hierarchy. Jaques defines "accountability" as "a system of roles in which an individual in a higher role (manager) is held accountable for the outputs of persons in immediately lower roles (subordinates) and can be called to account for their actions," whether collectively as a team or as individual contributors, or both. Jaques defines "authority" in terms of the powers that those who are accountable can use to ensure that these outputs are produced on time and meet the required specifications. Modifying Jaques' work a bit, authority for a set of outcomes is a function of the following four specific powers:

Accountability
A worthy constraint that everyone else in the organization must demonstrate to a far greater extent than they do today. Not to be confused with *authority*, which is what I need more of.

Authority A form of power of which I need more if I am to do my job properly. Not to be confused with *accountability*, the discipline that everyone else in the organization sorely lacks.

- degree of input regarding the definition of the outputs to be produced and/or regarding the priorities, work areas, and/or work plan for producing these outputs;

- degree of input into the performance evaluations actually used to determine the future compensation, assignments, and career progression of the people working within the unit or team to produce these outputs;

- ability to veto a newcomer to the unit or team who, in the judgement of the manager, does not meet the minimum standards for performance; and

- ability to initiate the process for removing a member of the unit or team for poor performance.

Mapping out who is accountable, for what, and with what authority is the first step in assessing the utility of any particular hierarchy. Going back to the McKinsey example, in my experience the system of accountability and authority was reasonably straightforward. Collective accountability, on the part of the team as a whole, was established by the proposal letter or other confirmation of the engagement, which specified the charter and deadline for the project. Individual accountability was defined by the work plans, which assigned specific responsibilities and deadlines to individual team members. In a corresponding fashion, each level of accountability had roughly appropriate authority—EMs for organizing the work plans, supervising the day-to-day work and interactions with the clients, and drafting the evaluations of the junior members of the team; EDs for guiding the efforts in these areas, assuring their overall quality, and bargaining for who should—and should not— be members on their client service teams. All things considered, it seems to me, the McKinsey system of accountability and authority was appropriate for its particular situation; its hierarchy suited the services it produced within its competitive environment.

Hierarchy Unmanaged Is Hierarchy Out of Control: The Hidden Risks of "The Molasses Syndrome" and "Animal Farm-itis"

When hierarchies are left unmanaged or are managed badly, they tend to spin out of control in ways that cause the timeliness and effectiveness of the organization to plummet. At one extreme of out-of-control hierarchies is "Judgmentus Interruptus," the condition of having so many more points of accountability than needed that each individual's exercise of judgment is unnecessarily and destructively impeded. This is the kind of organization typically highlighted when theorists talk about the ills of hierarchy, and this is where "de-layering" can be particularly effective. At General Electric, for example, from the period 1981 to 1992 the number of formal layers from the shop floor up to chairman, as shown on the org charts, was cut from nine to somewhere between four and six, depending on the business unit, as calculated by GE's corporate biographers, Noel Tichy and Stratford Sherman. Simultaneously, the number of business unit managers with profit-and-loss responsibility was cut from about 150 to less than 50.

At the other extreme is "Pseudo Empowermentia," a condition that typically results when a company attempts to annihilate or dramatically upend its hierarchy without careful attention to the effects on the system of accountability and authority by which it produces its products and services. The negative effects of such empowerment are quite serious, and every bit as detrimental as having too many levels on the org charts. When the points of accountability become unclear, *accountability dissipates* and soon no one is accountable for anything. By contrast, when the rules of accountability by which authority is exercised become murky, *authority migrates* and soon someone is effectively exercising the powers that shape how the work will be done . . . but not necessarily the person or people who should be or were intended to be.

At best, this lack of clarity about who is accountable and with what authority results in the "Molasses Syndrome," in which the organization becomes so stuck in the sweet goo of process that substantive progress could hardly move more slowly. At worst, the result is the "Animal Farm-itis," in which, as in the George Orwell novel, lack of clarity about accountability and authority leads to intense subterranean politicking and power grabbing, all covered with the nicey-nice rhetoric of the "flat" organization. The difference between the two, as far as I can observe, has to do with the internal game: if people who make power grabs are not rewarded with promotions and pay increases—and may even find their careers slowed, you are more likely to see the organization slide into molasses vat; if, on the other hand, they are rewarded for such behaviors, then it's off to the Animal Farm. In either case, the people at the top of the organization are unlikely to see what is going on and will describe their organizations as empowered, flat, team-oriented enterprises. This should not be surprising, since those at the top of an organization already have all the powers they need and they therefore often find it difficult to see what other people will do to gain similar powers.

> "Unused power slips imperceptibly into the hands of another."
>
> —Konrad Heiden (1901–1975), German author

The profusion of task forces, committees, and teams intended to substitute for the old, hated hierarchy do not prevent either "The Molasses Syndrome" or "Animal Farm-itis." Rather, such work groups can exacerbate both ailments simply because these groups are so often structured without adequate attention to the dimensions of accountability and authority. Typical of the impediments to effective, timely action faced by such temporary work groups are the following: unclear or nonexistent charters (no shared understanding of the end products to be produced or the problem to be solved); lack of deadlines and interim milestones (no reasonably clear articulation of what is to be achieved by when and by whom); lack of accepted processes for breaking stalemates or for assessing quality (no accepted procedures either for elevating problems that have become deadlocked in the internal deliberations or for critically reviewing the outputs of the group); and, finally, weak or nonexistent authority (no mechanisms by which the people nominally in charge can set the boundaries for the work, evaluate the performance of the participants, veto newcomers to the group, or initiate proceedings for removing poor performers).

The new bizbuz of "self-directed work teams" (often called SDTs in the academic literature) is not, in my estimation, the antidote to the problem of unmanaged hierarchy. The Levinson Institute, a Waltham, Massachusetts, training institute for senior executives, hears a number of claims for self-directed work teams that have been effective without worrying about these troublesome issues of accountability and authority. But as Levinson Institute CEO Gerry Kraines explained to *Training Magazine* editor Jack Gordon, "I've yet to hear anyone explain satisfactorily what 'team accountability' means. Every time [the Levinson Institute] has checked out a claim of an extremely effective SDT, we've found there's always an accountable manager involved." My observation is that it is possible for teams to manage their own operations and to do so superbly, as long as they ultimately report to someone who is accountable for their results and who therefore is also accountable for ensuring that the team works within the appropriate framework for action. (For more on the tasks of setting the framework for action, see both "Judgment, Empowerment, and the Parable of the Talents," pp. 93–105, and "Mission Indecipherable," pp. 15–24.)

Nor is the answer, in my view, allowing the real power structure to evolve while insisting on the use of nomenclatures and

District Attorney: [motioning to the jury] "Defense Counsel is accountable to you."

Defense Counsel: "Judge, I object to that. I object to him referring to me as a cannibal, Judge."

Judge: "He said accountable."

Defense Counsel: "A what?"

Judge: "He said accountable, not a cannibal."

Defense Counsel: "It sounded like cannibal to me and I object."

—an actual court transcript, cited in *Disorder in the Court*

organization charts that imply that the organization has no hierarchy, or that all the participants in the organization have the same powers. Take the word "associate." It is said that John D. Rockefeller, Jr., was one of the pioneers of applying the term "associate" to his subordinates. Nonetheless, it is also likely that the dozens of Rockefeller associates who worked for him were never in danger of confusing their status with that of the world's richest man. Today, all other things unchanged, calling people with entry-level jobs "associates" and those who evaluate them "sponsors," and banning language about "lower" and "higher" levels and about "subordinates" and "bosses" does not change the real lines of authority and power that have developed through the organization. Similarly, drawing the pyramid upside-down, on its side, or inside out will not obliterate all hierarchy within the organization, though it will obscure *who* now holds the *real* power, thereby confusing the less savvy players.

Bringing hierarchy to heel in fact requires actions much more difficult than simply changing the names and locations of the boxes on an org chart or simply declaring that boxes on an org chart are no longer needed; it requires clarity about the obstacles to effective action and attention to the points of accountability and the parameters of authority within the organization. By this standard, Bower was successful in his organizational design for McKinsey. He sought to create a flexible organization, not one locked into rigid procedures, and he achieved that organizational flexibility through the use of temporary work teams. He also wanted an organization in which open discussion was the norm, and he largely achieved that as well; team meetings commonly included all members of the team—from the most junior associate to the most senior partner—in open, problem-solving discussions, as Bower had advocated.

In short, the real challenge posed by hierarchy is thinking through how to distribute accountability and authority throughout an organization to achieve a given set of outputs for a particular firm with its particular market and its particular needs. Many organizations have let these elements get out of alignment relative to their environments and now have hierarchies characterized by some or all the problems listed at the beginning of this chapter. For these organizations, substantial, sometimes even radical, change is in order: from cutting the number of layers in the hierarchy, to overhauling the human resource and

"We have repeatedly stressed the need for reduction in hierarchy. . . . Does this mean that hierarchy will disappear? There are two responses. One is "That depends on what you mean by *hierarchy*." The other is "Not yet, and most likely never."

—Edward E. Lawler et al., *Organizing for the Future*

compensation policies, to fundamentally redesigning how the enterprise is organized and radically restructuring how people work within that new organizational design. But what will never be useful will be to try to obliterate hierarchy entirely. Those who try to do so would do well to keep one point in mind: without overall precepts that govern the system, accountability dissipates and authority migrates, often in ways that harm the morale and effectiveness of any organization.

In organizations, the hard reality is that hierarchies evolve whether you want them or not. The job of the manager, therefore, is to ensure that any given hierarchy is healthy and suitable for her organization, or to revise it and manage it so that it is. Those who think they can obliterate hierarchy by denying its existence only increase the odds that the hierarchies in *their* organizations will create so much process and/or such mean politics that people are effectively blocked from contributing their best efforts. Renaming or redrawing the boxes on an org chart without sufficient attention to who is accountable and with what authority may make great pictures, but it's no way to run a company.

CHAPTER 5

DECODING THE CORPORATE CULTURE

Time to Say Good-bye to the Excuse for All Seasons

Corporate Culture 1: *The way we do things around here, our combination of shared values and group norms;* 2: *An excuse for not making desperately needed changes in the way a company conducts its business.*

In 1982, Terrence E. Deal and Allan A. Kennedy published a groundbreaking book, *Corporate Cultures*, which coined a name for a phenomenon that many people had noticed but didn't know how to describe: "corporate culture," the tendency of organizations to develop their own, idiosyncratic ways of doing things.

In the years since the publication of Deal and Kennedy's book, "corporate culture" has become the excuse for all seasons. Everyone has observed organizations that describe bold plans for change while continuing to conduct business as usual—and that then attribute the resulting lack of change to the intransigence of their "corporate culture." The conclusion that many people reach is that such organizations will change only if they invest in a massive "cultural transformation" effort or "change management" program, preferably one designed and implemented by outside experts.

Change Management: The process of paying outsiders to create the pain that will motivate insiders to change, thereby transferring the change from the company's coffers into those of the consultants.

But while societal cultures have tremendous inertia, corporate cultures are, relatively speaking, far more malleable. Consider one of the biggest behemoths in the corporate world: General Electric. This is what Deal and Kennedy had to say about GE in 1982:

> Take an up-and-coming executive at General Electric who is being wooed by Xerox—more money, a bigger office, greater responsibility. If his first reaction is to grab it, he's probably going to be disappointed. Xerox has a totally different culture than GE. Success (and even survival) at Xerox is closely tied to an ability to maintain a near frenetic pace, the ability to work and play hard, Xerox-style. By contrast, GE has a more thoughtful and slow-moving culture . . .

When I read this quote to a manager who joined GE in 1984, only a few years after Jack Welch became chairman in 1981, and who rose quickly through the senior ranks, he burst into gales of laughter. First, he informed me that I had misread the quote and had somehow transposed GE and Xerox. When I assured him that I had not, he laughed even harder. "Where did they get that bullshit? It's outlandish! It makes GE sound like a gentlemanly place, refined. That's not GE. What you do at GE is you kill yourself, work hard, fall on your sword and hope someone notices— and then you hope that they don't raise the bar five times more. *At GE, you perform or you die.*"

This manager's view is not anomalous. Noel Tichy, coauthor of *Control Your Destiny or Someone Else Will*, which chronicles Welch's first ten years as chairman of GE, had this perspective when he signed on for a two-year stint as a manager at GE's training center in 1985, several years before he wrote his book: "By the time I accepted the job, I'd been consulting for GE long enough to know that I had to establish my credibility fast . . . GE's performance driven culture is so powerful that when you start a new job as a manager, you want to demonstrate your self-confidence and leadership right away . . . I felt I had just one turn at bat—and I'd better hit a home run. If I missed, I feared, GEers would lose respect for me, maybe forever."

Both the quote from the Deal and Kennedy book and the two quotes from the two GEers provide accurate reflections of GE's corporate culture. The difference is in the timing; Deal and Kennedy were describing the GE of the Reginald Jones era, which ended in 1981. The GE manager and Noel Tichy were describing the GE of only several years later. The intriguing question is, how did Jack Welch create such a massive cultural change so quickly in a company that, as of 1981, had more than 400,000 employees? A large part of the answer, I believe, lies in one aspect of corporate culture that is rarely discussed: what I call "the internal game," the set of implicit, unwritten rules about how to survive and excel within the organization.

Many people feel that they have only two alternatives when confronted by a strong corporate culture: throwing their hands up in despair or embarking on full-blown, consultant-driven programs for "cultural transformation" or "change management." I think the better alternative is to uncover the objectives and rules of the internal game and change *them* as a first and fundamental step in transforming the culture. This belief is based on the following three observations:

> "In the main it will be found that a power over a man's support [compensation] is a power over his will."
>
> —Alexander Hamilton (1755–1804)

1. Every organization has an internal game that sets the rules for how to survive and excel within the organization; if you want to change the culture, part of your plan must include changing the internal game.

2. The rules people use for navigating the internal game seldom look anything like the rules in the policy books; if you want to change the internal game, you first need to uncover the real rules.

3. Those who excel at the internal game are not always those who contribute to performance; if you want to fine-tune the game, you need to find ways to assess the true contributions of the participants and reward the worthy.

A closer look at these three observations, with some help from Robert Graves' account of the gods of Olympus, and Tichy and Sherman's account of the gods of GE, follows.

1. Every Organization Has an Internal Game That Sets the Rules for How to Survive and Excel within the Organization (or, How Hermes Played the Game and Came to Be Added to the Olympian Council of the Gods)

In 1980, Harvard Business School professors John Gabarro and John Kotter wrote an article called "Managing Your Boss" in which they argued that effective managers "take the time and energy to manage their relationships with their bosses." When the editors of the *Harvard Business Review* reissued the article thirteen years later as an "HBR Classic," they also included a retrospective commentary by the authors. Gabarro noted that when they wrote the article, "the idea of managing your boss was an illegitimate notion." Then Kotter added an interesting note. "If we were writing the article today," he said, "I would worry a bit about managers who pay too much attention to managing upward."

> "Well, for one thing, I find that I no longer win every golf game I play."
>
> —George Bush on life after the presidency

A multitude of people in organizations around the world would agree with both assessments. For while it is true that before Gabarro and Kotter's thoughtful article the academic literature paid scant attention to managing up, it is also true that skilled insiders have always been extraordinarily attentive to managing the people who control the rewards and punishments, well beyond what Gabarro and Kotter proposed and not always to the benefit of their organizations. And thus has it been for millennia, at least since the time of the gods and goddesses who, according to the ancient Greeks, met in the Council Hall of Olympus and determined the course of mortal affairs.

Consider the story of how Hermes came to be included as part of the Council of the Gods. As myth-teller Robert Graves recounts the tale, the Olympian Council originally consisted of eleven deities in all, five gods—Zeus, Poseidon, Haphaestus, Ares, and Apollo—and six goddesses—Hera, Demeter, Athena, Aphrodite, Artemis, and Hestia. Then Hermes decided that he too wanted to be on the Council of the Gods. The son of Zeus and a lesser goddess, Maia, Hermes started his campaign early—the day he was born, to be exact. After climbing out of his crib when his mother wasn't looking, he stole Apollo's herd of white cows and slaughtered two of them, using the newly purloined cow guts to invent an amazing new musical instrument, the lyre. Apollo, enraged at the theft, stormed down to earth, scooped Hermes up and brought him to Olympus for trial. And that's when Hermes began a masterful job of managing up.

First came the explanation—"I was too young to know right from wrong yesterday. Today I do, and I beg your pardon." Second came the expiation—"I killed only two, and cut them up into twelve equal portions for sacrifice to the twelve gods." And then came the close—the request for the order—which Hermes managed with the delicate finesse of a truly skilled insider. Since, as all Olympians knew, there were only *eleven* members of the council, Hermes simply waited for the inevitable inquiry as to who the twelfth god was and, once the question was asked, politely replied, "Myself." To seal the deal, he settled his accounts with Apollo by demonstrating the beautiful music that could be played on his cow-gut-and-tortoise-shell invention, then making a present of the lyre to Apollo, who was, after all, the god of music. And finally, he offered to Zeus to be his herald, hence the winged sandals associated with Hermes' image. Having demonstrated his cleverness, his initiative, and his deal-making abilities, Hermes won the prize he sought, being named by Zeus as the god of business, and gaining the twelfth seat at the Council Hall.

Modern organizations are filled with people like Hermes, active participants in the internal game who play to win, and thereby garner the rewards of winning—including promotions, power, prestige, pay. Changing the culture therefore requires changing the objective of the internal game and the rules by which it is played. At GE during the Jones years, for example, the objective of the game was to grow at about the same rate as the overall economy, and playing the game required both putting together beautiful plans and then meeting the commitments in these plans, no matter what. Welch, according to Tichy, was a master at this game. Though he set higher than GNP targets for his businesses, Welch became adept at submitting beautifully produced and custom-bound reports to his bosses at headquarters and always delivering on his promises.

"Dear Santa: Tell me something: Do you watch everyone all the time, or do you miss behavior sometimes?"

—excerpt from a child's letter to Santa, as reprinted in *The Boston Globe*

As soon as he became chairman, however, Welch changed the game. The objective was no longer GNP-level growth, but for each business to be "number one" or "number two" in its industry and increase its quarterly earnings consistently and substantially—or be out of the GE portfolio. Plans were now judged more on content than on packaging. Managers whose plans passed rigorous testing from the chairman and his lieutenants gained access to much needed capital for their businesses and the chance for career advancement; those who did not, found their businesses on the block and their own careers stalled.

No one watching the new CEO could have doubted that he meant what he said or that the internal game had been irretrievably changed; in the first four years of his chairmanship, 117 business units were sold and almost 20 percent of the workforce, or just under 80,000 people, left GE as the company "closed, fixed or sold" businesses that didn't meet the new criteria. As Tichy and Sherman comment, "by the end of 1984, the old GE no longer existed. Welch had cleared it away." He did it in part by changing the goal of the internal game and the rules by which it was played, using his control of the goodies—access to capital and career advancement—to reinforce these changes.

2. The Rules People Use for Navigating the Internal Game Seldom Look Anything Like the Rules in the Policy Books (or, Why a Classical Music Critic for a Major Newspaper Interviewed a Topless Cellist)

Though the gods of Olympus didn't have a policies and procedures handbook, the rules they espoused for Olympian conduct probably didn't match with the internal game by which Hermes garnered his seat. After all, Hermes had filched the prize possessions of another deity and had lied about being sorry. But Hermes had also understood what the gods valued: the lyre for Apollo, and great cleverness in making deals for Zeus. By understanding the rules of the real internal game, Hermes knew how to manage up to get what he wanted.

The same kind of internal games exist in modern organizations around the globe. Typically, the first rule of the internal game is to say that you follow the rules as espoused; usually, the more apparent sincerity with which this is said, the more potent its effect. And, typically, the second rule is to disregard all those espoused rules that don't match up with the way the game is really played. If you want to find the areas where the espoused rules are honored mainly in the telling—but only rarely in the doing—look first at what it truly takes to survive and then to thrive in your organization, quite apart from what the rule-books say.

Consider the fabulous topless cellist caper. Newspapers use a number of surveys to determine readership of their features. As a current classical music critic for a major metropolitan daily tells the story, classical music articles are not high draws, typically pulling somewhere between 5 and 7 percent of that paper's readers. Which may explain why one of this critic's predecessors, having heard that a reader survey would be conducted, decided to write a story about a topless cellist. Not surprisingly, the survey showed a much larger proportion of the respondents had read *this* article on classical music—reportedly more than ten times as many. The espoused rule was about journalistic integrity. The implicit rule—at least from the former participant's point of view—was at least in part about the readership numbers. Today the newspaper has a policy of not announcing to its staff when it is about to conduct one of these surveys.

More typical is the experience of the California unit of a telephone company. Worried by results of an internal survey showing that its employees thought speed in getting customers off the lines was more important than resolving customer problems, the company spent almost $170,000 on training programs and pep rallies to train the 850 customer service reps that "when you pick up the phone, you own the problem." The employees loved the program and, initially, were thrilled to have been given the scope and the training to do their jobs well. And then they became confused. The reason: even with all the training and pep rallies, they were still being measured on their time per call. As a result, as one disillusioned customer-service rep later explained to *The Wall Street Journal,* taking a few minutes to resolve a problem, though saving time for the system as a whole and leaving customers infinitely happier, "shows up bad on your talk time." The stated rule was "you succeed when you put the customers first." The real rule was "you succeed when you get all those time-wasting customers off the phones as fast as possible (but always remember to say—especially on surveys—that your goal is to 'solve the customers' problems')."

> "That which is honored is produced."
>
> —Plato (c. 428 B.C.–c. 348 B.C.)

> "What gets measured gets done; what gets rewarded gets done repeatedly."
>
> —Barcy C. Fox, Saint Louis University

In extreme cases, the gap between the stated rules and the real rules can produce severely dysfunctional results. That's what appeared to have happened at the Massachusetts Institute of Technology, which uncovered a massive cheating scandal in its 1990–1991 first-year introductory computer-programming class. MIT has long stood for the integrity of the scientific process and the hard work of its students and faculty. So how could such a scandal have happened? According to *The Boston Globe,* the vast majority of students found the course so difficult that they believed they would fail if they did not cheat. Said Professor Sheila Widnall, then chairman of MIT's Committee on Discipline, "many MIT students see the Institute as an obstacle course set up by the faculty . . . [and] feel the required work is clearly impossible to do by straightforward means and that any means that makes survival possible are allowed." The stated rule was "the system is tough but fair, so your best strategy is to work hard and abide by the honor code." The real rule, as many students perceived it, was "the system is rigged against you, so do whatever you need to do to meet the requirements."

Such gaps between the espoused rules and the real rules are not that unusual. Here are some of the ones commonly observed:

THE RULES OF THE INTERNAL GAME BALANCE SHEET

espoused rule (sounds like a corporate asset)	real rule (functions as a corporate liability)
Quality comes first	Get the tons out no matter what
Never sell the customers something they don't need	Get the order; he who books the most revenues gets the most goodies
Innovate! We need innovation and we celebrate honorable failures	No matter what, a failure is a failure; it's far, far worse to have tried and failed than never to have tried at all
We take the long-term view of our businesses	Miss your budget numbers and you're dead meat
We have an open environment; speak up if you ever have a concern	Accentuate the positive and just sublimate the negative (unless you have a death wish)

THE RULES OF THE INTERNAL GAME BALANCE SHEET *(continued)*

espoused rule (sounds like a corporate asset)	real rule (functions as a corporate liability)
Teams are our lifeblood	Promotions go to individual contributors
Developing our people is one of our most important tasks	Managers who spend time developing their people are weenies, neither tough enough personally nor strong enough analytically to do a good job around here
We are a learning organization; help us improve continuously	Don't rock the boat
Compensation is a private matter between you and your boss; do not discuss it with others	Share comp numbers with peers; it's the only way to create a reliable ruler for measuring how well you are really doing
We are a nonhierarchical collegial organization and we follow the golden rule of reciprocity in our treatment of each other	Golden rule, schmolden rule; I kissed up to my boss to get where I was going and now you're going to kiss up to me
Run this business as if it were your own; manage for the long haul	Fast trackers never stay in the same job for more than two years so go after actions that look big initially (but someone else has to implement) or that give great initial results (no matter what the long-term costs)

The bottom line of this balance sheet: no matter what the rule books say, and no matter how piously such official sentiments are repeated, in their actions the savvy players will always swing to the right of this ledger and follow the real rules for gaining rewards and avoiding punishments. But when leaders see and understand these gaps, they can change the real rules. At GE, for example, Welch set out to instill GE's managers with the value of acting as though they "own" the businesses they work in. Then he discovered that, on average, the top 248 managers in the company changed jobs every 2.2 years. To deter managers from talking about the long haul at the same time that they manage for the short term (while devoutly angling for a new job), GE is now working to keep managers in their businesses longer, so they will live with the consequences of their managerial decisions.

3. Those Who Excel at the Internal Game Are Not Always Those Who Contribute to Performance (or, What the Story of Hestia Tells about the Nonplayers of the Internal Game)

The good news about the role of the internal game is that those who wish to change their corporate cultures can get a significant head start by modifying the objectives of the game and its rules within the constraints provided by a particular environment and work force. The bad news is that, in the process of doing so, one can easily assume that those who learn to play by the new rules are contributing to the enterprise. Since the essence of being an effective player is managing the person who controls the goodies, it shouldn't be surprising that the people at the top can't always see through the snow job they are getting from their subordinates. The classic example: the kiss-up, kick-down manager, who speaks convincingly of "empowerment" and "trust" when talking with his boss, and then accords his subordinates little consideration.

Conversely, there are those participants who do not wish to—or are not good at—playing the internal game and whose positive contributions are therefore routinely underestimated or neglected. And since the idea of the nonplayer is counterintuitive to expert players who can decode the internal game and relish playing it, it's worth taking a detour to look at a classic example of a nonplayer who nonetheless was a great contributor: Hestia, goddess of home and hearth.

According to the continuation of the ancient Greek myth about the composition of the Council of the Gods, after Hermes became the twelfth member of the council, a new crisis arose. Dionysius, having invented wine, argued that he too should be on the Olympian Council. The Olympians agreed, but were stymied, since the addition of Dionysius would have given the council thirteen members, a number they regarded as unlucky. The Goddess Hestia solved the problem by volunteering to step down. This was an easy decision for Hestia, who cared only about doing a good job as goddess of home and hearth and therefore assigned little worth to the machinations of the gods and their incessant infighting for perks and power.

Hestia was the archetypal nonplayer. She carried out her duties with diligence and devotion, and paid scant attention to the internal politics of Olympus. Her disinterest in the trappings of power was evident even in her throne. As in many corporations today, the gods and goddesses of Olympus tried to outdo each other in the appointments of their offices, constructing their thrones out of costly materials ranging from solid gold and solid silver to black marble and creamy ivory, and decorating them with all manner of precious jewels and intricate, beautiful carvings. All but Hestia, that is, who chose a simple wood chair, unadorned by decorations or carvings of any type. (Perhaps not surprisingly, when Dionysius took Hestia's place, he did not also take her throne. Instead he had his own built of gold-plated wood, with carved grapes made of amethysts, snakes of serpentine, and animals of jade, onyx, carnelian and other semiprecious stones.)

Zeus and his colleagues probably thought of Hestia as at best a "B-teamer"—not part of the real power elite—and likely were not deeply distressed when she left the inner circle of the gods. Yet Hestia was dedicated to her job and, of all the gods and goddesses, was the least likely to create mischief on earth due to some vendetta against another Olympian or as part of a plot to gain some earthly possession she desired. As a classic nonplayer, Hestia never stopped doing her job, she just stepped out of the game.

People like Hestia aren't the only kind of "outer-circle" players found in organizations; also out of the game are the many people who would like to play but find the real rules too difficult to decode. Consider the experience of Dieter, an up-to-then fast tracker at a global services firm, who was told that an "out of office experience" was an important ticket to play for promotion to the next level. Dieter therefore transferred from the Düsseldorf office of his firm to the Detroit office. Of course, though everyone at his level was told the same thing, the savvy players understood that the first rule of advancement was "thou shalt not stray far from the godfathers who feed you sales leads" and they therefore found ways to work with the foreign subsidiaries of current customers without changing offices. When promotions time came, Dieter's revenue base was smaller and the recommendations from his new office were cooler than those of his peers who had stayed in Düsseldorf, even though Dieter's skills were comparable if not superior. In consequence, Dieter's career progress slowed while his colleagues continued their climbs up the corporate ladder.

How can managers make sure that, in the process of assessing adherence to the new internal game, they don't inadvertently give too many rewards to players who excel at managing up but whose contributions are relatively small, while not giving enough rewards to the "outer-circle" players who nonetheless make consistent contributions to the goals of the organization? One way is to use survey instruments to solicit feedback from customers, peers, and subordinates. If the questions hit the important topics, are expressed clearly and unambiguously, and can be answered anonymously, management can learn a great deal about the real internal game in their organizations and its impact on its players. A pair of complementary analyses are to review the profiles of the people who received the biggest bonuses or the most sought-after promotions versus those who fared less well, and to compare the characteristics of the businesses and projects that received ample funding and other resources relative to their requests versus those that suffered a lower hit rate in the corporate sweepstakes; these analyses will provide a glimpse into what characteristics people in the organization correlate with success. Regardless of how you do it, though, the key is to remember that those who play the internal game well always look like they make important contributions while adhering to the official rules whether or not they actually do—and that those who don't play the game well may still embody the values and make important though less visible contributions.

----------------■----------------

Every organization has its own internal game, a set of implicit rules about how to survive and excel within the organization. And every organization has its "inner-circle" players, who can decode these real rules and actively manage up with varying degrees of effectiveness, and its "outer-circle" players, who either can't figure out the real game or don't care to play it.

It's no use trying to eradicate the internal game, however; it exists in the first place because it describes what's really required to succeed and it therefore drives the behavior of the participants. For this reason, a first step in jump-starting "cultural transformation" or "change management" is to start by identifying the factors that most closely influence actual behavior: what is permitted and what is rewarded, versus what is prohibited and what is punished, and what is funded and supported versus what is starved and ignored. Having uncovered the real rules of the internal game, one can then move to alter those rules that stand in the way of the needed changes. Such changes may not tap into the deepest emotions of the participants or transform their core values, but they certainly can establish a critical beachhead in the battle against corporate cultures that stand in the way of new corporate goals. Without such changes, on the other hand, managers may find themselves talking about driving the culture when in fact it's the game that is driving the culture—and driving the managers themselves.

"Risk in Mutual Funds Is Rising as Managers Chase After Bonuses: Many Invest in Derivatives, Spurred by Incentive Pay and Need to Stand Out."

—headline in *The Wall Street Journal*

CHAPTER 6

OPEN ENVIRONMENTS AND OTHER ORGANIZATIONAL FANTASIES

Who Knows Where the Information Goes?

Open Environment *A place where you can say anything you want as long as you don't rock the boat and where you can find out anything you want as long as you discover it by using the internal grapevine.*

Among the mantras of the fad-surfing age, those calling for "continuous improvement," "learning organizations," "paradigm shifts," and "loyalty-based management" are often chanted the most loudly. All have tremendous value. Organizations that improve continuously can outrace those who are complacently confident that today's ways are the best ways. Organizations that learn by identifying new relationships between what they do and the results they seek can further increase the gap between themselves and their competitors. Organizations that understand the sets of beliefs by which they operate and can shift them as needed are far more agile than those stuck in old paradigms no longer appropriate to their current environments. And certainly, all other things being equal, organizations with happy and loyal employees will serve customers better and compete more effectively than those with disloyal and disgruntled employees, who, feeling exploited, treat customers with sullen indifference and otherwise work against the interests of their employers.

It's also true that turning these fad surfing mantras into results requires a common foundation: an accurate and timely flow of information that easily makes its way up, down, and sideways throughout the organization. Many executives see this requirement as presenting no problem; their organizations, they say, are "open environments." But that's exactly the problem; *no* organization is an open environment, although some organizations are more open than others. Figuring out how open an environment is requires looking at the information flows from the perspective of those within the hierarchy, as opposed to those at the top. (For those who believe that organizations need not have tops and bottoms, please see "The Flat-Org Theory of Modern Management," pp. 39–50, for a counter point of view.)

In my experience, the degree to which an organization enjoys healthy flows of information is in turn determined by the degree to which people within the hierarchy volunteer their ideas and observations, and the degree to which they trust the official information provided by those at the top. All organizations have hidden reserves of corporate intelligence, but in less open environments, people withhold more of their knowledge and ideas both about what is going on within and outside of the company as well as about how to make improvements or parry threats. And all organizations have official sources of information, but in less open environments, people rely on the grapevine for a greater proportion of the information they consume, sometimes to the almost total exclusion of the formal communications with which they are bombarded.

A core challenge for continuously improving, organizationally learning, paradigm-shifting, loyalty-building executives, therefore, is to understand how the information *really* flows throughout their organizations.

The Disclosure Dilemma: What Is Observed or Conceived Is Seldom Disclosed—Due, in Most Organizations, to the Widely Shared Belief That There Is Nothing to Gain and May Be Much to Lose by Contributing Ideas and Observations

Information held inside an organization—observations, data, ideas about new ways to correlate the data, ideas about new ways to do things—is a valuable currency, perhaps one of the most valuable that any company can garner. Yet in many organizations, withholding information is often the route many employees choose to take.

It Helps to Ask . . .

In many cases, there's a simple reason people clam up. Consider the story told by former University of Pennsylvania professor Russell Ackoff about the unionized workers at Alcoa's Tennessee operations who implemented a new system for moving aluminum coils. The new process called for storing the coils on heavy quilted paper and then rolling them on their bottom edges across the paper when, for whatever reason, a forklift truck was temporarily unavailable and the old coils needed to be moved to make room for new ones coming off the line. Previously the coils had been stored standing on end directly on the factory floor and were moved by rolling them on their bottom edges across the floor. The idea was a big money saver since the old method resulted in crimped edges while the new method kept the edges unharmed, thereby reducing returns of damaged products from angry customers. When Ackoff went to congratulate the workers, he also inquired as to when they had thought of this idea. Fifteen years ago, one of the workers responded. Fifteen years ago! Ackoff exclaimed, why had they waited so long? The answer: *"Because those sons of bitches never asked us before."*

> "War is ninety percent information."
>
> —Napoléon Bonaparte (1769–1821)

Not asking for the information happens all too often. The goal of "loyalty-based management" provides a case in point. Picture what's happening in many companies today: managers talking about "empowerment" and "loyalty" to workers who, having survived multiple layoffs, are now told that they must do more for less. For some, doing more means more required overtime hours; for others, it means more tasks to be done no matter what the time required. Similarly, working for less means anything from changes in the compensation and benefits to changes in everyday policies—including, as two small examples, companies that have replaced their workers' offices with temporary cubicles or even with the new requirement that employees now work from their homes, or travel policies that require personnel to take connecting flights instead of direct flights if the former are cheaper, regardless of how many hours of travel time are added. Given these realities, perhaps it's no wonder that in a 1993 survey conducted by *Industry Week,* 60 percent of the 2,185 respondents said that they felt less loyalty to their companies than they did five years ago. The rhetoric and the reality will surely stay on a collision path if companies don't do the research to understand what is a good enough deal to earn the loyalty that they desire. After all, maintaining a happy and loyal workforce is no different from maintaining a happy and loyal customer base: you have to provide a good deal relative to the alternatives. (For more on the role of the good deal in customer satisfaction, see "Customer Dissatisfaction," pp. 109–119.)

Avon Products learned about the importance of finding out what their employees consider a good deal the hard way when, as part of a cost-reduction effort, in 1993 the company cut the incentives that the sales force—the famed "Avon ladies"—valued: awards, trips, even birthday presents, anniversary plates, and annual pins. The result was a drop in morale accompanied by a drop in profits. When, afterward, Brian Connolly, director of national sales incentives, commissioned internal focus groups, he found an overwhelming preference for awards, which he then reinstated. "It's part of the magic," as he later told *The Wall Street Journal.* Said one of the ladies, Carmelita Caburet, who generates $250,000 in sales for Avon, "I know it sounds picky, but I guess those things gave us the feeling we were being noticed." Connolly got the information that Avon needed because he created a legitimate way for the keepers of the information to express their concerns. If you want to open a flow of information, it helps to ask.

... *But Asking Isn't Enough*

Many executives say they *do* ask for a free flow of information. They point to speeches they have given, memos they have written, informal visits they have made, even formal idea programs they have sponsored. Yet, still they discover, belatedly, that great ideas or critical information, though available internally, never made their way to the appropriate places. The reason, again, is straightforward: asking isn't enough. If, at best, those who have the information or ideas have little probability of even small rewards, and at worst, face high risk of substantial penalties for offering their insights, why should it be a surprise that few people bother?

One can picture the barriers to the free flow of ideas and observations as a continuum. On the left end of this continuum is "lack of rewards," on the right end is "lack of rewards plus the existence of substantial (though sometimes subtle) penalties." Where the barriers to getting the needed information sit on this continuum depends on the kind of information being sought and the people to whom it must be told.

Consider continuous improvement programs. In the United States, when such programs are first put in place, an unexpected problem often arises: a deluge of ideas, more than anyone anticipated, and more than anyone knows what to do with. In the absence of procedures for identifying which ideas can and should be implemented by the person(s) who have submitted them and which need additional consideration, the procedures for reviewing the ideas submitted can take on a life of their own, taking so long as to render the ideas irrelevant. In Japan, where continuous improvement programs have been in place for years, are carefully structured and are integrated into the fabric of the work life, a high volume of ideas is expected and the resulting suggestions are exploited quickly; in 1987, for example, workers at Toyota's auto body division in Japan reportedly generated about 2,600,000 improvement ideas, of which almost 2,500,000 were implemented, mostly by the workers themselves. The challenge for companies outside Japan is not necessarily to copy the Japanese approach, but to develop their own, in which responses are speedy and even in which rewards are available—ranging from kudos to cash. For these companies, new to the practice of soliciting and acting on ideas generated from within, the obstacles to be overcome are on the left end of the continuum, "lack of rewards."

For other kinds of information flows, however, the obstacles people worry about are far more troubling than those presented by complicated, user-unfriendly idea forms and convoluted, time-consuming review processes. Rather, the obstacles sit on the right end of the continuum: the risk of penalties from volunteering information that might be unsettling to those higher in the hierarchy (read: have more power). Yet unsettling information is exactly what is often required to test existing paradigms, create new organizational learnings, or understand what employees consider a sufficiently good deal to earn their loyalty.

In some cases the information, because it is unexpected, is simply ignored, though sometimes with tragic results. That's what appears to have happened with the Swiss Red Cross which, in April 1985, sent a shipment of blood to the New York Blood Center. The New York Blood Center tested the shipment for HIV, the virus that causes AIDS, and found that a small portion of blood tested positive. Accordingly, the New York Blood Center destroyed the part of the shipment that appeared to have been contaminated, and then telexed the Swiss Red Cross to inform their sister organization of their findings. But the Swiss Red Cross ignored the warning. It did not institute testing of its own blood and, as long as a year later, did not recall the blood that might have been contaminated from the medical settings to which it had been sent. In consequence, it is now believed, the transfusions using the tainted Swiss blood infected 68 Swiss hemophiliacs plus an estimated additional 100–200 Swiss hospital patients. How could this have happened after the warning issued from the New York organization? The culprit appears to have been the belief on the part of Swiss Red Cross officials that AIDS was a disease ravaging other places—Africa, Haiti, the United States—but was not an issue for Switzerland. As a hemophiliac Swiss architect told *The New York Times*, "The response always amounted to this: we are very clean; we have few addicts; we have few homosexuals, we use mostly Swiss blood." The belief was stronger than the data.

> What the gardeners in the Red Queen's flower beds told Alice when she asked why they were covering the white roses with red paint: "Why, the fact is, you see, Miss, this here ought to have been a red rose tree, and we put a white one in by mistake; and if the Queen was to find it out, we should all have our heads cut off, you know."
>
> —from *Alice's Adventures in Wonderland*

But the risk is not just the barrier posed by the blinding power of beliefs. Far more worrisome to most people in organizations, and appropriately so, is the risk of sharing ideas or data that angers the recipients—especially when the recipients hold power in the real hierarchy. Those with the power can and do signal their displeasure in a variety of ways, from subtle ostracism to violent outbursts—not to mention the whole range of options for job diminution for the person who shared the unwelcome ideas or data. Often, however, the more powerful people opt out of this cycle entirely, simply by signaling the answers they wish to hear. Not surprisingly, these are the answers they usually get.

Consider the saga of Simple Pleasures ice cream, introduced to the market in 1990. Simple Pleasures, made with Simplesse, a "fake fat" developed by Monsanto's NutraSweet division, was expected to be a smash success. After all, it had the taste of a high-fat, super premium ice cream like Häagen-Dazs though with far fewer calories per serving. At least that's what the head of NutraSweet's Simplesse group thought. Before Monsanto introduced the product to the market, he went around to his subordinates with samples of the product prototype, asking them, "Doesn't it taste like Häagen-Dazs?" Not surprisingly, all of his subordinates agreed with him. Unfortunately, as one of these executives later confided to a *Wall Street Journal* reporter, they had shaded the truth. His honest, but at the time silent, assessment: "It tasted like chalk." The market agreed and Monsanto dumped Simple Pleasures in 1994.

Were the Simple Pleasures personnel wrong to shade the truth when asked a direct, if loaded, question? Given what happens in most organizations, I don't think they were. Telling the boss the truth clearly had more short-term risk for them than telling him what he wanted to hear; in that situation, most people, in my observation, will opt for the path of least resistance.

In many organizations, the suspicion that telling the truth is likely a CLM (career-limiting move) is reinforced by key managers, though perhaps not intentionally. This was vividly illustrated to me when I was invited to speak at a corporate retreat for about ninety members of a large division of a Fortune 500 company, including union leaders, line workers, foremen, and senior executives. The topic of the retreat was "communication," which management saw as critical to achieving the division's strategy of "customer-driven quality." As one part of the day's activities, the top executives organized everyone other than themselves into breakout groups, which they asked to "communicate" back on key issues relative to the strategy. Of the seven groups, six came back and reported the same root obstacle: in the battle between tons and quality, tons always won, despite corporate rhetoric to the contrary. Clearly nervous about telling it as they saw it, each group nonetheless carefully documented its concerns and presented thoughtful recommendations for change. When they were done, a senior manufacturing executive stood up and said angrily: "Quality has always come before tons here, and that's the last I want to hear about this." It was, at least for that day and likely for a long time thereafter. Few people volunteer to be the messengers of bad news under any circumstances and fewer still do so more than one time once they see how unwelcome such bad-news messengers are in their organizations.

It is possible to overcome the CLM syndrome, but it takes effort and commitment. Nine days after a sexual assault by a male cadet of a female cadet at the U.S. Air Force Academy, the director of the academy, Lieutenant General Bradley C. Hosmer, called a meeting for the 518 female cadets, ordered both his male aides and the male projectionists out of the room, took off his insignia of rank, and then asked for the "ground truth" about whether there were other problems of sexual harassment at the school. Four hours later, General Hosmer had a far more accurate picture of life at the academy for female cadets. As General Hosmer later told *The New York Times*, "We really had a problem, but it wasn't assault, which is a rare occurrence here. The bigger problem was the climate here. We knew we had to work on this, but we didn't realize the extent we had to work on it." The general also took action: not only has the academy investigated and adjudicated specific complaints that have been raised, it has increased the training provided to prevent such incidents from occurring and has instituted a twenty-four-hour, confidential phone line for reporting infringements of the academy's code of behavior. As the *Times* commented, General Hosmer "shows what a difference the top leader makes."

> "I well believe it, to unwilling ears; None love the messenger who brings bad news."
> —Sophocles, *Antigone*, lines 276–277

> "It's a pity to shoot the piano player when it's the piano that is out of tune."
> —French saying

When companies need information that may make them uncomfortable, it's critical to think through how to get the needed information—rather than organizational half-truths. When, for whatever reasons, those who hold the facts want to please the person to whom they are speaking or, more darkly, when they fear reprisals or being exiled to the corporate gulag, it takes more than just asking for feedback. In some cases, anonymity is needed; this is especially true for understanding the factors that go into employee loyalty. In other cases, the questions and the approaches to answering them must be structured carefully so that those with the expectations and preferences can tussle with the data rather than summarily dismiss it out of hand. In either case, freeing the flow of information starts with the personal discipline of the requestors.

> "Show me a man who claims to be objective and I'll show you a man with illusions."
>
> —Henry R. Luce (1898–1967)

The Grapevine Generator: What Is Unofficial Flows Freely—And Is Often Seen As More Reliable than the Official Information That Flows through the Formal Channels

But while the information that many executives wish would circulate more freely is often withheld, the situation is just about the opposite when it comes to the formal communications that these executives so carefully craft. Despite all the efforts—programs, speeches, memoranda, pep talks, newsletters, management walkabouts, press releases, announcements, posters, and the like—in most organizations, it's the grapevine that thrives as the preferred source of information. The result in these organizations typically is that executives overestimate the degree to which people pay attention to the official proclamations broadcast over the formal channels—and underestimate the importance of all the unofficial "info bits" relayed over the informal ones.

Yet it's hardly worth the energy to curse the grapevine. The grapevine is a fact of corporate life; there's no way to squelch it, and few secrets escape its reach. Those who wish to believe otherwise would do well to review both the myth of King Midas' ears and the parable of Chemical Bank's electronic bulletin board.

The Myth of King Midas' Ears . . .

Midas, according to the Greek myths, was the king of Macedonia who, in exchange for rescuing a satyr, received the power of turning whatsoever he touched into pure gold. That's the part of the story about King Midas that is best known. But, as myth-teller Robert Graves recounts the tale, the final installment in the King Midas story occurred when Midas, asked to judge a music contest between the Olympian god Apollo and a lesser Earth god Pan, rendered his honest opinion that Pan played more beautifully than Apollo. This was unfortunate: even though Midas made an accurate musical judgment, his organizational judgment was less sound since Apollo was the more powerful of the two contestants. In consequence, Apollo, the god of music, became very angry with Midas and turned his ears into those of a donkey, because, as Apollo so quaintly put it, Midas had acted like an ass—as indeed he had from the point of view of the politics of the situation. (For more on the savvy and non-savvy players of the internal game, see "Decoding the Corporate Culture," pp. 51–63.)

As Graves tells the story, Midas, deeply ashamed of his hairy, misshapen ears, wore a cap to cover them and never removed his hat except to allow his barber to cut his hair. To maintain his secret, he swore his barber to an oath of silence, on penalty of death. This presented the barber with an untenable dilemma, as often happens to those entrusted with organizational secrets. On the one hand, he understood the penalty for divulging the information. But on the other hand, he simply could not keep the secret. Thus constrained, the barber hit on an ingenious solution: he went down to the Pactolus river, scanned the horizon to ensure that no one else was about, dug a hole, and murmured his secret. Then he filled the hole.

"It is perfectly monstrous the way people go about nowadays saying things against one behind one's back, that are absolutely and entirely true."

—Oscar Wilde (1854–1900)

But the secret did not die. Instead, according to Graves, a reed grew where the barber had whispered his secret, and then that reed told the other reeds, and soon some birds overheard the rumor, one of whom told a man named Melampus, who in turn told so many people who told so many people that soon all of Macedonia knew about Midas's ears. When the rumor got back to Midas, the king, deeply ashamed and very angry, committed suicide—though not before he beheaded his barber.

Not all grapevines are as accurate as the one that ran from reed to reeds to birds to Melampus to all the people of Macedonia. But all grapevines are hardy, providing ready sources of nonofficial information throughout an organization. They thrive, despite the best efforts of monarchs and managers to kill them, because the people inside any organization, just like the people of Macedonia, want the information being broadcast over the grapevine, and often trust this information as more accurate than the information beamed over the official channels—if, in fact, they pay much attention to the official information at all.

One source of nourishment for the grapevine is the human need to make sense of events. It's the rare organization in which people deny themselves the pleasure of consuming and purveying bits of information that, when strung together, tell a story—usually a story that differs in significant ways from the official corporate line and, more importantly, is seen as more accurate than the official corporate line.

And there certainly is no lack of food to keep the grapevine going and growing. The info bits can come from anywhere: observation of a new car a manager has bought, an overheard snippet of a conversation, a secret told by a secretary, and so on. But regardless of whether these info bits represent an accurate picture, you can be sure that they will be turned into a story that makes sense out of what people know or guess. To keep the grapevine amply supplied, all anyone in an organization has to do is just watch the people above, just as their seniors did during their own climbs up the organization. That these top executives may no longer remember how much time they spent trying to read the tea leaves doesn't make this impulse any less strong in the people in the rest of the organization.

"Gossip: sociologists on a mean and petty scale."

—Woodrow Wilson (1856–1924)

The final source of nourishment is even more important: the usefulness of the grapevine to those who participate in it. The reason the office grapevine thrives is that it's usually a better source of information on how the internal game actually works than the corporate manuals and official speeches. Consider it the "organizational sociology" for the insiders. There's an important corollary, too: the more the real game differs from the espoused game, the busier the grapevine will be, using ever more speculative source materials—a prescription for erroneous and distorted rumors.

... And the Parable of Chemical Bank's Electronic Bulletin Board

If, as King Midas learned, one can't kill the grapevine, what's the alternative? The first step is to recognize that grapevines thrive because they provide information in a form that is believable and digestible to its users. How can this be with all the time that senior managers spend on "communications"? T George Harris, former editor of the *Harvard Business Review* and *Psychology Today*, points to the 1956 work of linguist Wendell Johnson on every person's "most enchanted listener"—which, of course is the speaker him or herself. As both Harris and Johnson point out, at every level, people listen more to themselves than to other people so that each of us is our most enchanted listener. The problem with such one-way communications is that, though they may be broadcast elegantly and efficiently, those to whom they are broadcast do not necessarily listen to or believe in them.

Given this inherent problem with communications, perhaps the best way to deal with grapevines is simply to feed them, with honest listening and candid responses. That's what Bruce Hasenyager, senior vice president at Chemical Banking Corp did when he invited employees to use an electronic bulletin board on the office computer network to ask questions—anonymously—to which he would then respond on-line. The exchange was unbridled, uncensored, unruly—and effective. Its effectiveness came not from the computer technology, but from Hasenyager's willingness to cede control of the forum to its participants, to allow the participants to ask their questions anonymously, and to respond honestly to the questions he received. As Hasenyager later told *The Wall Street Journal*, "It became a powerful tool for building trust. We could kill off the crazy rumors. When it was whispered around the water cooler that part of our group's work might be contracted out to IBM, I had a way to tell everyone at once that it was baloney."

That Hasenyager's path is a difficult one is unquestionable. Hasenyager's successor, uncomfortable with the lack of control and stung by barbs contained in some of the questions, shut down the bulletin board. Equally unquestionable is that the new executive did not shut down the grapevine, but rather forced it

> "The habit of common and continuous speech is a symptom of mental deficiency. It proceeds from not knowing what is going on in other people's minds."
>
> —Walter Bagehot (1826–1877)

deeper underground and increased the likelihood that it would broadcast inaccurate and demoralizing stories.

The new manager was not alone. Consider the CEO of a company that convened an electronic "town hall" meeting about a planned reengineering effort. As Michael Schrage, journalist and research associate at the Massachusetts Institute of Technology tells the story, the encounter created an informational meltdown when respondents asked very specific questions about the budget cuts and anonymously criticized certain managers. After two days, the CEO ordered the function that allowed anonymous messages removed from the system. Schrage argues that the electronic encounter should have been structured more carefully. This assessment is undoubtedly correct; the wild west nature of anonymous on-line communications sometimes produces electronic lynch mobs that can overwhelm more balanced assessments. Also true, however, was the reaction of some of the participants who claimed that "this was an organization that punished honesty, not rewarded it." Shutting down the anonymous electronic function while not providing some other means for confidential feedback merely ensured that certain views, including some that were dead accurate, would not be heard or addressed by top management. And while e-mail systems are not necessarily or always the best forums for such exchanges, the need remains for some kind of forum that is both accessible and protected.

From the Macedonia of millennia ago to modern money center banks, the moral for managers is the same: no matter what the threats, you can't keep a good grapevine down. The paradox is that the greater the effort you exert to control the informal information networks, the less control you will achieve. So perhaps those who want a free flow of information and ideas up, down, and sideways through the organization should be willing to be confronted by the issues and rumors going around and respond to them forthrightly as well, ass's ears and all. Then, with the trust earned, there's a chance that the many ideas and observations held within the organization will flow more freely, perhaps almost as freely as the unofficial info bits that make up a grapevine.

According to the ancient Greeks, Zeus liked to claim that the goddess Athena was born when she burst from his forehead, fully grown, gorgeous, superbly talented, and outfitted in full battle regalia. But Robert Graves, myth teller, says that no one really knew who Athena's parents were, though Athena thought that, given his power and status, it was fine for Zeus to take credit for her creation.

Athena's fate is not unlike that of ideas and observations in an organization. The obvious winners have many parents waiting to take credit, after the fact. But these few obvious winners usually aren't sufficient to constitute the information flow needed to turn goals like "continuous improvement," "learning organization," and "loyalty-based management" into a reality. The task for managers, therefore, is to create homes for the ideas and observations that, at first blush, may be uncomfortable or even unpleasant. For though it's nice to think about the free flow of ideas and observations, the natural flow of information opposes organizational goals: Upward information tends to get censored or suppressed, while downward information is frequently ignored or distorted. And though a few Athenas may come along, fully formed and ready for combat, most useful ideas and observations start out life as fragile infants in somebody's head, and then stay there or wither away for lack of organizational sustenance.

PART THREE

THE EMPOWERMENT CONUNDRUM

Enhancing Individual Action

"I am a second-year Brownie. I got a first-aid badge that really comes in handy. One time after school, Jimmy Lee got hit by a car and was bleeding all over the place. I remembered what to do. I sat down and put my head between my knees to keep from fainting."

—from Fanny Flagg's *Daisy Fay and the Miracle Man*

Empowerment sounds so wonderful in theory: employees find their work enhanced and enriched, and experience dramatic increases in their job satisfaction; employers find their employees more energized and creative, and experience dramatic increases in profitability. In actual operation, however, empowerment programs often fall far short of such promises, leading to disillusionment and bad feeling on all sides.

The reasons for these gaps between the promise and the practice are not hard to find. In some cases, the real operating structures of the organization make it difficult for even the most motivated participants to contribute to the collective goals, as described in the previous three chapters. But there are other impediments that cripple efforts aimed at "empowering" workers, and two of these are discussed in the following chapters.

Chapter 7, "Empower Them Please (But Not Too Much): It's the 'Power' Part That Creates the Rub," argues that in empowerment, as in other human endeavors, it's rare to get something for nothing. Chapter 8, "Judgment, Empowerment, and the Parable of the Talents: Why Judgment Is Essential to Empowerment," illustrates how companies can build shared judgment reservoirs and why, without such reservoirs, employees will make decisions, but not necessarily in ways that will further organizational goals.

Human beings are infinitely complex, each of us a bit odd to lesser or greater extents and each of us odd in slightly different ways, and all of us interacting with a constantly changing environment. Given this inherent complexity, empowerment programs only work when they meet the needs of a particular group of participants in their particular environment. Otherwise, though those to be empowered will surely take action, far too often the actions they take will not be the ones that management intended or expected.

CHAPTER 7

EMPOWER THEM PLEASE (BUT NOT TOO MUCH)

It's the "Power" Part That Creates the Rub

Empowerment 1: The result that ensues when employees understand what "doing a good job" means for their position, are motivated to do so, and are given the tools and autonomy for using their hundred decisions a day toward this purpose; 2: New name for what used to be known as "delegation"; 3: A process, now also sometimes called "employee involvement" or "employee satisfaction" (but never "delegation"), that when done well can scare the living daylights out of corporate chiefs and union executives alike.

Empowerment is one of the biggest waves of the fad-surfing age; management books prescribe it, mission statements proclaim it, corporate executives praise it to the heavens. And, beyond the pervasive jawboning, some companies even invest in it, backing their fine sentiments with formal actions, often packaged under the labels of "employee involvement programs" or "employee satisfaction programs." Yet in an increasing number of cases, the pronouncements and programs aimed at building an empowered workforce leave both employees and their managers cynical, angry, and thoroughly demoralized.

The root cause of the empowerment problem is embedded in the word "empower" itself. The verb "empower" is not new; the year of its earliest recorded use in English was over three centuries ago, in 1648. Nor, once you scrape away all the recent management elaboration, is its meaning hard to understand, now or three hundred years ago; *Webster's Third New International Dictionary* defines the verb as "to give official authority or legal power to." And therein lies the threat, for it's when the "power" at the center of "empowerment" has to be shared that the troubles often begin. And thus it has been since the days of Prometheus.

———————————■———————————

Prometheus the Empowerer: Power-Sharing at the Peak of Olympus

According to the ancient Greeks, it was Prometheus who was the forefather of today's empowerment movement. How this came to be has do with one of the ancient Greek myths about the creation of human beings.

In the Greek litany of deities, first came Mother Earth (Gaea) and Father Heaven (Uranos). Gaea and Uranos in turn sired the Titans, a race of monstrous, giant gods. Among the Titans were Prometheus and his brother, Epimetheus, and the king of the Titans, Cronus. Unfortunately, as sometimes happens in family businesses, Father Heaven and son Cronus didn't get along, since they both wanted to control the universe, leading to a violent battle from which Cronus and the Titans emerged the winners. The Titans, newly victorious, then sired the Olympic gods and goddesses, including Zeus, the son of Cronus. But once again, father and son, neither wishing to share power, didn't get along. In the ensuing battle, this one even more fierce than the previous one, son Zeus and his fellow Olympians vanquished his father Cronus and the other Titans. Among the factors leading to Zeus' victory was the assistance provided by Prometheus and Epimetheus who, though Titans, had sided with the Olympians.

Heavenly battles settled, the next task, according to the myth, was populating the earth with mortal creatures. In reward for their service to the Olympians, Zeus gave this highly important task to Prometheus and Epimetheus. But Epimetheus, whose name means "afterthought" in Greek, acted impulsively and immediately made a hash of the assignment, giving, according to classicist Edith Hamilton, "all the best gifts to the animals, strength and swiftness and courage and shrewd cunning, fur and feathers and wings and shells and the like—until no good was left for men, no protective covering and no quality to make them a match for the beasts." Looking at the results, Epimetheus "too late, as always" regretted his actions and turned to his brother for help.

Prometheus, whose Greek name translates as "fore-thought" (exactly as one would hope for the forefather of empowerment), considered the problem carefully, made his plan, and then swung into action. The solution, he decided, required humans to gain access to some of the same powers the Olympians had. Fire, up to then the sole possession of the Olympians, was the perfect candidate, since it would allow these otherwise defenseless creatures to learn crafts and fend for themselves. But the Olympians didn't like sharing power any more than the Titans had. Therefore Prometheus crept into Olympus, stole one white-hot coal from the hearth of the goddess Hestia, concealed it in a giant stalk of fennel, and brought it back to earth, still aglow. The gods still had the other coals in Hestia's hearth and could still light as many fires as they wished, but now humans could do so as well.

"And now, though feeble and short-lived, Mankind has flaming fire and therefrom learns many crafts."

—from the myth of Prometheus, as told by Hesiod, around eighth century B.C.

Zeus was not amused. Having fought a bloody battle in order to gain power, he was hardly pleased to find that Prometheus had, in the words of the fifth-century B.C. poet Aeschylus, "[given] to mortals honors not their due." Zeus therefore created a punishment to fit the enormity of the crime, causing his servants, Force and Violence, to bind Prometheus to a mountain where an eagle came daily, forever, to feast on the Titan's liver. The fact that Prometheus' actions, while empowering the humans, had neither diminished the gods of Olympus in any way nor reduced the powers of these gods, was irrelevant. Clearly, the gods of Olympus did not take kindly to empowerment if it meant sharing *their* power.

"Those who have been once intoxicated with power, and have derived any kind of emolument from it, even but for one year, can never willingly abandon it."

—Edmund Burke (1729–1797)

From Fights on Olympus to Fites in Peoria: Power-Sharing in the Corner Office

In modern organizations, the "power" at the heart of "empowerment" is decision-making power. Empowerment in such organizations therefore requires managers to share some of their decision-making power with subordinates, similar to Prometheus' sharing of the Olympians' fire with humankind. More specifically, it typically requires sharing the decisions for setting the goals of an effort or, for a given set of goals, for determining the means by which these goals will be met. Unfortunately, like the gods of Olympus, many modern managers find real power sharing to be impossibly difficult. Worse, unlike the gods of Olympus, modern managers can take back the decision-making power shared through empowerment programs, though at a high price: the demotivation of the very people whose energies and judgments are critical to the success of the enterprise as a whole. A lesson to be learned is that it's dangerous to play with the fire of empowerment if you aren't willing to share the power.

Consider the case of Caterpillar Tractor Co., whose Olympus is in Peoria, Illinois, and whose workers are represented by the United Auto Workers, and about whom some might say that the gods of both the executive suite and the union hall have no more fondness for the power sharing part of empowerment than did the gods that the ancient Greeks worshipped. Cat's experiment with wider sharing of decision-making power began in 1986, when the company launched an employee satisfaction program (ESP) to involve workers in decisions about running its plants. That the company and union agreed to attempt any sharing of decision-making power was itself remarkable. Only four years before, the company had weathered a bitter 204-day strike when, threatened by the strides being made by archrival Komatsu, management tried to hold the line on union wages. In addition, within the larger organized labor community, some were arguing that empowerment programs were manipulative, snares and delusions, nothing more than clever ploys to reduce union power and take advantage of workers.

Yet, as reported in *The Wall Street Journal*, Cat workers and Cat managers made the empowerment program a success. At the company's Aurora, Illinois, plant alone, employee ideas saved more than $13 million in three years, by improving processes, cutting defects, and minimizing downtime. Involvement in ESP soared; by 1991, about half of Aurora's 2,200 UAW workers were participating on 110 ESP teams. Recalled one member of management, an engineer: "When we went to [team] meetings, there wasn't any such thing as union and management." And from a member of the union: "For the first time, I felt when I came to work, I made some difference."

Five years later, on November 5, 1991, the program slammed to an abrupt halt. George Schaefer, chairman of Caterpillar when the ESP program started, had worked hard for better relations with the union. His successor, Donald Fites, who took over in 1990, saw the situation differently. Fites wanted to stop "pattern bargaining," which linked the labor contract at Caterpillar with UAW contracts at similar U.S. companies like John Deere. Believing it counter to the company's interest to build on the foundation created through ESP and seek solutions that would have elevated the power sharing from the plant floor to the executive suite, Fites chose a head-on confrontation. To Fites, the path was clear: "How much is it worth," he asked "to run your own company?" The union responded by suspending all ESP activities, and going back to its old adversarial methods. Commented a union official, the whole experience taught "a simple lesson that we should have learned a long time ago: not to trust management."

Since then, many of Cat's U.S. workers have reverted to the classic behavior of workers who, in response to the many decision points they face each day, choose not to go beyond what the rule books say. So, as later reported by *The New York Times,* Lance Vaughn, at Cat's Decatur, Illinois, plant, went back to the rulebook way of attaching the large hose first in the off-highway trucks he helps assemble, and then reaching behind the large hose to attach several smaller hoses, instead of the other way around which he knows is faster. Morris Delbridge, at the same plant, stopped calling the repairmen himself when his equipment malfunctioned and stopped helping to diagnose the cause of the breakdowns; the rule book gives those jobs to the foreman and Delbridge went back to working by the rules. Rich Clausel, one of the UAW workers who helped lead the ESP program at the Aurora plant and who had harbored great dreams of what Cat workers and management could do together, summed up the post-ESP environment at the Aurora facility this way: "[Now] all you see is people doing the minimum to get by."

The Cat program had led to significant achievements—deeper understanding of the connection between individual action and collective success, better decision-making, and increased trust across levels and constituencies within the organizations—and still the end result was less commitment, less involvement, and less trust.

Will Cat be hurt by this loss of employee involvement in its U.S. operations? Short term, probably not. Its tough stance in the union negotiations yielded significant savings in labor costs. In addition, its investment of nearly $2 billion in improving the efficiency of operations during the 1985–1990 time period, when the company was faring poorly, especially against Komatsu, has led to substantial savings in operating costs; as just one example, the days required for producing a tractor dropped from twenty-five to six. The results of these savings, combined with the recovering worldwide markets for earthmoving equipment and the weakening dollar (helping Caterpillar's U.S.-produced exports) and the strengthening yen (hurting Komatsu's Japan-produced exports), put the company back in the black again in 1993, after several years of severe losses.

Long term, though, the costs to Cat in its U.S. plants are likely to be substantial, though these costs will be difficult to quantify, as they will reflect missed opportunities and lost ideas. The nearly invisible source of the harm is the hundred or so times over the course of a day each person faces the opportunity either to take an action that changes the status quo or to do nothing. This is what I called in my first book, *How Corporate Truths Become Competitive Traps*, the "hundred decisions a day" of every worker in every company, from the pinnacle of the pyramid to its base. The classic studies of the average number of work activities are one indicator of the number of times each person has the opportunity to make a decision either to do nothing or to intervene: Mintzberg's study of CEOs showed 15 work sessions with other people, plus review of 36 documents per day; Choron's study of the presidents of smaller companies tallied 77 activities of various types per day; and Guest's study of foremen recorded 583 discrete activities per day. Multiply a hundred decisions a day by all the workdays by all the workers at Cat's U.S. plants, and you can begin to see the likely gap between what could be and what will be.

"They say that power corrupts and perhaps it does. What I know, in myself, is quite a different thing. That power corrupts the people it is exercised over."

—Raymond Williams, British academician (b. 1921)

"The world is moved along, not only by the mighty shoves of its heroes, but also by the aggregate of the tiny pushes of each honest worker."

—Helen Keller (1880–1968)

Let There Be Lux: The Upside of Power-Sharing Beyond the Normal Bounds

The gap between "what could be" with empowerment and what will be lost when a workforce is turned off is often wider than many people imagine. Consider what happened in Kodak's ailing Black & White Film Division during the late eighties and early nineties. At that time, Kodak was under assault. Lower than expected quarterlies, the specter of Polaroid's lawsuit claiming patent infringements, labor issues, and environmental problems all had Wall Street turning up the heat on the company and its management. Kodak responded by reorganizing the company into "flows" that cut across the company's traditional functions with the goal of improving performance. Needing improvement in particular was Kodak Park, the company's major manufacturing site in the United States, where performance had been abysmal. And among the worst performers at Kodak Park was the flow for making black-and-white film.

When Stephen Frangos was put in charge of Black & White's turnaround, he found high waste, mountains of inventory (much of which was used as a hedge to ensure quality), long cycle times, an on-time record of only 33 percent—and the real risk that, without drastic improvements, B&W's work would be transferred to other Kodak plants around the world. Frangos's conclusion, as described in his book *Team Zebra*, was that the only possible foundation for the turnaround was the division's 1,500 employees. He therefore set the goal of creating an environment in which people could share in the power to create the required solutions. Within a year, Black & White had improved significantly on all key dimensions.

Black & White was able to rack up this impressive record because of the power shared with, and accepted by, people like Paul Lux. A twenty-seven-year Kodak veteran, Lux had started out at the company as a floor-sweeper operator. He eventually trained to become a process analyst, a job known internally as a "PA," responsible for ensuring that the chemicals used to make the light-sensitive emulsion "cooked" properly. The difficulty of this job was that the melt took place in giant sealed kettles. And though the kettles were fitted with instruments that could measure some aspects in any one melt, no one could predict whether the batch would be usable until it came out of the kettle.

Though his new job as a PA was to control and troubleshoot the melting process, Lux decided that his mission would be to create a system that would provide a window into the kettles in real time. His reasoning was that real-time measurement would allow adjustments to be made while there were still ways to save the melt, thereby preventing the costs associated with the labor and ingredients lost in a wasted batch as well as the downtime incurred by operations left idle until the new batch could be delivered. The commitment of Frangos and his management team to share their power gave Lux the authorization he needed. After learning about a T30 Allen Bradley terminal scheduled for the dumpster, he and two fellow workers, Jimmy Culmone and Bill Zinner, spent their lunch hours and coffee breaks wiring the computer to the mixing kettles. Two months later, the "data highway," as Lux dubbed it, was in operation.

Lux's data highway, though made of crude parts, stunned the engineering staff, normally the people who would design and requisition such a system. But unlike Zeus, the engineers were thrilled with the results of their power having been shared with Lux and his friends. Inspired by the data highway, these engineers then proposed and received funding for a state-of-the-art system for monitoring the kettles. And Lux was thrilled with the results of having shared in the power to transform an organization: "We had two cans and a string by comparison to the new system. But they never would have thought to design a system if it wasn't for the old data highway. I feel like we were pioneers on the frontier—we opened a path to the future."

> "Soldiers win battles and generals get the credit."
>
> —Napoléon Bonaparte (1769–1821)

Though these stories about Caterpillar and Kodak represent two extremes of empowerment in the workplace, both show the collective wallop packed by the many decisions made by many individuals at all levels in an organization and how that wallop can work for or against the enterprise in question. T George Harris, former editor of both *Psychology Today* and the *Harvard Business Review*, points out that Count Tolstoy wrote *War and Peace* to demonstrate the same idea. Excited by the Theory of Limits used by Leibnitz to build differential calculus—wherein an infinite number of infinitely small areas add up to measurable space—Tolstoy's story showed how an infinite number of small human acts add up to war or peace.

Taking Tolstoy's argument one step further, unit executives like Stephen Frangos and corporate executives like Donald Fites may make the big moves, but the hundreds of daily decisions by people like Paul Lux, Jimmy Culmone, and Bill Zinner at Kodak—and by Lance Vaughn, Morris Delbridge, and Rich Clausel at Caterpillar—add up to opportunities created—or opportunities forgone. Jawboning about "empowerment" but doing nothing more than mouthing kind words and fine sentiments, or enacting empowerment programs without a fundamental commitment to finding ways to consider decisions jointly, are each great ways to ensure that the path of forgone opportunities will be the one that most employees will travel.

The Mess in the Middle: Power-Sharing in the Trenches

One of the most common barriers to empowerment is not the people at Fites's or Frangos's levels, but rather by those in the midsections of the pyramid. Or as a union member at Weirton Steel told me after the company became employee-owned, the real obstacle to the progress that needed to be made in the mills was "the mess in the middle."

The observation that it's the middle managers who generate the most resistance to empowerment efforts shouldn't be surprising, since the power that senior executives decree will be shared in many empowerment efforts is not their own power but rather the power of their middle managers. And it's therefore the middle managers who most typically see their authority diminished when those who they (used) to supervise are given greater latitude for choosing how work in their areas can better be done.

Both Cat and Kodak appear to have handled this part of their empowerment program well, but many companies

What OSHA did after two employees of a plumbing company jumped into a trench, which their company had not dug, to rescue a workman buried alive by a wall of the trench that had just collapsed on him:

Fined the company of the rescuers $7,875 for:
• entering the trench without wearing the regulation hard hats, and
• not taking the prescribed steps for trench wall reinforcement and water seepage prevention

The fine was reversed after Senator Dirk Kempthorne, R-Idaho, intervened.

—stories in *The Idaho Statesman*, reporting on the May 11, 1993, incident

falter when they throw their frontline managers into a new, "empowered" environment. Imagine Zeus as a frontline manager. Here's a guy who is used to getting things done by yelling, threatening, and punishing his subordinates (not to mention letting loose a thunderbolt or two, Zeus's traditional reaction to events not to his liking). Now tell this manager that he needs to be like Prometheus; a coach, a helper, the kind of god who thinks about how to help his team members achieve their goals, works to make sure they have adequate resources to support their efforts, and contributes the kind of farsighted judgment that complements the day-to-day expertise of his new colleagues. And, to make sure that our Zeus-like manager will fail, tell his subordinates that their scopes have been enlarged, but neither redefine the role that Zeus now finds himself in, nor provide him with appropriate training, nor revise the measures by which his performance is judged, nor modify his compensation plan. In this scenario Zeus is likely to use his hundred decisions a day to block change, not to encourage it.

For some Zeus-like managers, of course, the Olympian habits of command and control are so ingrained that no amount of other changes in the system will allow them to cope productively with subordinates with whom they now have to share some of their powers. These managers, no matter what their rhetoric, will only create barriers unless they are reassigned— and if they are not, their obstructionist behavior will create a greater sense of disappointment and betrayal than if the E-word had never been uttered at all.

But others can make the change, as long as the company puts its money and organizational muscle firmly behind its romantic words about its empowered workforce, just as the frontline managers in both Caterpillar's Aurora plant and Kodak's Black & White plant did. And for managers who make the transition, there is a bonus: the opportunity to take part in an expanding scope of decision-making—and to take part in the satisfaction and pride that come from being part of a team that generates and executes more successful ideas than would be possible had their power not been shared as widely. Power-sharing can pay—even for those whose power is shared.

------------■------------

I was asked recently by an industry association to run a workshop on employee empowerment for the top executives of its member companies. After I told the story of Prometheus, one CEO leaned over to another and said, "I thought she was going to talk about empowerment. She's talking about power sharing. I'm not going to share my power with anybody!" But there's no way to promise empowerment and get around the root word of the term. Those who espouse empowering their subordinates (or have been instructed to do so) but who do not wish to share their power—no matter how high up they sit in their hierarchies and no matter whether their hierarchy sits within the company or within the union—will inevitably sabotage any empowerment program, even the most beautifully designed. In so doing, they will also reduce the flow of initiatives and ideas that can contribute to a company's advantage. For those managers, the better course of action is to avoid speaking the lingo of empowerment so they don't set false expectations—while making sure that they provide other compensation for those employees who would otherwise derive psychic income from participating in a broader scope of decision-making.

In the end, though, managers cannot eliminate the decision-making activities of subordinates. Decreasing the scope of legitimate decision-making to a fraction of what it could be doesn't reduce the hundred decisions a day—it merely tells employees that a variety of areas are off-limits to their expertise, regardless of how valuable their inputs could be, and motivates them to respond to each of the choice points they do confront daily with the least effort and enthusiasm possible. In addition, not giving them tools and information to support their efforts to do their jobs well just increases the odds that many of the "daily hundred" will be made poorly and indifferently. The more important question, therefore, is not whether to empower but how to make the sharing of decision-making power work well and profitably. The ancient Greeks might have agreed that sharing power is the way of the world. After all, Prometheus did get the fire to mankind despite Zeus, and at the end of the story, Zeus did allow Hercules to both kill the eagle nibbling at Prometheus's liver and release Prometheus from the rock, thus demonstrating that even the gods at the top of the steepest hierarchies can find ways to live with the realities of power-sharing.

"When I resist . . . the concentration of power, I am resisting the processes of death, because the concentration of power is what always precedes the destruction of human initiative, and, therefore of human energy."

—Woodrow Wilson, in 1912, when he was governor of New Jersey

CHAPTER 8

JUDGMENT, EMPOWERMENT, AND THE PARABLE OF THE TALENTS

Why Judgment Is Essential to Empowerment

Judgment The basis for every decision that every person in an organization makes every day and therefore, often though unaccountably, a matter that receives little attention.

Empowerment programs are big business. As one indicator of how big they have become, consider a 1994 survey conducted by CSC Index in which, of the 497 U.S. firms and 124 European firms responding, 84 percent and 70 percent respectively said that they had some sort of "employee empowerment" program in place. Many of these programs will not succeed nearly to management's expectations, however, due to insufficient attention to one vital prerequisite of empowerment: ensuring that the judgment used by those empowered is appropriate to the decisions entrusted to them. The parable of the talents, from the Book of Matthew, provides a perspective on why this is so.

In the parable, Matthew 25:14–30, a master who was about to go on a trip entrusted his wealth to his three servants for safe-keeping until his return. The master's wealth was in the form of eight "talents," with each talent the equivalent of more than fifteen years' wages for the average laborer. The master gave five talents to the first servant, two talents to the second, and one talent to the third, apportioning the talents "to each according to his ability."

When the master came back from his travels, he summoned the three servants to settle the accounts. The first had invested his five talents and now had ten talents to return; the second had done the same and now had four talents. To each the master said: "Well done, good and faithful servant, you have been faithful over a little, I will set you over much." Things did not go as well for the third servant, however. He returned the *original* talent he had been given, with this explanation: "Master, I knew you to be a hard man, reaping where you did not sow, and gathering where you did not winnow; so I was afraid, and I went and hid your talent in the ground. Here you have what is yours." To which the master responded: "You knew that I reap where I have not sowed, and gather where I have not winnowed? Then you ought to have invested my money with the bankers, and at my coming I should have received what was my own with interest." And with that, the master "cast the worthless servant into the outer darkness; there men will weep and gnash their teeth."

In its Biblical context, this parable has a clear moral; those who are faithful and apply their talents diligently are rewarded for their faithfulness and diligence. But, if you can, imagine this story having taken place in an average corporation, anyplace in the world. And now consider this question: *in a corporate setting, how was the third guy to know that he was supposed to invest the talent?*

What happened in the late 1960s when the MIT Artificial Intelligence Laboratory designed its first robot to build a tower of blocks: The robot was unable to build the tower, because it kept trying to construct the tower from the top down. Despite all the hours of programming, no one had remembered to put in the decision rule that towers have to be built from the bottom up.

In many companies, managers often feel like the master in the parable of the talents: having delegated more decisions, they find themselves looking at the results through a haze of what they think the decision-makers "should have known" and "ought to have done." Yet, the third servant had not violated the instructions he had been given; he had guarded the asset that had been entrusted to him and returned it to his employer when requested. (And had the story been set in the United States just after the Savings & Loan crisis in the early 1990s, he might have even looked like a hero in the context of the performance of his two colleagues.) The difference between the three servants, all of whom were given the same instructions, was judgment; the ability to forecast the likely consequences of one's actions and then to assess the fit between these likely results and some larger goal.

In a corporate setting, managerial mutterings about the "should have knowns" and "ought to have dones" similarly indicate a judgment deficit. Responsibility for this deficit does not start with the frontline decision-makers, however. Rather, its source is the managers who have assumed that each person's knowledge of his or her work environment provides a sufficient base for good decisions. The flaw in this common managerial assumption is that it ignores the importance of what I call the "judgment reservoir," a pool of judgment, widely and deeply shared, that informs the decisions made by everyone throughout the unit or organization.

Building the judgment reservoir for any company that believes it will profit by the broader empowerment of its employees starts at the top, with the core beliefs of the leader of the organization or unit. These core beliefs often have nothing or little to do with what is written on paper, official policies or corporate pronouncements. Rather they reflect a person's deepest convictions about the kind of actions that will lead to corporate success, about how competitors operate and what customers need, and, most profoundly, about the nature of human beings and what makes them tick. It is these beliefs that drive, directly or indirectly, the processes and criteria used for hiring and training employees, for assigning tasks and designing jobs, for evaluating performance and providing feedback, for deciding how to motivate and compensate personnel, for determining how much and what kind of information to share, and for defining what "doing a good job" means. And it is the actions that come out of these core beliefs that, in turn, are a prime determinant of the size and depth of the judgment reservoir within the organization.

Restaurants are great places to observe the judgment reservoir and how it can contribute to creating a competitive edge—or to reinforcing a competitive impediment. Restaurants are interesting because almost all of them say they are in the business of delighting customers, with virtually every high-end restaurant emphasizing its superlative food, its attractive ambiance and, of

> "Someone defined horse sense as the good judgment horses have that prevents them from betting on people. But we have to bet on people, and I place my bets more often on high motivation than on any other quality except judgment."
>
> —John W. Gardner, writing in *Stanford Magazine*

course, its thoughtful service. But providing thoughtful service requires good judgment on the part of every frontline worker in the restaurant, a nearly impossible condition to meet when the organizational judgment reservoir is shallow. Consider the experience that my husband and I and two guests had at a trendy, upscale restaurant I will call The Chez Tres Chic, a disguised name in a true story.

The Parable of the Tainted Potion

The Chez Tres Chic, a Boston-area institution for some years, is an expensive restaurant, famous for its food. If it had a motto, which of course it doesn't, it might choose the tag line "cutting-edge cuisine." The night we were there, which was several months after a new owner had taken over, the food was far from stellar, however. The poultry dish was nearly raw, and the soft-shell crabs, ordered by a native of Maryland where this dish is a specialty, had not been properly cleaned, leaving some hard, salty, inedible substance where there should have been sweet crabmeat. The final insult, however, was the dead cockroach floating in my water glass. And that's when our lesson in judgment as the hidden ingredient in the recipe for effective empowerment began.

First, the waitress came over to clear our dishes. After we pointed out the cockroach, she apologized and asked if I'd like another glass of water. And that was it. The waitress did not go to the maitre d' to find out what she should do. Nor did she take it on her own to offer any recompense for the situation. This was a lost opportunity for The Chez Tres Chic because at that point it would have taken relatively little—say, a bottle of sparkling water, after-dinner drinks on the house, or cancellation of some small part of the bill—to have left us feeling like we had been treated well despite a rather obvious mishap.

When we arrived home, we called the maitre d' and explained the situation. This time there was no apology; instead she retorted, quite disdainfully, that had we brought this situation to her attention in the restaurant, she would have ripped up our check, but since we had waited until we arrived at home (only minutes away

Diner: Waiter, waiter, what's that fly doing in my soup?
Waiter: It looks like the back-stroke, sir.

—Vaudevillian joke

from the restaurant), she would only reduce our check by half. Again this was a lost opportunity, for though it would have taken more than when we were at the restaurant, we still could have been placated by a sincere apology and some recompense that was not accompanied by a gratuitous lecture on why it was our fault that the amends were "only" one amount and not another.

Progressively more irritated by the treatment we had received at The Chez Tres Chic, the next day I called the new owner, mentioning the name of mutual friends who are also restauranteurs. Again there was no apology. Instead, in tones of great hauteur, the owner informed me that "*most* people love The Chez Tres Chic," and further, that since he was busy at that moment, he would call me back the next day. He did not. We later learned that he did telephone our mutual friends to inquire as to whether they thought the complaint was legit; perhaps he entertained the notion that one of us was the kind of customer who carries a pillbox of various dead insects to restaurants. Whatever the reason, the charge never came through on our credit card bill. We also, despite the owner's promise, never received any further communication directly from the restaurant; no telephone call, no letter. This was a more costly fix than the other options, not only due to the revenues the restaurant lost from us for that meal, but also due to the future revenues lost, for though we had been regular patrons of The Chez Tres Chic, we have never been back since our unfortunate entomological interlude and its unsatisfactory aftermath.

A bug in the water glass at a fine restaurant or a wayward bolt on an assembly line are the kind of problems where empowering the people closest to the situation almost always provides the best and least expensive solution, since the further away the solution occurs, the more expense it involves—in current costs (for rework, repairs, or refunds) and, even more importantly, forgone future revenues (loss of customers and reputation). The judgment used by the waitress and the maitre d', though deviating from this principle of fixing a problem as close to its source as possible, were consistent within the

Colonel Hall: "Waitress!"
Polly: "Yes."
Colonel Hall: "There's a *hair* in my mousse."
Polly: "Well, don't talk too loud or everybody will want one."

—dialogue from the "Gourmet Night" episode of John Cleese's *Fawlty Towers*

"The question 'Who ought to be boss?' is like asking, 'Who ought to be the tenor in the quartet?' Obviously, the man who can sing tenor."

—Henry Ford (1863–1947)

internal environment of The Chez Tres Chic; the decisions made by both of them fit within the core beliefs held by the owner of the restaurant. The judgment deficit at The Chez Tres Chic started at the top.

The Parable of the Frontline Heroes

In contrast to the experience at The Chez Tres Chic, the miraculous can occur in organizations where the shared reservoirs of judgment honor both what the consumers seek and what the employees can (and are proud to) provide. Federal Express and Boston's Beth Israel Hospital (known throughout Boston as the BI) are classic examples.

Consider two of the frontline heroes from Federal Express:

- When the van that Mark Horton, a courier in Oklahoma City, broke down, he radioed for a second van. When the second van, having been transloaded, wouldn't start, Horton walked to a fellow courier's home, borrowed a bicycle and a backpack from his friend's son, made the nine-mile delivery loop on the bike with his packages stuffed into the backpack—and completed his route on time.

- When Alonda Martinez, a service agent in Los Angeles, received a call from an infuriated customer whose sealed bid had not yet been received and couldn't find another company to expedite the package, she jumped into her own car, drove the 115 miles to the delivery site, and arrived just barely in time for the bid opening, thereby saving this FedEx customer millions of dollars in what otherwise would have been a forfeited bid.

Similarly, the heroes at the BI, a Harvard teaching hospital which is justly renowned for its physicians, include *everyone*—and not just the physicians—who works on the frontlines serving patients and their families. Patient testimonials highlight just a few of these frontline heroes:

- from an outpatient who had pointed out a problem in a waiting area, "I wanted to let you know how impressed I was at the speed and sensitivity with which the problem was handled . . . In particular, Dr. Klapholz's assistant Michelle, Dr. Niloff's assistant Kim, and Dr. Niloff himself showed a tremendous level of concern and caring—both for me and the patient who was directly affected. Most importantly, they showed a complete willingness to rectify the problem for the good of everyone."

- from the daughter of an elderly patient who died in the ICU, "The nurses, two in particular, took every possible measure to ensure that my father's comfort was maintained and that his dignity was respected. They were beautifully sensitive to my mother. She was made comfortable and received support throughout the night she spent in the ICU room with my Dad. I can't describe how important it was to her . . . that the nurse saw her through her most painful moments."

- and, from a new patient who wrote this to the director of his former hospital, "the contrast between [the BI and your hospital], two large city hospitals, is so great that I write to urge you to visit Beth Israel and find the secret of their astounding success. . . . My experience at [your] hospital over the past 10 years is that not only are the staff persons uninterested, but unable to give directions, slovenly, on occasion rude, and with no sense of urgency or keeping timely appointments."

What's important about these heroes is that they are *not* the exceptions; they are the *rule* at both FedEx and the BI, creating for both companies reputations for service that outstrip their competitors. And among the reasons for the effectiveness of these empowered employees is not only the fit between the judgment used and the core beliefs of their senior managers, but also the heavy investments both organizations have made in the innate judgment and the developed judgment of their people.

Of Innate Judgment and Developed Judgment

Building on strength is always easier than building on weakness. This would seem an obvious proposition were it not for the many companies that talk about an empowered workforce and then don't obsess about—and invest heavily in—the processes and criteria for recruiting and hiring decisions, designing jobs and compensation schemes, evaluating performance and giving feedback, and deciding on promotions and work assignments. Both FedEx and the BI make these investments, which in turn create a self-reinforcing cycle; people with similar values and standards of judgment are attracted to, and are attractive to, these organizations. Conversely, people whose judgment doesn't match the corporate values and standards of judgment will neither be attracted to, nor be attractive to, such an employer. Imagine a waitress with a strong orientation toward ensuring that the people she waits on have a good experience interviewing for a job at The Chez Tres Chic. It's unlikely that The Chez Tres Chic management would see her as a special find, and it's also unlikely that she would see The Chez Tres Chic as her first choice for her new job.

But such processes and criteria for maximizing the innate judgment available to the organization are not sufficient to create the entire judgment reservoir. That's where developed judgment comes in. In some companies, this development is inadvertently subverted by managers who punish and ridicule those who don't make the same decisions as their managers would have (or think they would have.) Since judgment grows by making mistakes and learning from them, this management style typically leads people to be as conservative as possible, severely constraining the options for action they will consider. Scott Adams, creator of the comic strip *Dilbert*, experienced this when, early in his work life, he took a job as a bank teller: "We were constantly told, 'You have to use your judgment.' But then if we cashed a bad check, which happened every day, we'd get yelled at. But there were so many rules that if you followed them all . . . the line [of customers] would literally go out the door and wrap around the building. . . . The point is that if I . . . hadn't feared that my supervisor would call me stupid when I made a mistake, I would have tried harder to do the right thing and would have been much more efficient."

Conversely, companies can actively invest in developing the judgment within their organizations. One place to start is with the creation of frameworks for action based on a shared understanding of the organization's goals and overall strategy for reaching these goals. Mission statements, when carefully crafted and clearly communicated, are one mechanism for creating such frameworks. (For more on the mysteries of mission statements, see "Mission Indecipherable," pp. 15–23.) So are corporate measures and formal training programs, especially when buttressed by generous sharing of information. But though most organizations have a welter of metrics and documents and programs that are intended to guide behavior, at many the result is a communications traffic jam; a surplus of numbers and words and courses but little forward progress. Both FedEx and the BI have cut through the clutter, though in quite different ways.

At FedEx, CEO Fred Smith set out to differentiate his company from the competition by guaranteeing that FedEx will "absolutely, positively" deliver its customers' packages on time. The company has had clear statements of its purpose and highly effective training programs. In 1988, the company did even more, and amplified and clarified this goal with its "SQI"— service quality indicator. Federal Express's Total Corporate SQI is the sum of the average daily failure points for the following components:

problem to be avoided	weighted failure points
Domestic SQI:	
Lost Package	10 points
Damaged Package	10 points
Wrong Day, Delivered Late	5 points
Complaint Reopened (not resolved)	3 points
Traces	3 points
Late Pick-Up Stops	3 points
Invoice Adjustment Requested	1 point
Missing Proofs of Delivery	1 point
Right Day, Delivered Late	1 point
International SQI	1 point

The construction of this measure makes it evident what problems are most important, providing a hierarchy of priorities that is clear for everyone who works at FedEx. (For more information on the effectiveness of FedEx's SQI, see "Total Quality Mayhem," pp. 173–182). And the SQI, combined with FedEx's tough hiring standards, clear communications, exuberant celebrations of its heroes, and rigorous training program, creates a framework for action that supported Alonda Martinez's judgment that, even though the problem of the infuriated customer on the other end of the phone was only worth one point in the SQI system, it was worth millions of dollars to the customer and therefore worth a heroic effort on her part.

Similarly, at the BI, CEO Mitchell Rabkin and his top management team have always been clear that the BI always puts its patients and their families first. Hiring standards at the BI have always been high and rigorous, with an enormous investment in finding people with the innate judgment that will fit in and contribute to this patient-centered environment. And though the BI has had neither an SQI nor a customer-service training program, its way to create its clarion call, in my view, was its "Statement on the Rights of Patients," published in 1972, six years after Rabkin became president. This "patient bill of rights" was a pioneering declaration, considered radical by some, the first such manifesto for a U.S. hospital. Excerpted here are the preamble of the 1972 document, the first three of its seven articles, the beginning of its fourth article, and its last several sentences:

> Beth Israel Hospital, its doctors, nurses and entire staff are committed to assure you excellent care as our patient. It has always been our policy to respect your individuality and your dignity. This listing is published to be certain that you know of the long-standing rights that are yours as a Beth Israel patient.
>
> 1. You have the right to the best care medically indicated for your problem, that is, to the most appropriate treatment without considerations such as race, color, religion, national origin or the source of payment for your care.
>
> 2. You have the right to be treated respectfully by others; to be addressed by your proper name and without undue familiarity; to be listened to when you have a question or desire more information and to receive an appropriate and helpful response.

3. You have the right to expect that your individuality will be respected and that differences in cultural and educational background will be taken into account.

4. You have the right to privacy. . . .

If you feel that you are not being treated fairly or properly, you have the right to discuss this with your doctor, nurse, unit manager, other health worker, or the Administrator-on-Call. You may also write a letter to the General Director, Beth Israel Hospital, Boston 02215. All correspondence will receive prompt and personal attention.

This message reflects the interest and philosophy of the entire staff of Beth Israel Hospital.

Mitchell T. Rabkin, M.D.
General Director

Many hospitals now have similar statements, and many of these are honored more in the breach than in the practice. But at the BI, this "patient bill of rights" added to the momentum of the organization because it *reinforced*, by articulating more clearly than ever before, the framework for action that Rabkin and his colleagues were *already building*: the best care, delivered with respect. It added to the judgment reservoir, by providing a clear statement of what "best care, delivered with respect" means—and then providing that statement to the consumers of the care. In consequence, the patient experience at the BI really is different than what typically happens at other health care systems; problems are resolved quickly by frontline people; nurses and doctors do spend extra time to make patients and their families more comfortable; and there really is an atmosphere of caring and helpfulness that permeates the place.

"Thank you, Beth Israel, you've given me the right to think positive."

—Albert L. (Dapper) O'Neil, Boston City Council President, commenting on his experience at the BI for treatment of a serious illness

When the Definition of Judgment Has to Change

Organizations like FedEx and the BI are inspiring examples of why creating and building the judgment reservoir is a prerequisite to creating and building an effective empowered workforce—and of how such empowered workforces can in turn become competitive weapons when their actions are linked to the strategies of their organizations. But even among the best, and no matter how well communicated, the task of maintaining the judgment reservoir requires constant reinforcement, review, and revision. Environments change—whether for delivery of packages or of babies—sometimes with monstrous leaps. The new world of health care delivery in the United States, for example, is requiring providers to cut costs relentlessly and create new alliances never before needed. The challenge for an organization like the BI, perhaps the largest challenge it has ever faced, is to revise its framework for action to meet this new environment while maintaining its reverence for its patients and their families.

> "If we could first know where we are, and whither we are tending, we could then better judge what to do, and how to do it."
>
> —Abraham Lincoln, 1858, the opening sentence of his "house divided" speech

And although health care is an extreme case, even in stable environments it's still important to keep learning and, based on the new understandings, refine the framework for action to make it easier for everyone to know what "doing a good job" really means. That's what Jan Carlzon of Scandinavian Airlines System learned when he found that SAS's newly empowered frontline employees were "delighting the customers"—but not raising SAS's market share. The reason: SAS employees defined customer satisfaction as extra service: holding planes to wait for connecting passengers, missing meals, or late-arriving flight attendants above the minimum complement required. But business passengers want to get where they are going on time. With this information, Carlzon subsequently defined the SAS framework for action this way:

> Our first priority is safety, second is punctuality, and third is other services. So, if you risk flight safety by leaving on time, you have acted outside the framework of your authority. The same is true if you don't leave on time because you are missing two catering boxes of meat. That's what I mean by framework. *You give people a framework, and within the framework you let people act.*

Creating and maintaining a judgment reservoir that is widely and deeply shared is the secret weapon of many organizations that seem to bring a competitive advantage to every encounter in their market place; their advantage truly is their people. One way to test the judgment reservoir in your organization is to start with a rigorous review of your own deepest beliefs about what you think the people you work with "should" know versus what the evidence suggests they do know. Every instance of a shortfall against this standard is a warning sign of a judgment deficit in your organization, one that can lead to many people acting like the third guy in the parable, hiding their talents in mounds of dirt, no matter how many employee empowerment programs you have in place.

PART FOUR

THROUGH A GLASS DARKLY

Determining What the Customers Really Want

"A great many people think they are thinking when they are merely rearranging their prejudices."

—William James (1842–1910)

For all the talk about delighting the customer, one factor is often neglected: the incredible difficulty of seeing through our own prejudices to what the customers *really* want or could want and how they make their choices among the alternatives available to them. And this is true whether the customers in question are employees on the other side of corporate paychecks or buyers on the other side of corporate invoices. The reason stems from a core problem in human perception: even with deep commitment to the various mantras of serving the customer and heavy investment in associated research, one tends to see what one expects and prefers, rather than what the *other party* expects or prefers (or, given the right circumstances, could expect or prefer in the future).

The three chapters that follow explore this dilemma further. Chapter 9, "Customer Dissatisfaction: Three Myths of the 'Customer-Sat' Movement," suggests some ways to keep the essentials of customer loyalty from getting lost in the rhetoric and surveys employed in the name of customer satisfaction. Chapter 10, "The (Inharmonious) Voice of the Customer: Seeking the

Irritating Whine That Must Be Heard," delves further into some of the requirements of conducting market research that actually clarifies what the customers want, rather than further clouding the corporation's view of the market, as more typically happens. And Chapter 11, "'Customer Focus' and Other Product Development Delusions: What Love Has Got to Do With It," explores ways to circumvent one of the most formidable barriers to attaining true customer focus: falling so deeply in love with one's own products and services that true customer focus becomes impossible.

It's a good thing to espouse the gospel of customer delight, especially in categories in which customers have many alternatives from which to choose or in which new alternatives are appearing. But it is an even better thing to learn how to keep from rearranging one's own prejudices in order to increase the odds of accurately determining what the customers want—or could want.

CHAPTER 9

CUSTOMER DISSATISFACTION

Three Myths of the "Customer-Sat" Movement

Customer Satisfaction: 1: *New name for the oldest premise in business—that unless customers are more satisfied with your product than they are with their next best alternative, they won't be your customers for long; 2: New name for one type of standard market research, often designed in rote compliance with guidelines, thereby limiting actual thinking about how to provide customers with a better deal than the competition offers; 3: New job-creation program, leading to legions of new experts, within companies and consulting firms.*

"Customer satisfaction" has been so ballyhooed that one might think it represents a revolutionary line of business thinking. But what could be more fundamental than the idea that, all other things being equal, companies that satisfy their customers do better than those that do not? What *is* new is the reemphasis on the importance of satisfying customers and the boom market for customer satisfaction tools. Both the reminder and the tools indisputably have tremendous value when used thoughtfully. When used blindly, however, investment in the "customer-sat" movement is no guarantee of results that lead to increased customer loyalty—or to fatter corporate profits.

Contributing to such blind but ineffective pursuit of increased customer satisfaction are three misconceptions that I call the three myths of the customer-sat movement:

CustomerSat Myth #1: We are organized for the convenience of our customers. (The reality: Despite CustomerSat-speak, many companies put their own convenience far ahead of that of their customers.)

CustomerSat Myth #2: A satisfied customer is a loyal customer. (The reality: Customers can be satisfied and disloyal, and often are.)

CustomerSat Myth #3: If we research it, we will know. (The reality: Customer-sat studies often yield surprisingly little useful data, and often obscure the real levers for improving customer satisfaction.)

A closer look at how adherence to each of these myths can block great customer-sat results follows.

"You pounce in here expecting to be waited on hand and foot, well I'm trying to run a hotel here. Have you *any* idea of how much there is to do? Do you ever think of that? Of course not, you're all too busy sticking your noses into every corner, poking around for things to complain about, aren't you?"

—English innkeeper Basil Fawlty to his paying guests in the "Waldorf Salad" episode of John Cleese's *Fawlty Towers*

CustomerSat Myth #1: We Are Organized for the Convenience of Our Customers

Today's talk is that "the customer is king." Despite this rhetoric, however, it's more typical to see companies put their own convenience and systems first, ahead of the customer. My all-time favorite example of this reversal of priorities comes from the British bus company whose managers, in response to complaints that its drivers were zipping past waiting passengers, issued the following formal response: "It is impossible for drivers to keep to their timetable if they have to stop for passengers."

Though speeding bus drivers might represent an extreme, examples of customer-unfriendly products and services abound. Consider the phone-answering systems that force customers into seemingly endless loops of syrupy sentiments ("your call is important to us"), followed by convoluted instructions punctuated by periodic prerecorded requests to please continue holding; hospital admitting procedures that, while fulfilling the information needs of insurers and providers, require seemingly endless and often frightening delays for patients and their families; mail-order catalog services that require customers to give their credit card information before they will check to see if the articles to be ordered are in stock; merchandisers who affix bar-code labels to their products with virtually irremovable glue; and retail outlets that require shoppers to make gargantuan efforts to find the items they seek or to locate sales personnel (including the Manhattan computer store that reduced the risk of potential customers asking questions—as opposed to immediately placing their orders—by pasting this index card on its locked front door: "Customers: If you want to *buy* computers, call this number").

Even more alienating to customers are companies that attempt to mask self-serving changes in the language of customer sat. Members of an upscale health club in Boston encountered this twist in a letter informing them of a change made for the "convenience" of its customers. According to the new policy, the added "convenience" was that henceforth the club would require all members to pre-authorize use of their credit cards for the payment of their monthly dues; checks and cash would no longer be accepted. (Other policies were similarly inflexible; as one customer commented to a *Boston Globe* reporter, after she had talked with the club's owner about another issue: "He didn't care. He isn't interested in customer complaints." Responded the club's owner: "I don't bite my tongue. You can only bend over so much. This is a business." Perhaps not surprisingly, a number of customers, finding no satisfactory solutions to their concerns, defected and gave up their memberships. The club's owner subsequently sold the business).

CustomerSat-speak of this sort is especially dangerous when it keeps managers from seeing the real impact of the choices they have made about how the company conducts its business. But even though the managers may miss the impact, the customers hardly ever do. Instead, such rhetoric increases the cynicism that results

"For contributions to the deceased's favorite charities, press 1. For information about the reading of the will, press 2. If you're the ex-wife of the deceased, please hang up and try again later."

—voice mail for the dead, as imagined by Harry Schwedock, California-based telecommunications analyst, as reported in *The New York Times*

"I feel that being a microcelebrity is the best of both worlds. I get enough recognition to feel good, but I can go to stores and still be treated rudely by the sales staff."

—Scott Adams, creator of the cartoon *Dilbert*

when consumers hear the "customer delight" mantra being chanted while they experience the reality of customer neglect. The result: increased motivation on the part of customers to search for more satisfactory (and more satisfying) alternatives.

One way that companies can check the tendency to slip into such an "us first" orientation is to experience their products or services as a customer or user would. Yet at many companies, executives have little idea of how user-unfriendly their products, services, or procedures truly are. An extreme example is General Motors, where for many years executives received new cars every several months and where the executives' cars were re-fueled, serviced and maintained during the workday by company employees. In consequence, these managers never had to negotiate with car salesmen, hassle with service departments, or deal with the realities of aging—and deteriorating—vehicles. Some companies do break out of such "us first" orientations, but only due to fortuitous happenstances. That's what appears to have happened when the president of a North Carolina bank attempted to call his office from an airport and became enmeshed in the bank's phone mail system. The bank's phone mail system reportedly became history shortly after he returned home.

Far better, of course, is to gain the customer's per-spective intentionally. That was the goal of Denny Sullivan, president of the $2 billion Industrial and Auto-motive Division of Parker Hannifin Corporation. Sulli-van asked his secretary, Sue Novak, to order a particular Parker product—without using her internal contacts. Here's what happened: Novak called directory assis-tance and asked if there was an 800 number for Parker Hannifin. She was given three. The first one connected her to a tool supply company that was a *former* sub-sidiary of Parker Hannifin. The second one connected her to the nurse at Parker's Huntsville plant. The last one connected her to a Parker hose plant in Iowa that could answer questions only about that subset of Parker prod-ucts made at that facility. Based on Novak's experience, Sullivan and one of his vice presidents, Mike Marvin, established a central product information center with its own 800 number (1-800-C-PARKER) and trained all employees to refer customers with product questions they couldn't answer immediately to this number. Eight years later, 1-800-C-PARKER gets 7,000 calls per month—and, Parker's data suggest, about 50 percent of the people who place calls to 1-800-C-PARKER subsequently place orders.

Insiders-turned-incognito-customers are great catalysts for boosting customer satisfaction. The shock of experiencing how little consideration is accorded to the customer's time and convenience—and the willingness to act on this shock—can do more to delight the customer than a gross of customer-sat surveys.

> Proportion of dissatisfied customers, according to researchers, who will bother to initiate a complaint to tell you that they are unhappy (rather than suffering silently or taking their business elsewhere): two to six percent

CustomerSat Myth #2: A Satisfied Customer Is a Loyal Customer

As paradoxical as it may sound, even the most highly dissatisfied customers may still be loyal; that is, despite being dissatisfied, they keep coming back to the same vendors, order after order, year after year. And, conversely, the most highly satisfied customers may still be disloyal; that is, despite being satisfied, they share their business with a number of sellers.

How can this be so? Consider my dissatisfaction with our local dry cleaner. These are a few of the reasons for my unhappiness: Smashed buttons. Suit lapels that often come back looking as if they have been pressed to the specifications of the Hunchback of Notre Dame. Fragile fabrics pierced by safety pins and plastic filaments because it's "too time consuming" to fasten the order numbers to the labels inside the garment. And recently, when I requested that they try not to tear out the shoulder pads in my blouses, I was informed that, to avoid this problem, most of the customers at this dry cleaner clip the pads out *prior* to dropping the blouses off and then sew them back in *after* the clothes have been cleaned.

Clearly I am a dissatisfied customer. I am also a fairly loyal customer. Why? Simple: I can't find a vendor that is much better, though not for lack of searching. Given equivalent insensitivity to consumer concerns, this dry cleaner can retain perpetually disgruntled customers like me as long as it is more convenient than its competitors, or less expensive (potential motto: "We ruin your clothes for cheap")—or until some vendor figures out how to deliver the basic unmet needs that I and customers like me have.

The converse is also possible: customers who are both satisfied and disloyal. A customer can be "delighted" at Restaurant A, and still choose to go to Restaurant B for his or her next outing—even if both restaurants serve the same kind of food at the same price points. In the presence of many acceptable alternatives, variety often rules.

The customer-sat lesson that crosses both dry cleaners and restaurants is that the satisfaction that matters is satisfaction *relative to alternatives,* those available today—or those that a clever competitor can make available tomorrow. Talking about an absolute standard of "customer satisfaction" without reference to what competitors offer can raise unrealistic expectations on the part of customers. At the same time, ignoring unmet needs on the grounds that no one else fulfills them is an invitation to future competitors. The best alternative is to view your customer satisfaction efforts in the context of the actions your competitors are taking or could take—exactly as your customers do when making their purchase decisions—and then revise your strategy accordingly. This can be a more difficult way of thinking about customer sat, but it has an essential virtue: it makes the customer satisfaction effort an integral part of the company's strategy, rather than a secondary, tag-along activity.

How to make sure that you will absolutely, positively turn customers who would have been satisfied with your products and services into customers who are dissatisfied: tell them that "we will exceed your expectations"

CustomerSat Myth #3: If We Research It, We Will Know

Market research is an important tool for understanding markets, including current customers, former customers, competitors' customers, and even those people who don't purchase products in this category (but perhaps could, if we understood their latent needs better). Customer-sat surveys, as one type of market research, can be a particularly effective way to look at one slice of a market: how *current* users view *current* products. Earning a return on this kind of market research, however, is far from automatic; many companies have made significant investments in customer-sat surveys only to find that the results provided surprisingly little information that they could act on. For this reason, possibly the most important issue to be addressed before putting a customer-sat survey into the field is what you could (or would) change in your business *if* you knew the answers to each of the questions. If you couldn't (or wouldn't) change much regardless of the answers, the question probably isn't worth including in the research instrument.

But even if the questions are focused on areas where appropriate action can be taken, other problems can diminish the usefulness of the research. Among the other issues that are useful to investigate before fielding a customer-sat survey are the following five:

• *Is the survey easy to complete and worth taking the time to do?* A case in point: soon after I bought my car, I received an eight-page customer-sat questionnaire that contained, by my count, 190 questions in microscopic type, printed in faint green ink on tissue-like paper. Most of the questions had many subparts, twenty-five in one case. I also received a quarter. The questionnaire went directly into the trash bin, and all subsequent ones from the company went there too.

I love my car, but like many customers—in both consumer and industrial markets—I am feeling the pains of QFD: questionnaire fatigue disease. In consequence, unless I can see that the company designed the questionnaire with some focus and some consideration of my time, I will either toss it out or not pay sufficient attention to the questions as I fill in my answers. In either case, the company would have recouped its investment severalfold had it taken the time to prune the laundry list of items included in the survey.

• *Does the survey show your customers that you understand their basic needs?* Consider the Macintosh PowerBook. If you have one and it breaks, you can send it back to Apple for repairs and you will receive, by return mail, the computer and an "Apple PowerBook Service Customer Satisfaction Survey." The first half of the survey asks all sorts of good questions about how satisfied you have been, in general and along a number

The question I'd like to see on a telephone company customer-satisfaction questionnaire: "Do you enjoy it when, having dialed a number incorrectly, you are greeted by three extremely discordant tones broadcast at more decibels than the average person, ear pressed up against receiver, is likely to want to hear?"

One of four questions on a bright yellow postcard-sized survey that Ben & Jerry's hands out to see if its Flavor of the Month is delighting its customers:
"Flavor:
—Totally Awesome
—Real Cool
—About like Brand X
—No way José"

of specific dimensions, including turnaround time, ease of conducting business, and cost of repair. You won't see a question asking specifically about whether the repair worked, however, until midway through the questionnaire.

The risk in situations like this is that the customer will think that the company has lost sight of the core benefits the customer is paying it to deliver. In Apple's case, for example, unless the box is fixed, the rest is secondary. For this reason, the survey instrument Apple uses would itself make a larger contribution to customer satisfaction if it started with the question about whether the repair worked, and then positioned the rest of the questions as the *remainder* of Apple's "service customer satisfaction" equation.

• *Does the survey allow you to identify the "differentiators" customers use to distinguish among products and vendors?* In some categories, like dry cleaning and computer repair, core customer needs remain unmet—buttons come back smashed, computers come back unrepaired. In many other product categories, however, some core needs are routinely met by all vendors; we expect the car engine to turn on the first time we turn the ignition key, just as we expect our hotel room to have a bed (although once, at a four-star hotel in Tulsa, I was given a room furnished with a conference table and eight chairs—and nothing else).

Most customer-sat surveys ask respondents to rate the relative importance of all the variables being tested, typically using a scale that ranges from "absolutely essential" to "not very important." The analytic problem arises when there are variables, like the bed in the hotel room, that customers rate as "absolutely essential," but don't use to discriminate among vendors because they take performance on these variables as "givens." One solution to this situation is simply to ask respondents both to rate the overall importance they place on each of the attributes as well as indicate which attributes they use to discriminate among vendors as they make their purchase decisions. Then you will know which variables to work on to get the biggest return for your improvement efforts. (For more on differentiators, see "Procrustean Strategies: Why the Real Question Is, How Differentiated and at What Costs," pp. 159–169.)

• *Will the survey allow you to find out how satisfied users are with the competition?* In some categories, the competition is not very relevant; for example, customers with cars under warranty don't usually go outside of the dealer network when they need a repair. But in most other categories, customers choose among vendors and often use products or services from more than one vendor. In these categories, it's important to include former customers and customers of the other vendors as well as current customers, and to get the respondents to evaluate the company's products and services vis-à-vis its competitors. Yet many customer-satisfaction surveys focus only on current customers and only on evaluating the vendor's products. This is often true even when the company is losing share to competitors.

One way to include the competitive dimension and still not cause more "questionnaire fatigue disease" among respondents is to use the format of a report card, just as Baldrige award winner Granite Rock, a California ready-mix concrete company, does. In this format, customers are invited to be the teachers and grade the company and its competitors on the same scale used when they were in school; in the United States, this usually means using the letter scale of A, B, C, D, and F or the word scale of Excellent, Very Good, Good, Fair, and Poor. The results can provide a view on the competitive threat today—for example, when you receive B's and your arch-rival receives A's on attributes respondents say are important in their decisions. The results can also give you perspective on the potential competitive threat of tomorrow—if you score C's and your competitors score D's on these same attributes, then you would see that even though you have an advantage now, the real opportunity is to figure out how to earn A's or B's—before someone else does.

• *Have you thought about how the instrument can be "gamed" or otherwise rigged by insiders?* In May 1994, a Ford Taurus owner received this letter from his dealer: "You will soon be receiving a questionnaire in the mail from Ford Motor Company. This questionnaire is how Ford Motor Company grades it's [sic] dealers on customer satisfaction. We respectfully ask that you . . . grade us the perfect 10 scores that we work so hard to earn from you! . . . I look forward to reading your completed survey when Ford Motor Company returns it to me!" The customer, who had not been to the dealer since the time, a year and a half before, when he was told that the service department had no idea why the car made loud noises and then decelerated suddenly when pushed to speeds of 50 to 60 mph, just shook his head in stunned disbelief, more convinced than ever of his choice to use a neighborhood gas station for his car maintenance and repair needs. (And for those readers who think this story can't be true, I can only say that I've seen the letter and have quoted it here verbatim.)

All customer-satisfaction instruments can be gamed. One way stakeholders rig a customer-sat instrument is to design the questionnaire so that the customers' real concerns will not be readily evident. Another, as in the above example, is simply to tell the respondents what you want them to tell you. The losers, in both cases, are the companies, since they will not receive the information they need to identify and fix deficiencies. Any company that uses its customer-satisfaction surveys to determine pay or other perks is therefore well advised to check behind the scenes to see if those who stand to gain or lose from the results are trying to rig the results. (For more on those who game the espoused rules, see "Decoding the Corporate Culture," pp. 51–63.)

And a final reminder: because customer-satisfaction surveys are aimed at understanding how *current* users view the benefits the company *currently* provides, they by definition will seldom provide clues about how to attract *new* users or spotlight *latent* customer needs. As in all market research, you gain answers only to the questions you ask. Customer sat is a great place to start building a deeper understanding of your markets, but it is by no means a one-stop-shop of the consumer's mind.

"Perhaps the next time you do this survey, you should not advise your dealers until after *the survey is completed, in order to avoid dealer efforts to influence the results."*

—last sentence of the letter to Ford from disgruntled recipient of the "customer satisfaction" survey

---

Talking the talk of customer satisfaction and then using surveys to measure this satisfaction represents an implicit promise to consumers: that you *will* take action to serve them better. You must therefore keep in mind that neither customer-service rhetoric nor fancy research instruments is sufficient for meeting this commitment. The payoff, instead, comes from challenging how you do business, keeping the competition in your "customer-sat" equation, and (if you use surveys) taking the time to design questionnaires that will give you information that you can use—*and then acting to improve the deal you give your target market relative to what the competitors do (or can) offer.* Otherwise, you might as well save your money and not make promises to your customers that you don't mean to keep.

CHAPTER 10

THE (INHARMONIOUS) VOICE OF THE CUSTOMER

Seeking the Irritating Whine That Must Be Heard

Voice of the Customer That irritating and incoherent whine of people who are never satisfied and yet who can't dream very well either; most effectively countered by market research that tells us exactly what we expect and then validates what we think we have already heard.

One might think that the "voice of the customer" (sometimes abbreviated as "VOC") is the new choral music of successful businesses today. The good news in this reemphasis on listening to the market is that the message about the importance of hearing what current and potential customers have to say always bears repeating. The bad news is that the current reflexive homage often does not take into account two key inherent risks. The first of these, which we can call the "Filter Factor," is that since customers often speak in tones that are less than melodious, the voice of the customer is often heard—and then disregarded as nothing more than irrational tirades or errant nonsense. The second, which we can call the "GIGO Effect," is that it's remarkably easy to design market research in accordance with the principle of GIGO (garbage in, garbage out), leading to deeply flawed research results that, nonetheless, are followed as gospel. Confronting both the Filter Factor and the

GIGO Effect is therefore critical to raising "listening to the voice of the customer" from reflexive fad to competitive weapon.

———————■———————

Facing The Filter Factor; or, Beware of Expecting the "Voice of the Customer" to Sound Like the "Voice of the Turtledove," Thereby Allowing You to Miss the Harsh Notes You Need to Hear

The phrase "the voice of the customer" has a lovely, poetic ring. It reminds me of "the voice of the turtledove" from the Song of Solomon, 2:10–12:

> My beloved speaks and says to me:
> "Arise my love, my fair one, and come away;
> for lo, the winter is past, the rain is over and gone.
> The flowers appear on the earth, the time of singing has come,
> and the voice of the turtledove is heard in our land."

Unfortunately, the voice of the customer typically sounds nothing like the voice of the turtledove. For where the voice of the turtledove is melodic and soothing, the voice of the customer can be disharmonious and profoundly irritating. The challenge for companies, therefore, is tolerating the annoying unpleasantness while distilling the market intelligence—whether from the external market (purchasers) or the internal market (employees).

And customers often do speak in disharmonious and harsh tones, even when they are served by the best in the business, as the experience of Marks & Spencer shows. The most profitable retailer in Britain, with 1992 earnings of £737 million ($1.25 billion), M & S garners almost one of every five pounds spent there on clothing, a clear indicator of the company's exceptional track record in understanding and responding to the customers in its market. As described by researchers Jacques Horovitz and Michele Jurgens Panak, the company's approach to market research goes something like this: "If the customers don't buy it, get it off the shelf. If they buy it, restock it immediately."

One of Marks & Spencer's encounters with the less-than-dulcet side of the "voice of the customer" occurred when a laudatory article on the company in *The Economist* ended with the following comment: "Margaret Thatcher bought her underwear at Marks & Spencer. So should Mr Major." Next to the comment was a nickel-sized line drawing of men's Y-front underpants with the M & S "St. Michael" label shown at the back of the garment.

It was the drawing that produced the rub. Sir Graham Hills of Laigh Threepwood, Ayrshire, wrote a letter to *The Economist,* complaining that "You should know (and it is no small matter) that the label is in fact on the right-hand side, there to act as a minor irritant to those who wear their pants inside their vests rather than the other way round." Mr. Keith Appleyard, of Brighton, responded by saying that the real problem was not the location, but that "the label is now more than 2 inches (5 cm) in length, stitched at one end, and . . . made of a rather unyielding material, itself a further irritant." Mr. Donald King, of Swanley, Kent, weighed in with this threat: "Makers seem determined that the labels will outlast the pants. They must take this matter seriously, or men will give up wearing underpants." The last word came from Mr. Bill Boyd, of Johannesburg, South Africa, who offered the solution of wearing the pants inside out, which, he noted, requires some ambidexterity on the part of the wearer in order to be implemented successfully.

Marks & Spencer's financial results indicate that it listens to enough customers well enough to beat its competitors—and the Y-front letters indicate that, even so, some customers, believing that their views have gone unnoticed, will speak in less than euphonious tones. I don't know how Marks & Spencer officials responded to these letters (though Sir Graham's previous complaints had gone unheeded) but I do know that companies can use such unpleasant and inconvenient comments to find new opportunities, even in men's underwear. That's what Fruit of the Loom did recently, using heavier fabric and more comfortable waistbands in its redesigned undergarments—and then refined them further based on the complaints of long-haul drivers, like 240-pound Ralph Hendrikson, who test-wore the briefs for a week.

Unlike Fruit of the Loom, however, many companies go out of their way to disregard the harsh notes, and in

"I have tried without success to persuade M & S to return the offending label to where it once was. . . . Correspondence with M & S and, recently, a face-to-face discussion with its managing director have failed to persuade this invariably user-friendly retailer to remove this tiny flaw from their portfolio of garments."

—the conclusion of Sir Graham's letter

consequence only hear those customers who coo like turtledoves. Consider the experience of Christie's, the famous auction house. At the beginning of the twentieth century, there was no contest for dominance in the auction house world: Christie's reigned supreme. One of the factors that allowed Sotheby's to gain market share was its willingness to embrace the Impressionists well before Christie's did. But as Sotheby's increased its participation in the strong and growing market for Impressionist paintings, Christie's hung back. The reason: despite Sotheby's increasing Impressionist sales—surely the clearest indication of "the voice of the customer"—Sir Alec Martin, Christie's managing director from 1940 to 1958, couldn't fathom why anyone of taste would bother with such paintings. As Anthony Lousada, one of Christie's lawyers, later remembered: "My personal recollection is of going up to Christie's one day and walking around the rooms with him [Sir Alec] when there was a considerable number of important works by Picasso, Braque and others on the walls and Alec referring to them as we went past as 'this 'ere filth.'"

The Great Y-Front Debate and the Great Impressionist Debacle illustrate the basic principle of the Filter Factor: the "voice of the customer" is often heard as the whimpers of ingrates who are never satisfied or as the proclamations of louts who have no taste. Being confronted with such whines and grumbles can occur whether or not you do formal market research; if you are lucky, you will hear these unpleasant noises through any one of a number of mechanisms: complaints called into your 800 number, feedback from vendors of your products, comments at trade shows, trends in your warranty data, notes transmitted over your e-mail system, results of formal market research programs, offhand remarks from neighbors—even letters to the editors of *The Economist*.

Such unpleasantness is easy to spot: if you hear or read something that makes you angry, indignant, or incredulous, that's exactly when you have to stop and ask whether there could be any validity in the whining or any way to meet the concern. This takes courage and discipline, since your every instinct will be telling you to ignore what you have just heard. But if companies collect the information and their managers disregard it as only so much twaddle, they will never benefit from "listening to the voice of the customer" no matter how reverentially they laud this goal. The question is, therefore, when customers speak, do you hear whines that you feel justified in ignoring—or do you discern market intelligence you can use to enhance your position with your customers?

Confronting the GIGO Effect; or, Beware of Research That Tells You Exactly What You Expect, Thereby Allowing You to Ignore What You Really Need to Know

In the early days of computers, it was frequently noted that data printed on computer paper held far more credibility than the exact same data written out by hand or typed out on a typewriter. Yet those who played with the data knew that faulty algorithms lead to faulty results, giving rise to the acronym GIGO: garbage in, garbage out.

The GIGO effect is equally applicable to market research. Most customers don't tell vendors the whys and wherefores of how they see a market; instead they let their checkbooks do the talking as they switch to the vendors they see as providing better deals. Being able to anticipate such behavior is, of course, where market research and all the related rhetoric about "the voice of the customer" come in to play. But when the GIGO Effect is operative, flawed research designs actually block out important information. Three particularly pernicious forms of the GIGO Effect in market research are prevalent today: 1) searching where one wishes the data to be, rather than where the data are; 2) talking with the people you would like to think represent your market rather than the people who actually do; and 3) asking questions in a way that the respondents will either be unwilling or unable to answer correctly.

"Because the light is better here."

—punch line of the old joke about the guy who continues to search for his house keys under the street lamp, even though he knows he had dropped them somewhere in the dark alley some hundred yards away

Searching Where One Wishes the Data to Be

One cause of the GIGO Effect is looking only at the variables one hopes will explain the market, excluding all other variables that may be inconvenient to consider. For example, many companies invest heavily in research to tell them how their target markets break out in terms of their demographics (e.g., how

What Harry
Warner
(1881–1958),
head of Warner
Brothers, said
after Edwin Land
demonstrated
3-D movies: "Not
bad, but I don't
get it. What's the
big deal?"

What Edwin
Land didn't
know: Warner
had a glass eye,
and therefore
could not see the
stereoscopic
effect

old you are and what your income is) and findographics (e.g., what you read and what television shows you prefer). At the same time, they avoid looking at the psychographics of these markets (e.g., what you believe and how you feel about a group of products), since these data are messier and more difficult to translate into marketing plans.

Take car purchases, for example. The great insight of Alfred P. Sloan, who led General Motors from 1923 to 1958, was that the socioeconomic status of buyers drove the car-buying decision, allowing the automaker to segment the market on the basis of demographics; Chevrolets for those with less money, Cadillacs for those with more. But, as Peter Drucker points out, the key criteria for segmenting the market shifted to "lifestyle," a psychographic variable that "is as elusive and qualitative a concept as socioeconomic segmentation was tangible and rigorously quantitative." Drucker's conclusion: the root of the problem with the American automotive industry has not been its "fat" manufacturing or its "short-term vision," but its continuing insistence on using *demographics* to identify the target customers for each of its cars, long after it needed to shift its attention to the *psychographics* of its market.

Many companies fall into the same trap. Demographic and findographic data are "actionable"; that is, if we know the demographics and findographics of our market, we know how to estimate the size of our prospective market as well as how to reach it. But when the factors that separate one group of customers from another include their beliefs, their expectations, their hopes, or their values, the tasks of estimating market size and reaching target customers become far more difficult. This is unfortunate, of course, because taking into account such squishy factors stands in the way of *efficient* marketing. They are, however, also the reality in a number of industries, from financial services to computer equipment to men's apparel. In the interest of *effective* marketing, therefore, those who wish to hear the voice of the customer need to be very clear about what needs to be discovered, even if this requires looking at areas beyond those they wish would define their markets and their opportunities.

*Talking with the People You Would Like to Think
Represent Your Market*

A second cause of the GIGO Effect is talking with the people you would like to think represent your market, rather than people who actually do. Consider the saga of Xerox and personal computers. Xerox invented the Alto—and with it, most of the attributes now associated with the Macintosh line of computers—years before Apple was even founded. Why didn't Xerox pursue the Alto, its wonderful invention? One factor was the voices that Xerox chose to listen to. As one of the inventors of the Alto told Douglas Smith and Robert Alexander, chroniclers of the Xerox saga, the reactions to the Alto prototype when it was presented to Xerox executives and their wives provided one important part of the answer: "What was remarkable was that almost to a couple, the man would stand back and be very skeptical and reserved, and the wives, many of whom had been secretaries, got enthralled by moving around the mouse, seeing the graphics on the screen, and using the color printer. The men had no background, really, to grasp the significance of it." The voices of the executives may have been wrong, but theirs were comfortable, familiar voices—and the ones to which Xerox paid attention.

Women's apparel provides another example of this form of the GIGO Effect. Until recently the implicit assumption held by many apparel manufacturers was that women who bought nice clothing were no larger than a size 12, with maybe a few size 14's and size 16's thrown into the target market for good measure. With whom could the manufacturers have been doing their market research to reach such a conclusion? Sixty percent of American women wear a size 12 or larger; fully 31 percent wear a size 16 or larger. Equally important, many women who are larger than a size 12 want—and are willing to spend their money on—clothes that fit and look good. A look at the figures for women's large-size apparel documents this latent demand: from 1980 to 1990, revenues zoomed from $2 billion to $10 billion. (And it's not just women's apparel; the exact same trend is occurring in men's apparel as well, as demonstrated by the 275-store chain of Casual Male Big & Tall stores. Says company executive Jerry M. Sokol, "The big guy wants to look like everyone else. That was the misunderstanding. Everybody thought the big guy wanted to wear dumb clothes.")

In almost every case that I have seen of this second form of the GIGO Effect, the culprit has been managers who wish their market looked like them, or like people they admire. Unfortunately, not all markets accommodate this personal desire. Listening to the voice of the customer not only requires hearing the words, but also acknowledging who needs to do the talking, and then adjusting the product/market strategy accordingly.

What many respondents to an epidemiological study, administered by telephone, were willing to answer: detailed questions about their sexual habits

What many respondents to the same epidemiological study indignantly refused to answer: general questions about their income levels

Asking Questions That Will Not— Or Cannot—Be Answered Accurately

A third cause of the GIGO effect is asking questions in a way that the respondents will either be unwilling or unable to answer accurately. Do consumers lie deliberately? I'm not sure. But I am sure that many market research questions invite people to lie. Are there people who would tell a focus group that they prefer to watch *Masterpiece Theatre* on public television, when they really watch *Roseanne* on commercial television, because they think they will look more intellectual? (I watch *Roseanne* myself.) Or who would tell you, in response to a question on a questionnaire, that your prices are *not* too high? (Even if they are willing to pay your current prices, some will still see the question as a way to lobby for price reductions.) In each case, the question itself will provide the stimulus, for some people at least, to shade the truth.

Even more common than inviting respondents to lie is market research that poses questions that consumers *can't* answer accurately. At the most prosaic level, even for products that consumers know well and even when consumers want to be helpful, they can't give accurate information on what's most important to them for the simple reason that they often aren't fully conscious of the tradeoffs they make as part of their purchase-decision process. For example, do you place more value on style or color in your clothing purchases? On mouthfeel or flavor intensity in your ice cream selections? On sound systems or safety systems in your choice of cars? These are the kinds of tradeoffs that all consumers make intuitively when they make their purchase decisions, but typically don't think about explicitly on a factor-by-factor basis. A simple checklist on a questionnaire therefore often is inadequate for capturing the real decision-weights consumers use as they make their purchases.

And the further the products or services in question are from those available today, the more difficult it is for consumers to respond to questions about what they want or could want. Most people can't imagine how or whether they would use products and services that they have never thought about before, much less ever seen or touched or experimented with. Who could have predicted that the first Polaroid camera, unveiled in 1948 at $89.75, over *thirty times* the price of a Kodak Baby Brownie, would incite a near riot among shoppers the first day that it was introduced? Or that, when Fred Smith introduced Federal Express, consumers in 1973 would pay twenty-two dollars, almost *150 times* the price of a first-class stamp, in order to gain guaranteed overnight delivery of their letters? And this difficulty of imagining new products occurs even with less dramatic innovations; consumer research showed that telephone answering machines would bomb: too rude. Ditto for hairstyling mousse, which got a big thumbs-down in test markets: too goopy.

Grade that Fred Smith received, as a student at Yale, for a paper in which he first proposed the idea that became the foundation for Federal Express: C

Many techniques exist to help overcome the GIGO tendency of asking questions that the respondents cannot or do not wish to answer accurately. Among these is conjoint analysis, which asks the respondents to make selections among a set of products, and then allows the researchers to "back out" the implicit "weights" the respondents applied to the component benefits of these products. Another is the focus group; with gifted leaders, such groups can help consumers to dream. One can also do as Marks & Spencer and many Japanese electronics firms do: simply put the products out there and see which ones the customers buy. And there are lots of other ways as well. Regardless of the technique used, however, it's essential to play the game in your own mind about whether the respondents will be willing to—or even able to—respond accurately to the question you ask.

Learning what the customers want or could want is the foundation for good strategy. But listening to the "voice of the customer" will not amount to much if the messages one doesn't wish to hear are discounted or otherwise deemed unworthy of attention, whether these messages are coming from the external customers, the purchasers of the company's products and services, or from the internal customers, the company's employees. Likewise, the results of research undertaken to obtain vital market intelligence will be worth little if you don't invest the time to figure out what needs to be discovered, who has the desired information, what techniques will be best for uncovering it, and why you will be better off with the information once obtained. And these requirements in turn sometimes mean talking to different kinds of people, covering different topics, and using different techniques than the company or the market research department is used to or comfortable with, rather than working furiously to replicate past findings or to measure distance from an increasingly irrelevant baseline of past data.

So, it's true, the voice of the customer is often irritating, misleading, and unimaginative. So what? It's not their job to tell you what they want and why they want it. Making it *easy* and *enticing* for customers to give you the information you need is *your* job—no matter how jarring, "uninformed," or peculiar the message might be.

CHAPTER 11

"CUSTOMER FOCUS" AND OTHER PRODUCT DEVELOPMENT DELUSIONS

What Love Has Got to Do with It

Customer Focus   That which is seen when one looks into the customers' eyes to see what is desired and observes one's own image of the ideal product.

"Customer focus," it is said, is the key to developing products and services that will "delight" the customer. Accordingly, techniques for the development and launch of new or improved products and services typically start with some formalized method of capturing customer input and then translating it into product specifications.

Consider quality function deployment (QFD), perhaps the most highly structured approach to combining "customer focus" with efficient processes for the development and introduction of new or improved products. Formalized at Mitsubishi's Kobe shipyard in 1972, the QFD process starts with a detailed analysis of customer "wants." With this analysis as its foundation, the process guides the participants from customer requirements to product planning, and from product planning through the various production stages to product launch. Each step is linked to the next, causing the original read on the customers to be channeled through the process so that, in theory at least, customer focus is maintained from the first gleam in an inventor's eye to the final touches on the advertising and packaging.

Adherents of QFD and other product-development techniques point to the potential for dramatic reductions in times-to-market and in preproduction and startup costs. What's tricky, however, is ensuring that the products so quickly delivered will, in fact, be the products customers *actually want to buy*. As anyone who has worked with a simple spreadsheet model knows, a single faulty core assumption at the beginning of any calculation can cascade through the computations and then produce wonky results at the finish line. With a highly structured approach like QFD, it's possible to misread the customer at the start and then launch the wrong product, but more quickly and at lower costs than ever before. As Lawrence Sullivan, one of the early American experts on QFD points out, QFD "makes it more difficult to change direction once a project is underway because all the interrelated elements of the system must be revised."

More to the point, no matter what the process is or what mechanisms are built into it for "listening to the voice of the customer," customer wants are often misread due to one of the most basic of all human experiences: falling in love. More specifically, the source of this particular problem is falling in love with one's own products and services, or with the technologies on which those products and services are based.

The ancient Greek myth of Narcissus sheds light on this modern predicament. According to the myth, Narcissus was a young man so beautiful that he fell in love with his own reflection when he knelt down to take a drink of water, and then died by the water's edge, heartbroken that he could not embrace his beloved. In modern organizations, when people fall in love with their own products and services, the results can be just as deadly. The cause of death: blindness to virtually all data that suggest their ideas and creations are less than perfect.

The ghost of Narcissus haunts many companies today, striking any time in the evolution of a new or improved product, from original concept to final launch. At its heart, however, keeping the ghost of Narcissus at bay is not a matter of methodologies or

> "They say that when his spirit crossed the river that encircles the world of the dead, it leaned over the boat to catch a final glimpse of itself in the water."
>
> —Edith Hamilton on the last passage of *Narcissus*

> "A belief is not merely an idea the mind possesses. It is an idea that possesses the mind."
>
> —Robert Bolton

mechanisms, but rather one of the personal resolve to consider the possibility that what you love may not be what your customers love—and that what your customers love may not be what you see as terribly attractive. For this reason, a good though often neglected place to start consideration of product development strategies is with a close look at the symptoms of corporate narcissism.

"Auto"-eroticism: Narcissus in the Fast Lane

Corporate narcissism is a risk for any company; not just those with mediocre managers but also those whose people are capable and dedicated, where the understandings of the most important projects are widely shared, and where the processes used for developing and launching new products are thoughtful and appropriate. As an example, consider what happened to Volvo when it introduced the 850, its first front-wheel drive car, into the United States market in late 1992.

A successful launch of the 850 was a top priority for Volvo. The company was retiring the 740 series, which accounted for 43 percent of Volvo's sales in the United States. The new model, the 850, was the result of a fourteen-year effort to create a new car platform that would carry Volvo into the twenty-first century. The work began in 1978, when Volvo initiated its "Galaxy Project," one result of which was the basic concept for the 850. Development of the 850 was the largest industrial project in Swedish history, requiring 16 billion Swedish kroner—about $2.5 billion. The way Volvo presented the car to the American public was therefore critical to the car's, and the company's, future. Faced with this "you bet your company" challenge, Volvo unveiled its first 850 (in its nonturbo form) in a prime-time television campaign as the smart buyer's alternative to the Porsche.

Porsche?!?

True, the cars featured in the Volvo ads were always "arrest-me red" and were always shown streaking across the screen at warp speed. It's also true that the automotive pundits proclaimed the 850 to be a great car. But while the new 850 was slightly smaller and a little rounder than other Volvos, it still looked just like . . . a Volvo. And while its ability to move from 0 to 60 miles per hour in about 8.5 seconds made it a lot zippier than its armored half-track-like predecessors, it was hardly in the league of the Porsche 911 (0 to 60 in five seconds) or even of the Porsche 986 (0 to 60 in six seconds). As a reviewer from *The New York Times* commented, the 1993 nonturbo 850 was exactly the right car for those buyers who sought "safe sex, automotive style"—not exactly the profile of Porsche-owner wannabes.

Volvo management must have arrived at a similar conclusion. After a few months of the first campaign, it yanked the original ads and replaced them with a new one featuring a man and woman riding on a tank and emphasizing that the new 850 is, well, a Volvo, but a Volvo with a twist: one that's fun to drive. Initial indications were that shifting to the new campaign was the right move; in 1993, Volvo sales of the 850 models accounted for approximately a third of the company's car sales worldwide, and 44 percent of the company's car sales in North America, exceeding the company's expectations for that market. And, with the jump-start provided by the 850, operating profit for Volvo's worldwide Car Group soared to 502 million Swedish kroner, the group's first operating profit since 1989.

———■———

"The course of true love never did run smooth."

—Lysander, in Shakespeare's *A Midsummer Night's Dream*

———■———

Why did Volvo management risk its important investment in the 850 with an ad campaign that promised benefits the car could not deliver, while at the same time ignoring the benefits sought by the people most likely to purchase the new model? My guess is that Volvo's managers fell in love with their own creation. With performance and handling so much better than the company's traditional cars, the 850 must have *felt* like a Porsche to them. Their logical conclusion was therefore to target those car buyers whose lust for a Porsche exceeded the depth of their pockets.

In reality, Volvo had the right car, but the wrong target customer. Money aside, the 850 appeals to people for whom safety comes first, then performance and styling; Porsches, to those for whom performance and styling come first, with safety far behind—if, indeed, safety even appears on the list of desired benefits at all. Moving to the new ad campaign required seeing the car as its target buyers wanted to see it, despite the internal perceptions and preferences.

Volvo was smart to convert its ad campaign so quickly, and lucky that its brush with corporate narcissism was brief and had a relatively minor impact. Good product, wrong target is a lot better than bad product, right target, the form of corporate narcissism that appears to have afflicted the Cadillac Allanté, one of my favorite examples of a product that only its creators could have loved.

A luxury two-seater convertible priced at $55,000 in 1987, the Allanté was conceived as GM's answer to the Mercedes 560-SL and the Jaguar X-JS. What Cadillac saw in its new model was a classic—and classy—European car: "body by Pininfarina," designed and manufactured in Italy and then shipped in a specially designed 747 for final assembly in the United States. But the romance of the car's Italian heritage must have blinded GM management to the car's blatant deficiencies. Critics blasted Allanté for its underpowered engine, its constant squeaks and rattles, its plastic-plastered interior, and its notoriously tricky mechanism for raising and lowering the top. Customers complained about the tendency of the car's automatic door locks to fail to release, its unreliable seat adjusters, and the often-unanswered "twenty-four-hour" Allanté phone line. The gold ignition keys were yet another source of dissatisfaction. As one customer wrote: "I think you are having a problem obtaining the image you are looking for . . . as long as the gold flakes off of the keys."

Even with improvements, too few customers calculated that the Allanté, including its body by Pininfarina and delivery via 747, was worth its price. Seven years after the car's introduction, Cadillac managers came to see the Allanté as their target market did—a poor value—and declared the 1993 Allanté as the end of the line.

Could a process like QFD have saved either Volvo or GM from their respective encounters with "auto"-eroticism? Sure, if the process had been followed perfectly. But that's just the point. Few new-product launches flop in the marketplace because their developers pushed projects that they knew were based on inaccurate assumptions about "customer desires." But many do flop—or need to be redirected—because their developers, blinded by corporate narcissism, couldn't see flaws in their own creations.

Technocentricity: *Corporate Narcissism in the Laboratory*

Technocentricity is a very specific form of corporate narcissism. The love that blinds in technocentricity is the belief that new technologies, *by definition, always* provide better deals than old technologies. To explore the dynamics of this form of corporate narcissism in a little more detail, take the following brief quiz:

1. All the products on the two lists below were introduced to the market with great fanfare and high expectations. Yet there is a consistent difference between the products in column A and those in column B. What is it?

A	B
stereo sound systems	quadraphonic sound systems
frozen food	dehydrated food
nylon (DuPont's artificial silk)	Corfam (DuPont's artificial leather)
microwave ovens	cool top ranges
Matsushita's VCRs for home use	RCA's videodisks for home use

2. Which set of analogies, those listed under "option R" or those listed under "option S," best capture the relationship of a new technology to an older technology?

   option R) New technology : old technology : :

           fax machines : telex machines

           electronic calculators : slide rules

           word processors : typewriters

           automobile components : buggy whips

   or:

   option S) New technology : old technology : :

           radio : newspapers

           television : radio

           instant photography : 35 mm photography

           microwave ovens : conventional ovens

3. A number of professional, general, and trade publications run stories predicting products based on new technologies. If you were to peruse the past three decades or so of such forecasts from credible sources, what percentage of roughly correct forecasts do you think you would see?

Answer to Question #1: The Difference between the Products in Column A and Those in Column B

Though many people have a difficult time at first detecting the difference between the products listed in the two columns, the difference is obvious once you spot it: the products in column A were commercial successes while those in column B flopped. More to the point, all the products in column A provided good deals relative to the available alternatives, while all those in column B provided miserable deals against the same standard. This may seem self-evident, except that products that end up in column B often receive investments and ink of equal magnitude to that received by the products in column A. That's because one element of the love a technocentrist feels for a new technology stems from "tenet #1 of technocentricity," which posits that new technologies *always* lead to better mousetraps and that better mousetraps *always* lead to increased sales. Or as the famous line from the movie *Field of Dreams* goes, the belief is "if you build it, they will come."

> "It's terrific if you're a computer."
>
> —novelist Rita Mae Brown on computer dating

This core tenet of technocentricity is flawed, however, since new mousetraps sell only when the deal (benefits relative to price) represented by the new technology is better than the deal represented by the existing alternatives. Sometimes continuing improvements in the underlying technology can change a poor deal into a great one. When fax machines were first introduced in 1968, for example, they were very expensive and could transmit only one page every eight hours, severely limiting their acceptance. Today, of course, fax machines, far cheaper and faster than they were twenty-five years ago, are ubiquitous. Still, even acknowledging the dynamic nature of new technologies, asking why and to whom the new products could provide better deals than existing alternatives can help weed out some losers early, before additional investments are committed to products that have little, if any, chance of succeeding in the market place.

(For those who are curious about the details of Question #1: quadraphonic sound was hurt by a lack of industry-wide standards for the technology as well as by the need for consumers to find places for yet two more speakers, both of which increased the costs and inconvenience to the potential buyers; dehydrated food, though convenient, didn't taste very good; Corfam, though less costly than leather, didn't breathe like the real thing, limiting the comfort of shoes made from this new material, and didn't look like the real thing either; cool top ranges required the use of special pots and cost much more than conventional ranges; and RCA's videodisk system, unlike the VCRs being introduced at the same time, didn't allow users to record programs off the air. Nonetheless, all five of these products received substantial investments as the "new and improved" mousetraps for their industries.)

"Kevlar was the solution. We just weren't sure what the problem was."

—Kevlar marketing manager, about a product that by 1987 had accumulated an estimated $200 million in losses

Answer to Question #2: The Set of Analogies That Best Captures the Relationship of a Newer Technology to an Older Technology

All of the above. The analogies in "option R" are often used in debates about a new technology, because they make the point that new technologies can render their predecessors obsolete, by *replacing* them. But the analogies in "option S" are equally valid; many successful technologies *supplement*, rather than replace, the older technologies. Even though both technology scenarios are valid, the love of a technocentrist also springs from "tenet #2 of technocentricity," which recognizes only the replacement analogies, arguing that the new technology will *always* conquer the old, as though what was true in the case of electronic calculators versus old-fashioned slide rules will apply to every other new alternative to an old technology.

Again, the tenet is not always true. The paradigm of technology replacement does not apply in every case and, when misapplied, leads to inappropriate investments. A textbook example is the American microwave oven industry, which poured millions of dollars into new features, like browning elements and programmed cooking sequences, intended to replicate the functions of conventional ovens. The expectation was that, with such features, microwave ovens would replace conventional ovens, a classic "replacement analogy" strategy. The industry lost out to the Japanese manufacturers, however, who produced smaller, cheaper microwave ovens with fewer features—the perfect product to coexist with conventional ovens. The Japanese strategy triumphed because the limits of the technology made microwave cooking a poor replacement for the conventional oven—but a great supplement.

A more recent example is the newspaper industry. Executives in that business are now used to hearing "replacement analogy" arguments, and being told that they are dinosaurs, linked to paper in an age of electronics. A common theme is that news on paper will soon no longer exist. One candidate for the replacement technology, according to this argument, is CD-ROM, described by a senior executive at one major newspaper as a "medium in the making." So, a few years ago, I asked a group of newspaper editors and publishers to tell me in what way CD-ROM provides a better deal for newspaper readers. The answer, after a thoughtful silence: for archival needs, as a way to store yesterday's newspapers, rather than as a method for delivering today's newspaper for today's reading. That new technologies are providing newspapers with extraordinary opportunities and threats is without question. All the more reason for people within this industry to go beyond blind acceptance of replacement analogies, and ask the hard questions about how good a deal, from the consumer's perspective, each new technology will deliver, and to which segments.

Conversely, of course, are those products to which common wisdom applies a supplement-analogy when a replacement-analogy is more appropriate. When automobiles were first developed, some saw them as supplements to horse-drawn transportation, not as replacements, which is perhaps why they were originally called "horseless carriages." But no matter what the product in question, it's important to identify, and then evaluate, the paradigm within the analogy. Analogies are powerful rhetorical devices for winning arguments but winning in the market-

Some of the comments directed at newspaper executives at their 1992 industry conference:

- "You guys are irrelevant. You are extinct."
  —a marketing consultant

- "Be prepared to decouple—decouple from paper. . . . Sometimes you look like Luddites. I recommend a cultural sea change—a 180-degree turnabout."
  —academic from a major institute of technology

- "There are lots of solutions out there that are begging for a mission."
  —president of a newspaper chain

place requires understanding whether the analogy reflects the right paradigm for the technology under consideration, and if so, why.

Answer to Question #3: The Percent of Roughly Correct Forecasts about Successful Products Based On New Technologies

According to Professor Steven P. Schnaars, who reviewed three decades of predictions of technological hits and published the results in 1989 in his book *Megamistakes*, only 20 to 25 percent of these forecasts were anywhere close to being on target.

Looking back through the incorrect forecasts, it's clear that many of these predictions could have been weeded out by a rigorous application of the good-deal test, examining why consumers might see this product as a better combination of benefits and price than the alternatives. It's equally clear, however, that for a smaller number, the technologies were so new that one could not make accurate forecasts about the success of the products they would spawn. This anomaly leads to "tenet #3 of technocentricity," which states that, for any radically new technology, understanding the new good deal requires a leap of faith because past trends are not reliable predictors of what users will want in the future. According to this tenet, those who are blind due to their love of a new technology are no worse off than the rest of us, since no one can really know in advance how the technology will change the way consumers will behave, and therefore the benefits these consumers will value in the future.

> "The problem with television is that people must sit and keep their eyes glued to the screen. The average American family doesn't have time for it."
>
> —*The New York Times*, 1939

Like the first two tenets, this belief is not true in all cases; but, again like the first two, it is true in *some* cases. When television was first previewed in 1939, it was pooh-poohed on the basis that few consumers would have the time to sit and watch it; similarly, few people in 1979 could imagine that executives would be willing to learn how to type in order to use personal computers. This third tenet reflects the most difficult dilemma that technocentricity poses: since technocentrists love virtually all radical new technologies, and since these technologies are rarely accompanied by a fact base sufficient to determine market acceptance, how does one decide which of these is worthy of a leap of faith? One starting place for resolving this dilemma, other than relying on luck or instinct alone, is pushing hard to understand to whom, and under what circumstances, the technology *could* provide a better deal—so that any leap of faith is at least an *informed* leap of faith.

Technocentricity is a particularly obstinate form of corporate narcissism. And although processes like QFD take care of technocentric biases in theory, one can imagine people who, deeply in love with a technology, define the "customer desires" in ways that apparently but incorrectly validate their choices about the specifications of the product to be developed. With technocentrists in particular, even more important than matrices and methodologies is the need to keep asking *what* specific benefits the new technology could provide to *which* specific groups of consumers, and *how* these benefits could compare in price and importance to other alternatives likely to be available.

> "Every child I know has an *Encyclopaedia Britannica* within reach as they watch MTV. Why is wiring them up to the Library of Congress going to change things? Get a grip!"
>
> —Scott McNealy, CEO, Sun Micro-systems

The Stages of Corporate Narcissism: Death by Love

A little dose of corporate narcissism can be a good thing; clearly, people who believe passionately in what they create will naturally inject great passion in the development, production, and marketing of their products and services. The trick is balancing this passion with a clear-eyed assessment of whether the market beholds the same beauty. That's what "listening to the voice of the customer" is supposed to do. Unfortunately, however, accurate customer feedback does not tend to penetrate far in organizations afflicted with corporate narcissism, no matter what processes are used to identify customer wants. For this reason, it's critical to know the symptoms of corporate narcissism before it reaches advanced stages. The course of the disease, which typically progresses through a set of beliefs that reflect increasing levels of denial along with increasing levels of financial investment, generally goes like this:

> "The bottom line? The bottom line is in heaven!"
>
> —response of Edwin Land at the Polaroid annual meeting, April 26, 1977, to an analyst's question about the "bottom line" of Polaroid's massive investment in Polavision, a non-video-tape based instant movie system

Starting belief: The superiority of our product is self-evident. (This belief is often buttressed by market research inadvertently designed in accordance with the GIGO Effect—garbage in, garbage out— that tells managers what they want to hear instead of what they need to know, as described in "The (Inharmonious) Voice of the Customer," pp. 121–130.)

Stage-1 denial: Some people inside our company are saying that the superiority of our product is not self-evident. They say some of the market research is raising red flags, or even that the market research supporting this product wasn't done correctly. These people are blockheads. Perhaps they aren't smart enough to work here. Keep to the original development plan without modification.

Stage-2 denial: All we need to do is put this product out in the marketplace; once people see it, the product will sell itself. Full speed ahead with the product launch!

Stage-3 denial: It's hard to imagine why the customers are being so stupid when this product would delight them, if only they were smart enough to buy it. Increase the advertising budget—we need to increase the frequency of our message.

Stage-4 denial: The competition, which is gaining sales for a clearly inferior product, has been lucky so far that the customers are so stupid. We'll ignore them.

Stage-5 denial: The market research showing that, to improve our sales, we need to make changes in our product or our marketing, was done incorrectly. Fire the incompetent who did the research. Put more money into promotions, advertising, and sales.

Terminal stage: Having escalated its investment with little potential for reasonable financial return, the company hemorrhages cash; in extreme cases, the result is organizational paralysis, sometimes leading to death.

———■———

Processes that systematize product development and launch, including the need for accurate knowledge about customers and market, are all to the good, of course. What such processes cannot do, however, is eliminate the human beings involved and their passions. People fall in love with their own products and services, or with the underlying technologies, all the time. When they do, their passion forms the lens through which the customer is seen, creating a distorting filter between a company and its customers. That's why corporate narcissism persists. And that's also why rigorous consideration and reconsideration of customer needs is critical to any process for developing and launching new or improved products and services. And if such effort seems unwarranted, just remember, while it takes investment to break out of the trance created by admiration for one's own products or technologies, Narcissus died for the love of his own reflection. No matter how painful, it's worth double-checking that your customers behold the same beauty in your new product or service that you do.

———■———

"You must kill your darlings."

—Ernest Hemingway on what writers must do, when, having crafted that perfect turn of phrase, they find that their words do not work with the intended audience

———■———

PART FIVE

FUZZY LOGIC
Moving from Customers to Strategy

"Ease your bosoms."

—rendering of the English expression "take a load off your chest," as displayed on the packets of the Japanese brand, City Oriental Coffee

It might seem that moving from market to market across national borders is the ultimate in cross-cultural challenges; most people who have worked in international marketing have their own pet examples of linguistic gaffs. In fact, however, the more difficult cultural challenge is translating the hopes, dreams and data that exist within an organization into strategies that produce what customers see as good deals—while still generating profits.

Perhaps it is this very difficulty that has led many companies to understand strategy formulation in Chinese-menu terms: pick out one pre-thought template from column A, some pre-designed management programs from column B, and then fill in the details. In consequence, one sees some companies selecting the "value" template, on the theory that shifts at the macro-economic level mean that customers have just recently become interested in getting the best deals they can, while others choose the "cost" or "differentiation" templates, as though these two variable were independent of each other.

As the next two chapters argue, however, such seemingly straightforward selections often don't translate into winning strategies. Chapter 12, "The Value 'Revolution' and the 'Death' of Brand Loyalty: Consumers' Revenge on Shortsighted Companies," makes the argument that customers *always* seek value—though their definition of what constitutes value is dynamic—and presents one approach for keeping track of the ever-changing value equation. And Chapter 13, "Procrustean Strategies: Why the Real Question Is, How Differentiated and at What Costs," goes a step further, showing why strategies based on the "either/or" thinking of "either" low cost "or" high differentiation typically leads to cutting the wrong costs, increasing prices foolishly, and/or adding trifling benefits, all of which weaken a company's competitive position.

If only crafting winning strategies required no more than selecting the "right" pre-thought template and then filling in the blanks. Then all companies could be winners and most of the heavy thinking could be done by lunch time.

CHAPTER 12

THE VALUE "REVOLUTION" AND THE "DEATH" OF BRAND LOYALTY

Consumers' Revenge on Shortsighted Companies

Value The completely new goal of consumers who, in the early 1990s, for the first time began making their purchase decisions by comparing the prices and benefits of available products relative to the money they have to spend, thereby causing the recent and completely untimely Death of Brand Loyalty.

We are, it is said, in the midst of a "revolution," created, apparently, sometime in the early 1990s, when customers suddenly discovered the idea of "value." As one consequence, according to this line of thinking, customers also became less attached to the brands to which they had previously been completely loyal. Or to put the argument in headline form, we are now at the crest of the transition from "The Age of Brand Loyalty" to "The Age of Value." Two products typically given as examples of this transition are Marlboro cigarettes and Kraft cheese, both of which ceded significant loses in share to their nonbranded brethren during the early 1990s.

Belief in the value "revolution" can lead companies to make significant changes in how they do business and what they offer their customers, as they redefine "value" to mean stripped-down products and services, with fewer bells and whistles and less investment in frills like brand names. But before you design your "value"-oriented products in accordance with this definition, it's worth understanding whether there truly has been a value "revolution" and if so, what has caused it and what it means for your company.

A good place to start this assessment of the value revolution is with a look in *Webster's Third New International Dictionary*, which defines "value" as "relative worth, utility, or importance." By this definition, customers *always* buy on the basis of "value" or the "good deal"; that is, they *always* look for the best combinations of benefits and prices they can get relative to the benefits they are seeking, the money they have or want to spend, the time they have to search for the product or service in question, and the alternatives they have identified. What changes in this equation is not *whether* customers buy on the basis of value, but *how* they define value.

This is not a trivial semantic distinction. A number of factors can affect how customers define value. One of these is the overall economic climate. When the economic climate becomes harsher, many people shift their purchase criteria, sacrificing certain product benefits in favor of lower prices. This observation was confirmed by a 1993 study, conducted by University of Chicago professors Stephen Hoch and Sumeet Banerji, which showed that, for the period 1972–1991, the share of the U.S. grocery market going to private-label products was inversely correlated with trends in personal disposable income. For example, in the relatively tough economic times of 1982, the share of dollars going to private-label products rose to about 16.5 percent; conversely, during the relatively good economic times of 1986, the share of these products dropped to about 13 percent. (To put these statistics in context: the U.S. grocery market for the year ending June 30, 1991 was $368.5 billion and a difference of 3.5 share points during that year would have amounted to about $13 billion in sales.) Or consider what a change in economic outlook did to one market for high-end goods—luxury cars. After the Dow took a nosedive in October 1987, the sales of these cars in the United States did too. One casualty, BMW sold almost 100,000 cars in the U.S. in 1986 and only about 65,000 in 1989.

Another factor is the competitive set. If competitors, current or new, cut a little out of the benefits provided and a lot out of the prices charged, and if customers don't care much about the benefits cut, the new definition of value will require substantially lower prices, as has happened in the airline industry. If competitors aggressively introduce new or improved products with lower prices while steadily adding to the benefits provided, the new definition of value will require either more benefits at the same price or the same (or even more) benefits at lower prices, as has happened in the computer industry. And if the demand within a product category suddenly exceeds industry capacity, the new definition of value will likely include a higher price, as anyone who has ever negotiated with the building trades after a major hurricane knows from experience.

But changes in economic climate or competitive conditions are not the only factors affecting how customers define "value." Also important are the actions taken by the producers of products and services themselves. And that's where we come back to Marlboro cigarettes and Kraft cheese. For while the downturn in the economy undoubtedly affected these two brands, the actions taken by the producers of these two products also had significant impacts on their fortunes. In combination, their two stories provide a cautionary tale about why it is so important to keep track of the specific value equation for any particular market, and to be able to estimate how actions taken by the company, moves taken by the competition, and other external forces are likely to affect the customers' evaluation of the various deals available to them.

Instigating the Value Revolution: Of Marlboro Friday and the Great Macaroni and Cheese Debacle

Cigarettes are the most frequently cited indicator of the transition from "The Age of Brand Loyalty" to "The Age of Value." In part, this is because the main event in the cigarette story is so clearly demarcated; on Friday, April 2, 1993, Philip Morris announced a forty-cents-per-pack price cut (about a 20 percent reduction) on its Marlboro brand, a day that quickly became known as "Marlboro Friday." One result of "Marlboro Friday": sharp drops in the 1993 operating profits for the tobacco giants, amounting to a $2.3 billion reduction for Philip Morris and a

$1.3 billion reduction for RJR Nabisco Holdings, maker of Camels and follower of Marlboro's price cut. Another result: as calculated by *Fortune* magazine, a $47.5 billion drop in the stock market value of the 25 top makers of consumer brands during the five months following Philip Morris's change in pricing. Yet, for all the pain, the price decrease did lead to one outcome that Philip Morris sought: in the fifteen months following its dramatic announcement, Marlboro's share soared, increasing by eight share points, from just over 22 percent of the market to almost 30 percent.

But the real story behind Marlboro's brush with the Death of Brand Loyalty began long before Marlboro Friday. Until 1980, no generic cigarette brands existed. Then, in 1980, Liggett & Myers, faced with sickly sales of its Lark and L&M cigarettes, introduced a discount brand—a strategy based on cheaper tobacco, deep cuts in advertising, lower prices, and slimmer margins than the industry had seen before. A year later came generic cigarettes, with even lower prices and thinner margins. Finally, all the players, including Philip Morris and RJR, joined the fray and introduced their own cheap smokes.

"The overriding lesson of this last year is that big brands are still popular and that the consumer will opt for them if the price is in line."

—Ellen Merlo, vice president Philip Morris

And what actions were taken on behalf of the premium brands like Marlboro and Camel? Two hefty price increases per year, averaging 10 percent per year throughout the 1980s. By 1992, RJR's product portfolio included both generics, such as Highway (private-labeled by RJR for British Petroleum's chain of 800 service stations) priced at sixty-nine cents per pack, and Camel—priced at around $2.10, a differential of 300 percent. The volume of nonpremium brands responded accordingly, skyrocketing from zero in 1981 to around 150 billion cigarettes, or 30 percent of the market, in 1992—and over 40 percent in 1993.

A similar story can be told about the skirmishes in the cheese world, and particularly about Kraft cheese. Acquired by Philip Morris in 1988, Kraft's revenues and profits didn't grow nearly as fast as Philip Morris had hoped. The official corporate explanation: the weakening economy and volatile raw material prices. But a review of management decisions shows an additional factor: Kraft's pricing policies. Through 1989 and 1990, Kraft kept raising the prices on its cheese brands—such as Kraft Singles,

Velveeta, and Kraft Macaroni & Cheese—and consumers hung on. Then in 1991, raw material prices dropped, and with them the prices of the private-label alternatives. Suddenly the premium for Kraft cheese slices versus the private-label versions rose from thirty cents a pack to sixty cents. Similarly, in some markets, a box of Kraft Macaroni & Cheese surged to as high as eighty-nine cents per box, more than twice the price of the private-label alternatives. As a result, in 1991 Kraft lost three to four points of market share, which translated into more than $150 million in lost sales. The company subsequently rolled back its prices by 8 percent.

The stories of Marlboro cigarettes and Kraft cheese reflect several interesting parallels. Both did, it's true, find competing more difficult as the economy soured. Both did lose share to nonbranded alternatives. And both did eventually roll back their prices. But just as importantly, both also helped to create their own problems by increasing the price differential between their products and the other alternatives without increasing the differential in benefits as well. Perhaps these manufacturers held the belief that their brand names were so strong that just the use of the name would justify the ever increasing price premiums. But such a belief often leads to a losing strategy when the companies offering the alternatives do not raise their prices at the same clip (or, in contrast, even reduce their prices and/or increase the benefits they offer) and when the customers aren't locked into one vendor by some sort of switching costs.

This is not to say that Philip Morris and RJR didn't find themselves in tough positions. The fat margins on the branded products were hard to forgo—before April 1993, the margin on a pack of Camels was about ten times that of a pack of generic cigarettes like Highway. Further, the culture of brand leadership had bred a kind of deadly complacency such that in some consumer goods companies, the verb "to price" had come to mean not "to *set* prices" but "to *raise* prices" as in, "the best way for us to ensure that we will meet the goals that Corporate has given us is to 'price.'" And finally, the lag times between price increases and consumer defections were in most cases long enough to confirm the companies' fervent wish that their customers were

"What'd he say? Blessed are the cheesemakers?"

—how some onlookers heard the "Blessed are the peacemakers" speech, according to the Monty Python movie, *Life of Brian*

indeed "price insensitive"—that their volumes would not de
cline (or would not decline much) as their prices increased.

But though the difficulties that Philip Morris and
RJR faced were real, they were also irrelevant since
the customers' concern is always about getting the best
deal they can relative to their standards and their constraints—and hardly ever about the short-term profit-
maximization issues facing the companies to which
they give their business. Companies that continuously
increase their prices relative to the alternatives while
providing no incremental benefits should therefore not
be surprised when significant numbers of consumers demonstrate that the brand names in question are
no longer worth the ever-escalating premiums being
asked.

> "Brand loyalty is
> very much like
> an onion. It has
> layers and a core.
> The core is the
> user who will
> stick with
> you until the
> very end."
>
> —Procter &
> Gamble CEO
> Edwin Artzt

The First Line of Defense: Keeping Track of the Alternatives

The first line of defense against the kind of consumer
revenge that Philip Morris, Kraft, and others have felt is
to keep track of the alternatives from which the customer can choose. And since each of these alternatives is
characterized by a set of benefits that it provides to consumers and its price, one way to track these alternatives
is to create a grid on which you can map the benefits-to-
price position of each product competing for the customer's purse. I call this grid the "Good-Deal Map."

The horizontal axis of this grid shows the benefits,
from the customer's point of view, of each of the alternatives, with the number or intensity of the benefits
provided increasing as one moves to the right. The vertical axis shows the price per unit or per usage, depending on how the customer calculates price, with the price
increasing as one moves up the page. The resulting pattern of points on the grid, moving from the lower left
to upper right in a rough band, illustrates how much
more some customers are willing to pay in order to get
more benefits. Products that are far above this "band of

> "The successful
> producer of an
> article sells it for
> more than it cost
> him to make, and
> that's his profit.
> But the customer
> buys it only
> because it is
> worth more to
> him than he pays
> for it, and that's
> his profit. No one
> can make a profit
> producing any-
> thing unless the
> customer makes a
> profit using it."
>
> —Samuel Barrett
> Pettengill
> (1886–1974), U.S.
> Congressman

Figure 2: Good-Deal Map #1

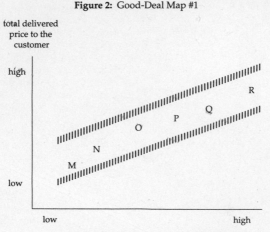

value" will likely struggle for market share unless they reduce their prices, while those far below will grab sales away from competitors.

Consider Good-Deal Map #1. This map could apply to a market for virtually any product—from cheese or cigarettes to concrete block or CAD-CAM systems. On this map, M, N, O, P, Q, and R define the value band and each of the positions within the band represents a point of value, or "a good deal," to its respective buyers. For this reason, no position within the value band is inherently better than any of the others. Rather, determining the best position depends on the context: the number of unit sales and margins associated with each point, market trends that will affect sales and margins, and the company's ability to protect its position. The best position, therefore, is the one with the superior profit dynamics, independent of the point that represents the product that the viewer happens to prefer or of whether the position is "high" or "low" on the map.

One advantage of thinking about the benefits-to-price position of each alternative on the Good-Deal Map is the ability to

Figure 3: Good-Deal Map #2

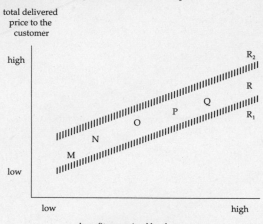

benefits perceived by the customer

anticipate how moves in the market will likely affect the share and overall profitability of any one product.

Take the company that makes product R as shown on Good-Deal Map #2. Trouble will likely ensue if R moves to position R_2—that is, increases its price per unit while not increasing the benefits delivered—*if* at the same time the competitive brands maintain their old benefits-to-price (or "value") positions. In these cases, you can predict generally what will happen: as the price premium for R grows, some consumers will shift to lower price/lower benefit alternatives, which is exactly what happened in the cases of Marlboro cigarettes and Kraft Macaroni & Cheese. Alternately, if R_2 is the old price and R_1 is the new price and nothing else changes, we would expect R at its new reduced price to increase its share of the market at the expense of lower-priced alternatives, just as Marlboro did in its post price-cut period of April 1993 through March 1994.

Of course, a tool like the Good-Deal Map is only helpful in tracking the alternatives if the data used are accurate enough to highlight likely threats and opportunities *and* the map is completed quickly enough that the insights are generated while effective action can still be taken. For these reasons, I like to start with a first draft of the Good-Deal Map based on best guesses and the internal data that are easily available, spending the bulk of my time not on detailed data collection but rather on getting the structure of the analysis right. More specifically, this means thinking hard about: 1) whether the right universe of alternatives has been included; 2) whether the measures for the vertical axis, price, reflect the way customers compare prices; and 3) whether the measures for the horizontal axis, benefits, capture the way customers compare benefits.

Step 1: Defining the Universe

The first step in creating a Good-Deal Map to track major trends in how consumers define "value" is to make sure that the map includes all the alternatives that consumers might consider as they make their purchase decisions. Imagine, for example, a Good-Deal Map for cigarettes in 1991 that included Marlboro and Camel and other branded cigarettes but didn't include discount brands and generics. Such a map would not have shown major threats among the brand leaders themselves—and would have totally missed the danger these leaders were creating for themselves by increasing the price premium they asked consumers to pay while not providing any incremental benefits.

Similarly, imagine the Good Deal Map for macaroni and cheese in 1991 that included products provided by Kraft and Borden but didn't include either the private-label alternatives or the novelty alternatives (including, at that time, "Teenage Mutant Ninja Turtles and Cheese Pasta Dinner," complete with bright purple box embossed with the four turtles in all their green glory). This map too would not have shown the wonderful price umbrella that Kraft was creating for both the private-label vendors, such as A&P, and for the novelty-item vendors, such as Primera Foods Inc, maker of Teenage Mutant Ninja Turtles and Pasta Dinner. In the absence of what the customers could see as relevant alternatives, a tool like the Good-Deal Map will not be terribly useful in tracking the customer's definition of value.

> "Consumer research showed that people wanted more contoured edges and didn't want the center to melt first when sucked. So we filled in the center and rounded off the edges."
>
> —response of a Velamints manager to a question from *Consumer Reports* on why its package of mints, having gone from .85 ounce to .71 ounce, was proclaiming itself to be "new improved"

Step 2: Estimating the Customer's Perspective
on Costs

The second step in creating a Good-Deal Map is estimating how customers calculate their costs when they make their comparisons among the alternatives available to them. Typically, this is more difficult than it may first appear for two reasons. First, in many product categories, the prices customers actually pay often bear little resemblance to the price lists used in the industry. In these situations, even rough estimates of comparative prices can involve considerable effort in order to factor in the effects of rebates, coupons, or discounts negotiated in the field.

The second complication in understanding how customers calculate their costs is that the sticker price per box or per widget or per service may not be the costs that the customers implicitly use as they do their comparison shopping. In some cases, the customers' calculations are straightforward, as when the package dimensions are the same for two products but the product counts or product weights are not. In other cases, the calculations are more complicated, as when a vendor convinces the market that its product or service has a higher initial price but saves the customer other costs. This is commonly true for industrial products but can be true for consumer products as well. For example, luxury car makers often compete on the basis that their higher sticker prices need to be evaluated in the context of their higher resale values and their lower maintenance costs. Similarly, Pine-Sol, a branded cleaning fluid, advertises that while its per-bottle price is higher than that of its nonbranded competitors, its more concentrated formula yields many more cleanings per bottle, more than making up for the initial price differential. Whether the product is a sedan on a showroom floor or a bottle on the grocery store shelf, the prices that matter are the adjusted prices that customers use as they choose among alternatives.

Step 3: Laying Out the Benefits

The third step in creating a Good-Deal Map is laying out the core "generic" benefits (or what I call the "tickets to play"), and the key "differentiated" benefits in the product or service. The key differentiated benefits are what pull a product out to the right on the horizontal axis and can be of many types, including: enhanced performance (any razor gives a shave, but Gillette razors give particularly close shaves); consistent quality (any roadside diner can flip you a burger, but McDonald's provides the same taste and nutritional quality in the same clean setting every time and every place); and amplified image (any new knit shirt can cover your torso, but the little pony on a Ralph Lauren polo shirt both clothes you and conveys a message about who you are and the way you live or wish to live your life). (For more on creating and managing differentiated benefits, see "Procrustean Strategies," pp. 159–169.)

Brands provide a shorthand for some of these differentiated benefits. Brands do one or both of the following two things. They extend promises—for example, about the benefits the product delivers or about the consistency of an attribute every time the product is purchased. And/or they broadcast information—for example, about the buyer and his or her economic status. When consumers feel they need the promises being made or care about the information being broadcast, these benefits go far to the right on the benefits scale, and can command a price premium. For example, the Hoch and Banerji study cited earlier showed that—all other things being equal—lower-priced private-label alternatives make less inroads against those branded products characterized by: 1) high technical complexity that translates into superior benefits or lower costs (as Gillette has done with its proprietary manufacturing technology for producing its razors); 2) relative consistency of quality in categories where the other alternatives are subject to more variability (as McDonald's has done with its worldwide network of restaurants); and 3) heavy investment in advertising their brand names, even when the economy slows down (as Ralph Lauren had done with its apparel).

A new frontier for brand names: information offered on the Internet.

Conversely, brands that charge a hefty premium to the customer but that, relative to their private-label competitors, provide little difference in the benefits to the consumers (and unattractive margins to the retailers), will find themselves in trouble. This is often a particular problem for brands that trail the brand leader in categories where stores have established their own credible premium private labels, as Great Britain's J. Saintsbury PLC has done with its Saintsbury store-brand, and

Canada's Loblaw Companies has done with its President's Choice store-brand. The root of the problem: relative to the store brands, the also-ran brands with their premium prices do not provide a sufficiently good deal. And, as retailers become increasingly able to extend promises about quality that are close in credibility to those made by the established brand leaders, some of the power—and some of the profit margin—of the brand names shifts from the manufacturers to the retailers.

Talking about a *new* age of value is preposterous. The "age of value" is a constant. What isn't constant is how customers define value and the alternatives from which they have to choose. In markets and categories where consumers learn that store brands or other private-label products can deliver close-to-comparable performance and consistency at lower price points and where the branded alternatives cut advertising—or where the price premium for the branded alternatives escalate out of control even with heavy advertising—the branded alternatives should not be surprised to see their shares erode. In short, the issue for any company is not whether customers have suddenly become interested in value, but whether those within the company can anticipate and respond to shifts in the customer's definition of value faster and more effectively than their competitors.

———————■———————

The saga of the cigarette- and cheese-makers is about neither the Death of Brand Loyalty nor the Rise of the Age of Value, but rather about the revenge of consumers on companies that take them for granted. Whether you call it "value" or "delighting the customer," the good-deal test is, and has always been, the customer's bottom line in considering any product or service. Delivering the good deal must therefore be the foundation for any strategy, total quality management program, reengineering effort, or customer-retention initiative. Vendors who forget this fundamental rule eventually pay the price, as once-loyal customers take their business elsewhere—to other vendors, brands, or even private-label products—that now provide a better deal according to the customer's criteria.

> "Your premium brand better be delivering something special or it's not going to get the business."
>
> —billionaire investor Warren Buffett

CHAPTER 13

PROCRUSTEAN STRATEGIES

Why the Real Question Is, How Differentiated and At What Costs

Procrustean strategies 1: *Those strategies that, in the process of aiming at cost and price leadership, miss all opportunities for providing differentiated benefits that customers seek, thereby forgoing incremental price premiums and volumes that could have been realized;* 2: *Those strategies that, in the process of aiming at differentiation and product leadership, miss all opportunities for cutting excess costs, thereby forgoing incremental product margins and volumes that could have been achieved.*

In 1980, Michael Porter, professor at Harvard Business School, published his landmark book, *Competitive Strategy*, in which he stipulated three "generic" strategies for "outperforming competitors in an industry": 1. *overall cost leadership* ("low cost relative to competitors . . . in its industry"), 2. *differentiation* ("creating something that is perceived industrywide as being unique"), and 3. *focus* ("focusing on a particular buyer group, segment of the product line or geographic market"). It is, said Professor Porter, "rarely possible" for a company to pursue more than one of these generic strategies.

Thirteen years later, two consultants, Michael Treacy and Fred Wiersema, published an article in the *Harvard Business Review* in which they revealed the three generic "paths to market leadership": 1. *operational excellence* ("lead its industry in price"), 2. *product leadership* ("offer leading-edge products and services"), and 3. *customer intimacy* ("segment and target markets precisely and then tailor offerings"). "Few" companies, said Treacy and Wiersema, can master more than one of these paths.

As all three of these business thinkers rightly conclude, strategies do vary in terms of the type of customer targeted, the benefits included in the product or service, and the cost structure the company needs to maintain. A McDonald's restaurant on the Champs Élysées would surely pursue a different kind of strategy than Restaurant Lucas-Carton, a three-star dining establishment on the same street. But as applied by many in businesses, these frameworks have created an unfortunate fad: Procrustean strategies.

Procrustes, according to the ancient Greek myths, was the uncompromising hotelier who maintained an inn along the main road to Athens. The distinguishing characteristic of this inn was that it had only one room, and that in this one room there was only one bed. Procrustes believed that all travelers who stayed at the inn should fit into this bed. In keeping with his philosophy, he therefore lopped off the feet of any traveler too long for the cot, and stretched those too short. Alas, in both cases, by the time Procrustes was done with his adjustments, his guests were dead.

Procrustean strategies work in much the same way. Managers who use the template of "overall cost leadership" or "operational excellence" as their Procrustean strategy tend to view their products or services as "commodities," with no real option for differentiation. Accordingly, these managers tend to see their strategic goal as almost exclusively a matter of producing only the base, commodity-level benefits and then keeping the costs of these core benefits as low as possible. Conversely, managers who employ the template of "differentiation" or "product leadership" as their Procrustean strategy tend to view their products or services as abounding in "differentiators"—benefits above and beyond the set of generic performance requirements for that particular category of goods. Given this perspective, these managers do not tend to manage the costs of these "differentiated benefits" very aggressively.

The cause of Procrustean strategies is Procrustean managers; that is, people who try to fit their businesses to the absolute standard of *"either* we must classify ourselves as a vendor of commodity products *or* we must classify ourselves as a vendor of differentiated products." This is an oversimplified and misleading way to think about strategy. Far more useful is to focus on to what degree a product or service can be differentiated in ways that target customers care about, while doing so at costs that keep the resulting prices attractive to these customers.

Replacing the absolute standard of "*either* cost *or* differentiation" with the relative standard of "to what degree differentiated and at what costs" is essential for capturing the profit opportunities associated with delivering more of what the customers want. Making this transition can, in turn, be helped by liberal application of what we might call "The Three Anti-Procrustean Propositions":

1. Virtually all products and services abound in the potential to use intangibles as differentiators; your job is to find them.

2. Virtually all products and services abound in the potential to use performance extenders as differentiators; your job is to create them.

3. No matter what the differentiator, costs always count; your job is to keep these costs low relative to the benefits they provide.

A closer look at each of these propositions and its consequences follows.

————■————

Anti-Procrustean Proposition #1: Virtually All Products and Services Abound in Intangibles; Your Job Is to Find Them

On a price/performance basis, Product "A," described below, is a bad deal relative to Product "B," also described below. Yet thousands have bought "A," and many more covet it.

attribute:	Product "A"	Product "B"
price:	$1,500+	$100
conformance to performance specs:	relatively poor	close to perfect
repair rate:	frequent	rare
maintenance requirements:	high	low

What are Product "A" and Product "B"? Why, a Rolex mechanical-movement watch and a Timex quartz-movement watch, respectively.

Rolex can achieve its prices, which on some models substantially exceed $1,500, because its watches do more than tell time; they also impart intangibles that are highly valuable to a certain segment of watch buyers. Among these intangibles are the aesthetics of the watches, the status associated with the Rolex brand name, and the message about the wearers that the watches broadcast. Nor are timepieces the only goods that can be differentiated on the basis of such attributes. As Harvard Business School professor Theodore Levitt has argued forcefully, virtually all products abound in intangibles, benefits that do not visibly or measurably contribute to performance but which consumers nonetheless factor into their purchase decisions. Consider vodka. By U.S. law, vodkas cannot have any distinctive taste, color, or aroma. Yet consumers discriminate vigorously among the competing vodkas on the market. If it isn't the taste, color, or aroma, there must be intangibles—including brand name and image—at work.

Or consider another beverage that, not so long ago in the U.S. market, was largely undifferentiated: water. A "Good Deal Map" similar to the ones shown in the section on "Value," for a glass of water to accompany dinner at home might look like that in Figure 4.

The intangibles in water include the brands, with their pedigrees, promises, and packaging. Ty Nant, a brand of imported water with U.S. 1993 sales of 8,500,000 eleven-ounce bottles, ascribes the growth of its Welsh water to its Welsh name—and its cobalt blue bottles. Says Alfonso Guerrero, owner of Ty Nant: "It's incredible, the power of this package." Brands, in fact, are the ultimate intangibles, since, by virtue of nothing more than their names and logos, they extend promises—about the product or service to be purchased—and/or broadcast information—about the customer and/or the consumer. (For more on brands and the price premiums they can command, see "The Value 'Revolution' and the 'Death' of Brand Loyalty," pp. 147–158.)

Figure 4: Good-Deal Map for a Glass of Water

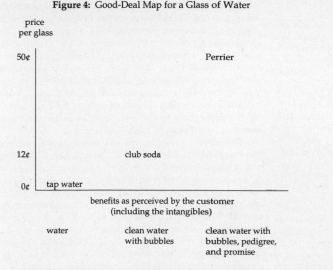

Looking at a product or service only in terms of its generic performance requirements is often a mistake; just because intangibles, by definition, are difficult for vendors to see or measure, doesn't mean that customers won't use them as part of their purchase decisions. Identifying and communicating the right intangibles can therefore be a substantial source of revenues from large segments of buyers, even for previously "undifferentiated" products like water or chicken, as Perrier and Perdue, respectively, have shown.

Anti-Procrustean Proposition #2: *Virtually All Products and Services Abound in Performance Extenders; Your Job Is to Create Them*

It's not just the intangibles that can differentiate a product or service. Benefits that extend the definition of performance of a product or service in measurable ways

An intangible in the rag trade: "Older women . . . still want to be a size 4 or 6 even though they're really an 8 or 10. We will cut a big size for the older woman and call it a 4 or a 6 and everyone will be happy."

—Bud Konheim, president of apparel manufacturer Nicole Miller Ltd.

can also be very important in the choices customers make. Consider ready-mix concrete. The generic performance attributes of this product include workability, pumpability, "slump" (a measure of the downward slide of the concrete), set time, and "psi" (pounds per square inch) strength. But as Granite Rock, a ready-mix company in northern California and Baldrige award winner, proved, it would be a mistake to think of concrete as a commodity, purchased only on the basis of the lowest price for a given set of specifications for these five basic performance attributes.

Through its customer satisfaction surveys, Granite Rock was able to determine which of a set of possible performance extenders—which included such attributes as "helpful dispatchers," "sales reps who understand their customers' needs," and "orders arrive on time"—were most important to the customers in their market. The company then used its findings to improve its performance on the attributes its target market cared most about. As a result, Granite Rock was able to increase its prices and its unit sales relative to its competition. In other words, Granite Rock's concrete is a differentiated product; the company used a set of performance extenders to differentiate its concrete from its competitors' concrete—and to achieve superior financial results relative to its competitors.

Browning-Ferris Industries, the second largest trash hauler in the United States with 570,000 industrial customers, also has found ways to extend the definition of performance for what is usually considered a commodity service: garbage collection. Recently, the company undertook a massive customer-satisfaction survey involving 30,000 accounts to determine why it was losing 14 percent of its customer base each year. The results revealed a set of benefits, beyond carting away the garbage at the contracted times and prices, that consumers used to distinguish one trash hauler from another. These include:

- Keeping the dumpsters in good working order, and repairing or replacing them quickly when they rust, pop holes, or when their lids no longer close properly (in contrast to the experience of the North Carolina veterinarian who complained to BFI three times about the hole in his dumpster and the resulting spills—and who was finally visited by a BFI team that made no repairs but did *paint* the dumpster, hole and all).

- Providing locks on the dumpster to keep other people's trash out (a benefit to customers such as the frat house in Georgia that wished to keep its refuse separate from that of "the brothers at those other houses").

- Ensuring that the drivers don't arrive late, make unnecessary noise, drive recklessly, deposit the emptied dumpsters in places other than where the customers have specified, forget to put the locks back on the lids, or leave leftovers from earlier pickups (leading the proprietor of a souvenir shop, whose trash pickup followed that for a seafood house, to complain bitterly to BFI about the driver who "spills shrimp juice . . . [which] smells so nasty we have to hose down the parking lot").

Based on the actions BFI took in response to the survey results, the company was able to cut its rate of customer loss by about 12 percent. The resulting 10,000 or so accounts that were saved by these efforts represent a significant savings over the costs of finding and selling an equivalent number of replacement accounts.

Granite Rock and Browning-Ferris Industries demonstrate the profit in expanding the company's definition of "performance" to give the customers more of what they want. The basic approach for doing so is straightforward:

- Step one: Discover what benefits, including those beyond the standard industry definition of performance, are most important to your target customers and how you stack up against the competition on these attributes. Granite Rock and Browning-Ferris did this using customer satisfaction surveys. Sometimes more qualitative methods, like focus groups or individual interviews are required, to identify the potential performance extenders, before moving to quantitative ways of measuring the company against its competitors on these attributes.

- Step two: Look at the attributes that are most important to customers when they choose among vendors. If you are ahead on these attributes, the task is to identify the sources of your success and the actions you need to take to protect and increase your lead; if you are behind, the task is to figure out the causes of the gap and how to close it or leapfrog the competition. This is the kind of tactical-level business blocking and tackling that, when applied to the differentiators customers care about, can bring strategic-sized returns.

- Step three: Set measures for defining improvement in the key attributes and use them to monitor progress. These measures can be simple or complicated, single or multiple, depending on the situation and the people involved. What they *must* be, however, is clear, so everyone who can affect them knows what they are, how they are calculated, and what progress is being achieved. (For an example, see the Federal Express "Service Quality Indicator," or SQI, as described in "Judgment, Empowerment, and the Parable of the Talents," pp. 93–108.)

Finding the performance extenders that customers value often requires thinking beyond the traditional industry metrics about performance. One way to find these extenders is to map the "usage timeline" for a product or service, and then look hard at the customer's needs at times other than when they are actually using the product or service in question. "Pre-use" aspects include such tasks as the time spent searching for the right product, making the purchase, arranging and taking delivery, and storing the product before it is used; "in-use" aspects include basic performance attributes in addition to such items as the time spent arranging for repairs, waiting for the repairs to be started, and waiting for the repairs to be completed; and "post-use" aspects include the time spent storing the product between uses, cleaning up after its use, disposing of the product, and reordering the product or its components. BFI's "repairs or replaces dumpsters quickly when needed" is an example of this kind of performance extender; it saves the customer's time both in following up on unmet requests for repairs and in cleaning up around the damaged dumpster until the repairs are made.

Another way to locate performance extenders is to look hard at how customers want the product or service to perform during usage. "Range of software available" is a classic measure manufacturers have used to define the performance of personal computers, for example. Yet I purchased my first Apple Macintosh in 1988 even though I knew it did not have as great a range of software available as the DOS-based machines and that it carried a much higher sticker price—simply because I wanted a machine that was easy and fun to use, and have been a loyal user ever since. (IBM ignored this way of thinking about the performance of personal computers for a long time, however, instead discounting the importance of "ease of use" for a significant segment of users. With the advent of Microsoft's Windows, ease of use is moving from being a clear differentiator to becoming more a part of the industry definition of PC performance.)

Anti-Procrustean Principle #3: No Matter What the Differentiator, Costs Always Count; Your Job Is to Keep These Costs Low Relative to the Benefits They Provide

Discovering the most important differentiators, both the intangibles and the performance extenders, that customers use to discriminate among products and services doesn't mean that vendors can then ignore costs. To the contrary, "differentiation" or "product leadership" strategies followed with little regard to costs merely invite competitors to create lower-cost products that preserve the differentiators that matter, and drop the ones on which customers place little value.

Consider the dilemma of the start-up company that has redesigned the traditional hospital johnny. Here's what's different about the redesigned gown: the back has an extra overlapping flap, and the flap closes with Velcro tabs instead of cloth ties; the shoulder seams open to provide access to the patient's torso without taking off the entire garment (an especially difficult process when the patient is hooked up to an IV or other apparatus); the cloth is softer and thicker than traditionally used; the gown has pockets for monitors or personal items and loops for attaching a drainage bag. Anyone who has ever been a hospital patient will

A question to consider: Why do fine restaurants instruct their wait staff to place each diner's napkin in his or her lap? And why do they think that this is an intangible of positive value to their diners who, presumably, are perfectly capable of this task themselves—or a good use of their waiters' time and attention?

instantly see the benefits of this gown—and instantly understand why the maker calls itself the No Moon Company.

The dilemma is not the differentiators but the price. At two to three times the price of a standard gown, the customers—hospitals—are not inclined to pay for No Moon's incremental benefits, even if they're desired by the consumers, the patients themselves. A product like the No Moon gown will thrive only if the company can line up its costs with the benefits *most* desired by its consumers and then deemphasize the others. Co-owner Anita Chafee says the benefits are "to give the patient some dignity and comfort." My bet is that the more important of these is the incremental dignity afforded by the gowns; keeping the innovations on the backflap and shoulder seams, and reducing the other benefits and their associated costs might provide No Moon with a cost/benefits profile that allows the gown to compete more effectively in the hospital market. (And, to the extent that patients today snag extra johnnies to wear, with the opening on the front side, as robes over their back-opening gowns, No Moons might even provide hospitals with a modest cost savings.)

No Moon is not an exception. Many companies fall into the Procrustean trap of thinking that their beautifully differentiated products or services exempt them from managing their costs aggressively. In 1992, for example, the Ritz-Carlton hotel chain won a Malcolm Baldrige National Quality Award. In 1994, *The Wall Street Journal* reported that of the thirty hotels in the Ritz chain, "only half a dozen are believed to be in the black." The challenge to companies like No Moon or like the hotels in the Ritz-Carlton chain, therefore, is not one of shifting from a differentiating strategy to a low-cost strategy, but to pick the right costs to cut and the right benefits to reduce. (The difficulty of this challenge should not be underestimated, as described in "Low-Cost Migraines: How to Cost Cut Your Way to Big Trouble," pp. 197–203.) No matter what the differentiator, costs matter.

———————■———————

Customers don't care what the textbooks say. They don't care about "operational excellence" products or "differentiation strategy" products or "customer intimacy" products. They care only about one thing: getting the good deal—the best combination of benefits (including the differentiators) and price according to their particular preferences and relative to the available alternatives—just as any of us operates when we are on the buying side of the counter.

Given the dangers of following Procrustean strategies, it's worth remembering that the original Procrustes eventually met his end when Theseus, cousin of Hercules and son of Aegeus, king of Athens, gave him a dose of his own medicine. As myth-teller Robert Graves recounts the tale, Theseus lashed Procrustes to the bed in which Procrustes had placed so many others, cut off both his feet and his head, and then, for good measure, wrapped his corpse in a blanket and tossed it into the sea.

Companies might profit from using Theseus as their guide for dumping their own Procrustean strategies. Whether a company focuses on microniches or sells across entire industries, makes steel or brews beer, collects trash or runs hotels, designs fashion apparel or redesigns hospital johnnies, it's the relative standard of "to what degree differentiated and at what costs" that pays—and not the absolute standard of "either 'cost' or 'differentiation.'"

"There's something sick about the whole thing. I personally have in my possession thousands of little shampoos from the thousands of hotels I've been to. And I don't even have hair."

—Jerry Della Femina, who, with an estimated net worth of over $20 million, can presumably buy his own shampoo, on the importance of a tiny, but important, differentiator provided by hotels

PART SIX

MORE INSTANT ANSWERS

Paddling Out to the Biggest Waves

*"There is no expedient to which man will not resort
to avoid the real labor of thinking."*

—Sir Joshua Reynolds (1723–1792)

When I was a student at Harvard Business School, what I found most challenging, and ultimately most satisfying, was that at the end of each case discussion we were left to determine for ourselves the lessons to be learned. This is no longer standard operating policy at HBS, I am told. Students now demand that the professors dedicate the last twenty minutes of each case discussion to outlining "the" school solution, preferably with prepackaged slides. Since student ratings are used in the evaluations of the professors' teaching abilities, many teachers now comply with the request, saving students the effort of trying to reason through their own solutions.

A similar dynamic seems to be present outside of the classroom as well. And there is certainly a ready supply of prepackaged panaceas since, if there's one eternal truth of fad surfing, it's that there's always another wave, always another promise of a school solution that, if followed without question, will lead to certain success in a prescribed area. Some of these waves are small, some of moderate size. But every once in the while there come tsunamis, monster waves that promise total success in virtually every area of every enterprise.

When used with forethought and tailored to a specific situation, these techniques can yield remarkable results. But when applied blindly or mindlessly, they can create organizational chaos. Chapter 14, "Total Quality Mayhem: When Cookbook Compliance Creates Quality Quagmires," examines how to keep the fundamental insights and tools of the quality movement from turning into a TPN (total process nightmare). Chapter 15, "Reengineering and the Labors of Hercules: There's More Than One Way to Leap to Breakthrough Results," explores a few of the many ways to create fundamental change, including reengineering. And Chapter 16, "Low-Cost Migraines: How to Cost Cut Your Way to Big Trouble," addresses an enduring and potentially lethal wave—the drive to become the low-cost producer—and illustrates how cost slashing, when done without adequate analysis of the benefits that the costs support, can lead to the weakening of loyalty among customers and employees alike.

There's no doubt that business is a complex endeavor. But while having someone delineate "the" answer may ease anxieties and even make it easier to prepare for business school exams, it is surely no guarantee of success on the ultimate test—winning, profitably, in the market place.

CHAPTER 14

TOTAL QUALITY MAYHEM

When Cookbook Compliance Creates Quality Quagmires

> *Total Quality Management (TQM)* 1: *A management philosophy based on the idea that quality is a prerequisite for improving the competitive position of any company rather than a cost-burden that only some companies can afford; 2: A set of tools that mostly predate the TQM label and that, when practiced as part of a TQM program, so totally absorb management in "process" that the process becomes an end in itself; 3: A process import thought by some to be an integral tactic in Japan Inc.'s secret strategy for destroying American enterprise.*

Edith Kelly, formerly Federal Express's vice president of Audit and Quality and now its vice president of Purchasing and Supply, tells the following joke about the three executives who, facing execution, were asked for their final wishes. The first, Fiona from the Finance Department, said: "Just let me finish this calculation so I can figure out why our total assets are two cents out of balance with our total liabilities." The second, Tom, a member of the TQM staff, in response to the same question said: "In honor of our total commitment to total quality management, I would like to give one last speech on quality." And then the third, Peyton, a product line manager said: "I don't mind waiting for Fiona to finish crunching her numbers, as long as you grant me my last wish—that you execute me before Tom . . . so I won't have to hear another speech on quality."

Kelly's joke captures a key element of current discussion about Total Quality Management: the polarization between TQM-champions like Tom and TQM-skeptics like Peyton. Before picking sides, it's worth a look at the data.

------◼------

The TQM debate follows a formulaic script. The TQM-skeptics view TQM as a mania from management hell, at best a waste of time and money and at worst harmful to organizations. They therefore dismiss TQM as just another fad, fanatically and irrationally supported by what they see as an army of "TQM-zealots." The TQM-champions respond in kind, defending TQM as manna from management heaven, essential to the future competitiveness of any organization. Accordingly, they disregard all criticisms as the efforts of "TQM-bashers" who they see as trying to destroy all that the quality movement stands for. There are ample data to support both views.

> "A fanatic is one who can't change his mind and won't change the subject."
>
> —Sir Winston Churchill (1874–1965)

Dueling Data: *Florida Power & Light and Federal Express (and Their Seconds)*

> "Without fanaticism we cannot accomplish anything."
>
> —Eva Peron (1919–1952)

In a debate where the combatants pick their facts the way duelists used to choose their side arms, the experiences of Florida Power & Light Company, winner of the Deming Prize, and Federal Express, winner of the Baldrige Award, are two weapons of choice.

The Deming Prize is Japan's quality award and the one on which the American Malcolm Baldrige National Quality Awards are based. In November 1989, Florida Power & Light Company (FPL Co.), a $4.6 billion subsidiary of the $6.2 billion FPL Group Inc., became the first U.S. company to win this prestigious prize. But even before the formal award ceremonies, staff of the Florida Public Service Commission began to complain that rate payers should not have to pay the tab for FPL Co.'s dash for the Deming. Then, on January 11, 1990, the commission ruled against higher rates for FPL Co. Given the costs involved in FPL's quality program, perhaps it isn't surprising that shortly after the commission denied the rate relief the company sought, the leadership of the company changed. On February 20, *The Palm Beach Post* noted that James L. Broadhead, the chairman of the holding company, had "quietly taken control" of the FPL Co. and "without any announcement" had succeeded John Hudiburg—the spearhead of the FPL Co.'s quality effort—as FPL Co.'s chairman and CEO.

Almost immediately, Broadhead set out to listen to FPL Co. employees, meeting with more than 500 of them over the next several months. In June 1990, four months into his new position and a mere seven months after receipt of the Deming, he unveiled the result of his investigation: a vastly stripped down and simplified quality improvement process, known as QIP within the company. In an open letter to all FPL personnel that was subsequently reprinted in *Training* magazine, Broadhead announced that he was, effective immediately, shutting down three departments (Quality Improvement Department, Quality Improvement Promotion Group, and Quality Support Services) and abolishing many QIP procedures (including the requirement that the "QI Story Seven-Step Process" be used for *all* problem solving, the three-level QIP review process, and quotas for QIP-related activities). Among the other changes described in the letter: a sharp pruning of the number of internal indicators tracked (to eliminate the many measures not contributing "in a substantial way" to FPL's objectives) and a major redesign of FLP's training program (to shift its almost exclusive focus on QIP to a broader menu of skills).

Florida Power & Light is not alone in the mixed results from its quality effort. Wallace Co. Inc., a Houston-based pipe-and-valve distributor, won a 1990 Baldrige Award. In February 1992, the company filed for Chapter 11. Wallace's quality programs had paid off in performance; on-time deliveries shot up from 75 percent in 1987 to 92 percent three years later, and the company's market share almost doubled, from a little over 10 percent to 18 percent over the same period. But these improvements came at a price—about $2 million in additional overhead costs on total sales of $88 million. When the company increased its prices to cover its new expenses and the industry hit a slump, a number of customers bolted. Wallace executives exacerbated this vicious cycle of higher costs and dropping sales by spending much of their time away from home, crisscrossing the country giving Baldrige Award speeches. Commented Wallace Co. CEO John W.

Wallace in a *Business Week* report: "We were so busy doing the presentations that we weren't following up and getting the sales."

Research on the effectiveness of TQM efforts shows that FPL and Wallace are part of a larger, disturbing pattern. Two-thirds of the 500 U.S firms in a 1992 survey by Arthur D. Little, Inc. said their quality programs had not had a "significant impact" on their competitiveness. Four-fifths of the 100 British firms in a 1992 study by A. T. Kearney, Inc. assessed their quality programs as not having produced "tangible results." And many of the 584 American, Canadian, German, and Japanese firms in a 1992 review by Ernst & Young reported that their TQM investments not only had failed to result in improved performance but in some cases had even hindered it.

On the other side, consider the experience of Federal Express. The winner of a 1990 Malcolm Baldrige National Quality Award and the first service company to receive this honor, Federal Express was particularly effective in using the principles and tools of total quality to accelerate achievement of goals already in place. As one example: "100 percent service performance on every package handled" is a long-standing ambition of Federal Express. The old way the company measured its performance against this goal was by tracking the number of packages delivered on time as a percent of total packages delivered. The new way, begun in June 1988, uses a "service quality indicator" (SQI), which FedEx created by delineating specific types of delivery failures (including "damaged package" and "right day, delivered late") and assigning weights to each (e.g., ten points for "damaged package" and one point for "right day, delivered late"). The company's goal: to continue increasing the number of packages delivered while reducing the absolute number of points in the SQI. (For the construction of FedEx's SQI, see "Judgment, Empowerment, and the Parable of the Talents," pp. 93–108.)

By 1994, six years after instituting its SQI system, FedEx's package volume had increased by 82 percent, to 1.8 million packages per night. Despite the increase in volume, however, the

absolute number of points in its SQI had decreased by four percent, indicating a significant reduction in the number of delivery
failures per 1,000 packages delivered. In addition, during a similar time period, from 1990 to 1994, FedEx also reduced its cost
per package by more than 20 percent. With ever improving performance and dropping costs, FedEx's investment in Total Quality has put even more teeth in its claim of "absolutely, positively"
on-time delivery—while still producing a profit.

Even more dramatic is the experience of Ford Motor Company. Ford likely would not be around today as a profitable,
independent company had it not embraced the principles of
TQM in the late 1970s. Nor, for that matter, would Toyota have
been a threat to the American automobile industry or Komatsu
been a threat to the American earthmoving equipment industry
had they not embraced these same principles years earlier.

In fact, the cumulative change created by TQM
efforts around the world—from companies such as Federal Express and Ford Motor in the United States to
Komatsu and Toyota in Japan—has been so great that
it's difficult to remember business policy before the
TQM revolution. But it wasn't so long ago that practices
considered foolish today were standard operating procedures at most companies: conformance to product
standards was "inspected in" and only at the end of the
production line; improved product reliability was seen
as a costly extra, unnecessary in most markets; and
involvement of line employees in improving processes
was rare, and generally viewed with suspicion. In short,
much of what we now think of as good management
was, in the pre-TQM days, regarded as nonessential,
extravagant, and possibly even dangerous.

With all these data in mind, the TQM-zealot conclusion that TQM must be followed without modification
or question and the TQM-basher conclusion that TQM
should be disregarded as yet another management fad
are both deeply flawed. Cognitive psychologists might
diagnose these flaws as the result of "all-or-nothing"
thinking (technically: "dichotomous thinking"), a way of
sorting and distorting data that leads to faulty conclusions that
in turn beget poor decisions. A more useful way of viewing the
data, in my mind, is to recognize TQM as a powerful, breakthrough

> "We . . . are sorry to hear about the problems you have experienced with your Corvette. Your comment eill [sic] help us to provide you with the quality you expect from Chevrolet."
>
> —1991 letter to a dissatisfied Corvette owner from the Chevrolet division of General Motors

management process that itself can be improved—just as James Broadhead did at Florida Power & Light.

What's Sauce for the Goose . . . : First, Find the Sources of Failure

A basic principle of TQM is that improvement starts with finding the sources of failure. Oddly enough, in some companies, practitioners apply that principle to every business situation except to TQM itself. For those willing to entertain the idea that even TQM programs must be subject to continuous improvement, here are three questions to consider:

1. Has process taken over purpose? For centuries, theologians have argued about how much of the path to salvation lies in following the rules versus the intent and outcome of the actions one takes. I don't know the answer for religion, but I am convinced that for business, process used with intent is far more effective than process used in the belief that "if we just do this, all will work as desired."

Some TQM practitioners do not agree with my conclusion, advocating instead a philosophy of "if you mind the process, the results will take care of themselves." In my view, in most situations this is a dangerous way to proceed. James Q. Wilson, professor of government at Harvard University, has argued that such an orientation produces "procedural organizations" in which *"how* the operators go about their jobs is more important than whether doing those jobs produces the desired outcomes." And while it is true that initially such processes can empower participants by giving them new skills and perspectives, when followed blindly they can become organizational straitjackets, preventing probing inquiries and creative solutions. In the case of TQM, over time this kind of process orientation can effectively prohibit problem-solving that doesn't fit the prescribed approach and forecloses any improvements to the TQM program itself. As destructively, it can wrap an organization in so much procedural

"We can't order them to work faster. We emphasize quality over timeliness."

—explanation from the director of the Baldrige Award, U.S. Commerce Department, as to why the report critiquing a company's Baldrige application arrived four months later than promised

red tape as to slow the process of innovation to a crawl and demotivate all but the most devoted bureaucrats. Such ill effects appear to have surfaced at Florida Power & Light before Broadhead enacted his changes. Or as Broadhead explained his actions in his June 1990 letter: "In the process of achieving [our] pervasive quality improvement, we have created an intense institutional emphasis on procedural requirements and processes . . . [which] has required enormous amounts of time and sometimes discouraged real innovation and creativity."

Broadhead's approach for assessing the balance of process and purpose is a good one: confidential conversations to understand how the process really works in practice. And his solution to the problem is equally commendable: pruning away the process overgrowth while recommitting to fundamental principles. Perfect adherence to process prescriptions may satisfy those who monitor compliance to the rules, but if it is achieved at the expense of nimble, timely, creative problem-solving, the organization will surely be the poorer for it.

2. Is the process being guarded by a TQM priesthood? TQM can transform an organization in fundamental ways. Whether it does so, however, depends on the people leading the effort, since it's their responsibility to set the purposes and ensure that the process serves the organization, rather than the other way around. Yet in some organizations, this leadership role is abdicated to the TQM specialists. In these cases, a TQM priesthood often develops, as the specialists come to see themselves as keepers of a sacred flame that, they believe, can only be kept lit by strict adherence to the process as handed down from on high. This problem is worse when the experts don't have much affinity for business (or even, as I have seen in some cases, actively dislike business) or they don't have a track record that demonstrates solid business judgment.

In established religions, priesthoods are essential for preserving the rituals and ensuring compliance among the faithful and typically are composed of people who have spent years mastering complex bodies of knowledge. In companies, process priesthoods—whether external consultants or internal experts— can slip over the line from those who coax, cajole, and coach the organization in new and better ways of doing business

"We guarantee
6-hour turn-
around on
documents
of two pages or
less . . . (does not
include client
subsequent
changes or equip-
ment failures).
We guarantee
that there will be
a receptionist to
greet you and
your visitors dur-
ing normal busi-
ness hours . . .
(short breaks of
less than five
minutes are not
subject to this
guarantee). You
will not be obli-
gated to pay rent
for any day on
which there is not
a [company]
manager on site
to assist you
(lunch and rea-
sonable breaks
are expected and
not subject to this
guarantee)."

—excerpt from the
"Quality Standard
Guarantees," from
an office services
company

to those who have themselves become obstacles to change.

3. Does the definition of purpose provide standards against which the process itself can be measured and adjusted?   Try this experiment: ask people what they see as the purpose of their TQM program (or, if they are TQM gurus, what the goal of TQM programs should be). Had you asked this question in the late 1970s in the United States, the answer you would have heard likely would have been "zero defects" or "hassle free." Today you are more likely to hear something about "com-pletely satisfying both internal and external customers" or "meeting or exceeding customer needs and expecta-tions, and hopefully, delighting the customer."

All of these answers are deficient. Mantras like "zero defects" or "hassle free" are irrelevant if they are not defined in ways that provide a better deal for a *specific* set of customers. And while the slogans of "customer satisfaction" and "delighting the customer" implicitly acknowledge the link between quality and a company's ability to offer a better deal to their customers than the alternatives do, they still aren't good enough. After all, anyone can offer a better deal if they don't have to worry about the "at a profit" portion of the equation.

For this reason, I like to link TQM and strategy via the idea of "appropriate quality," a moving target with the constant goal of giving customers what they see as a good deal relative to what the alternatives offer, at a profit, and over time as circumstances change (the "good deal at a profit over time" criterion is described further in "A Gambler's Guide to Setting Direction," pp. 25–36). Or as Edith Kelly articulates the goal of the quality process for Federal Express, "Total Quality is a people-focused management system that aims at *contin-ual increase of customer satisfaction and decrease in cost.*"

Undoubtedly, some will see this linkage between TQM and the "good deal at a profit" criterion as an unacceptable narrowing of focus. As David Garvin, Harvard Business School professor and former member of the Board of Overseers for the Baldrige award, argued in an article for the *Harvard Business Review*, "The Baldrige Award and short-term financial results are like oil and water: they don't mix and were never intended to. . . . Indeed, winning is neither a necessary nor a sufficient condition for financial success."

But financial success is not an optional part of business for either for-profits or not-for-profits. Generating healthy cash flow is in fact the inescapable and fundamental requirement for long-term survival and success in the marketplace. Beyond providing the potential for increased returns to the equity holders, cash flow is the source of reinvestment in bricks and mortar, people and systems, equipment and technologies, and research and development—all critical to future performance. A company may not need to link its quality to the "at a profit" part of the equation within the next quarter, but surely if the company cannot make this linkage in a conscious and disciplined way, it will increase the odds of losing to those organizations that do. Then all the TQM rhetoric in the world will not compensate for opportunities that need not have been lost had the organization kept its sights on staying ahead in the race to deliver appropriate quality—and on achieving the ongoing financial health essential for thriving, self-renewing enterprises.

"Quality is characteristic of a product or service that helps somebody and which has a market."

—Dr. W. Edward Deming in his last interview, given to *Industry Week* two weeks before his death

"But this *long run* is a misleading guide to current affairs. *In the long run* we are all dead."

—John Maynard Keynes (1883–1946)

Businesses are complicated organisms. They run, well or poorly, through complex interrelations between diverse people and multiple operating mechanisms—systems, processes, measures, rewards, structures, policies, beliefs, values, and strategies. The adoption of a total quality management approach creates changes in all these mechanisms; done well, and these changes will contribute to an enhanced record of pleasing customers profitably. If, however, you believe, as I do, that no one knows a priori the exact way for your organization to make these changes, then you cannot reasonably expect a cookbook answer to be satisfactory. In that case, the better way is to approach TQM as an iterative process, one in which you learn what others have done, make changes in your own organization, learn as you go, correct course, and make more changes.

" 'First Time
Right' Counts!"

—slogan on a 1930s
workplace poster

A motto of the TQM movement may be to "do it right the first time," but in crafting a TQM approach, as in any creative venture in uncharted waters, there is no way to do it right the first time. Maybe the new first principle of TQM should be "just do it" the first time, and then keep figuring out how to do it better.

CHAPTER 15

REENGINEERING AND THE LABORS OF HERCULES

There's More Than One Way to Leap to Breakthrough Results

Reengineering 1: *The process of taking a comprehensive, "clean slate" approach to an organization's work flows in order to achieve dramatic improvements in costs, time, and effectiveness; also known as "business process reengineering," "core process redesign," "horizontal organization," and "process innovation"; 2: In verb form, as in "to reengineer," an all-purpose word commonly used to describe virtually any cost-cutting or reorganization effort; 3: The Consultants' Full Employment Act.*

Hercules may have been the first reengineer. He gained that honor when he cleaned the Augean stables.

According to the ancient myth, Hercules found himself in the stables after the goddess Hera contrived a scheme whereby Eurystheus, the high king of Greece, set for him twelve tasks, known now as "the Labors of Hercules." Myth-teller Robert Graves says Hercules volunteered for these labors so that his stepfather, Amphitryon, might keep his kingdom; classicist Edith Hamilton says that it was in penance for a terrible crime Hercules committed when Hera caused a fit of madness to fall upon him; but both agree that Hera hated Hercules because he was the offspring of one of the many liaisons between her husband Zeus and various mortal women and that the twelve labors she finagled to set in his path were meant to be impossibly difficult.

The fifth of these twelve labors was to clean King Augeias' cattle yard. Cleaning the yard was more difficult than might first appear since Augeias had thousands of head of cattle and the yard had not been mucked for years. As if this were not enough, Eurystheus allowed Hercules only one day to complete the job. By Eurystheus' calculations, Hercules would sink deep into the refuse as he carted away basket after basket of dung and then, even with his superhuman strength, would still not be able to complete the task.

Hercules knew that he could not complete this labor if he attacked it by merely trying to speed up the old ways of moving manure. Instead, as we might say today, he "radically redesigned the process for stable cleaning in order to achieve breakthrough results in the dung department." His reengineering plan was a model of simplicity: first he took his club and knocked down the wall that surrounded the yard, then he borrowed a pickax and dug two deep channels from the yard to two nearby rivers. And voilà! The two rivers rushed through the yard, cleansing everything in their path.

As one might expect, after a reengineering feat of this magnitude, there was a certain amount of Herculean press. Edith Hamilton tells us that the Greeks regarded Hercules as their greatest hero. Millennia later, the afterglow of Hercules' achievement continues: in the 1976 case of *Sakraida* v. *Ag Pro Inc.*, the U.S. Supreme Court held as invalid Ag Pro's patent for a barn-flushing system on the grounds that Hercules had established "prior art." Wrote Justice Brennan for the Court: "Systems using water to clean animal wastes from barn floors have been familiar on dairy farms since ancient times," citing in particular the fifth labor of Hercules and quoting in its entirety an 1893 rendition of the story.

> "You've got to take the bull by the teeth."
>
> —Samuel Goldwyn, movie mogul (1882–1974)

Today the press is paying similar homage to reengineering. Prominent business publications from *The Wall Street Journal* to *Fortune* magazine have all dedicated major articles extolling reengineering as a fundamental innovation in management practice. Michael Hammer and James Champy, authors of the bestseller *Reengineering the Corporation*, go a step further, envisioning their book as the "seminal" work for the "postindustrial business age we are now entering"—the first book of such magnitude, in their view, since Adam Smith's 1776 masterpiece, *The Wealth of Nations*. Reengineering, Hammer and Champy claim, is "the single best hope for restoring the competitive vigor of American businesses" and for many companies "the only hope for breaking away from the ineffective, antiquated ways of conducting business that will otherwise inevitably destroy them."

Given such expectations, it's important to understand the potential risks as well as the promised benefits of reengineering and to take a second look at the assertion that reengineering truly is "the best single hope for restoring competitive vigor."

The Herculean Leaps of Reengineering: Recitals of Success and Tales of Woe

In the wake of Hammer and Champy's book, the term "reengineering" has become synonymous with any corporate cost cutting or run-of-the-mill "reorg." But Hammer and Champy are far more precise in their description of reengineering as the radical redesign of an organization's work flows in order to achieve dramatic improvements in cost, time, and effectiveness. Reengineering, they say, must be top-down in direction ("It is axiomatic that reengineering never, ever happens from the bottom up"), comprehensive in scope ("Reengineering, we are convinced, can't be carried out in small and cautious steps. It is an all-or-nothing proposition"), and sweeping in ambition ("Reengineering [derives from] the passion to reinvent the company, to . . . finally get it completely right").

Taco Bell provides a great testimonial for the power of reengineering to create dramatic improvements in performance. The starting point for Taco Bell was a basic fact about the economics of fast-food operations: few of the costs are related to the food. Explains John Martin, Taco Bell's CEO since 1983 and author of the Taco Bell case study contained in *Reengineering the Corporation*, the average fast-food operation spends about 25 percent of

"When I was in Washington, I noticed there was something called the Bureau of Efficiency. I inquired as to how efficiency could be increased, and was told it is nothing other than saving time."

—Tang Hualong, Chinese reformer, writing in 1918 about his visit to the United States

its revenues on its cost of goods sold—the food and its packaging; another 8 percent on marketing; and the remaining 67 percent on indirect costs and profits—and then focuses its profit improvement efforts on whittling down the first 25 percent. Martin decided that Taco Bell would do just the opposite and reduce all the costs, including advertising expenses, that *weren't* part of the first 25 percent.

With the effort grounded in the revolutionary idea that "our restaurants should *retail* food, not *manufacture* it," Taco Bell made radical changes. One was reversing the proportions of sitting space to kitchen space in its restaurants from a 30/70 ratio to its mirror image, 70/30, a shift made possible by moving much of the food preparation and cooking to central commissaries. Another was its 1990 introduction of its "value menus" with items priced at fifty-nine cents, seventy-nine cents, and ninety-nine cents. The result: though the average Taco Bell outlet in 1992 was the same size as in 1983, the reengineered restaurants had twice the number of seats and almost quadruple the peak revenue capacity ($1,500 per hour versus $400 under the old setup), at the same time that average prices to consumers had dropped by about 25 percent. In addition, the company grew, from about $500 million in revenues in 1983 to about six times that size nine years later. And in 1994, when significant downturns were plaguing the two other restaurant chains in PepsiCo's portfolio, Pizza Hut and KFC (once known as Kentucky Fried Chicken), Taco Bell was still growing: for first quarter 1994 compared to first quarter a year earlier, Taco Bell's profits increased by just over 8 percent while Pizza Hut's and KFC's declined by 18 percent and 23 percent respectively.

Taco Bell's reengineering efforts clearly allowed the company to take a Herculean leap. Other companies, however, have found that attacking their business practices in the comprehensive way specified by reengineering theory has significant risks. Listen to what a senior executive at another company, one touted as a classic example of reengineering success, has to say about reengineering within his division, which we will call the Campanilla Division:

> We started our reengineering with a part of our business that was antiquated; that no longer fit with the environment or met the

What all Taco Bell restaurant managers had to be able to do before John Martin's reengineering effort: assemble and disassemble all twelve pieces of a deep fryer . . . while blindfolded

needs of our customers. There our work with the reengineering consultants was a great success and worth every penny. But then the consultants came back and made a massive, sweeping proposal. It was too massive, far larger than could ever be achieved. Most of us [the senior management team] knew it, but the consultants just seduced our CEO. We watched as it happened; they knew what he wanted to hear and created this sense that this mega-reengineering would solve all his problems and then he'd be a leader, be "on the cutting edge of business management." He ate it up.

So then we had, oh I'd say somewhere between 20 and 35 consultants running around here, many of them with just a year or two of work experience it seemed, and then a half a dozen senior ones, you know, the ones that would talk to the executives at my level. And we assigned between 75 and 100 of our people to work on the project. But though there were more of our people than consultants, the consultants drove the process. They did it in a very interesting way. They have these "templates" and their rule is that you can't vary from the templates. That allows a couple of consultants to trigger a huge amount of activity and still claim that they were just "facilitating" the effort.

So within our company, there were only two or three people who could describe what was being done. Even the internal members of our Steering Committee didn't comprehend all the moving parts and for sure couldn't describe how all the pieces were to come together. People two to five levels down knew that the thing had gone out of control but they felt like saying anything would be organizational political suicide. And they were right too, 'cuz if anyone said anything, the consultants'd go back to the CEO, saying that Suzie "isn't a team player," or that John "is resisting change," or "isn't it too bad that old Bill can't get on board, that he's clinging to the past." And as this went on, our people lost confidence in their management.

And you know what? The pieces never did come together. No one pulled it all together. We kept generating more and more paper—you know, these consultants sure knew how to generate a ton of paper—and we kept spending millions and millions of dollars. But you couldn't see much return on our investment, either in net cost reduction or revenue growth, and eventually X [the executive to whom the division CEO reported] fired our CEO. The reengineering project

> "We trained hard ... but it seemed that every time we were beginning to form up into teams, we would be reorganized. I was to learn later in life that we tend to meet any new situation by reorganizing; and a wonderful method it can be for creating the illusion of progress while producing confusion, inefficiency, and demoralization."
>
> —Petronius the Arbiter, d. 66 A.D., as quoted in Robert Townsend's *Up the Organization*

was part of the reason; the primary reason was the lack of revenue growth. So beyond the first project, most of what was recommended was put on the shelf. The first project was a worthy attempt and had we stopped there we would have been in great shape. But the whole effort, it just overwhelmed the organization. We just choked on it.

Of King's Ransoms and Unintended Results: The Risks of Reengineering

The Campanilla Division is not an isolated example. In their book, Hammer and Champy themselves estimated that up to 70 percent of reengineering efforts fail. A 1994 report by CSC Index Inc., the firm with which Hammer has worked and of which Champy is chairman, provides more detailed data. Of the ninety-nine U. S. and European companies included in the study that had completed their reengineering efforts, 33 percent reported "extraordinary" or "strong" results—while 42 percent reported "mediocre to marginal" results and 25 percent reported "no" positive results.

The CSC Index report identifies a number of sources of such failures, including lack of high ambition, lack of highly committed senior management sponsorship, lack of effective internal communications, and, most especially, lack of excellent project management skills. Not discussed, however, are the intensified versions of what the Campanilla Division experienced: heavy fees that can outweigh the value received, and heavy emphasis on the *learned* knowledge of the outsiders about the *process* of reengineering that can overwhelm the *earned* knowledge of the insiders about the *substance* of their business.

That the fees for reengineered systems are high should be no surprise; this has been so from the time of Hercules when the price was literally a king's ransom. As Robert Graves retells the story, in exchange for Hercules' successful completion of his labors, King Eurystheus did cede the kingdom of Thebes back to Hercules' stepfather, Amphitryon, the king of Thebes. In the case of today's companies, according to Champy, the price is hardly less: fees of $100,000 to $700,000 *per month* for twenty-four to forty-eight months. Though steep, this can be money well spent if the results are produced, but leads to ever diminishing returns if the scope of the efforts exceeds the organization's ability to absorb the changes—as at Campanilla, where the bulk of the proposed changes remain in cold storage.

More worrisome, however, is the heavy emphasis on the *process* of reengineering. Even more than total quality management programs, reengineering efforts tend to be process driven. Or as one executive, involved with a successful reengineering effort commented to me, the thing that surprised her the most about the consultants with whom she worked was how exclusively they focused on process. "We're in a fascinating industry," she said, "But they weren't interested in that at all. All they were interested in was their templates and timetables."

This focus on process is not so much a problem for companies that have strong capabilities in managing process-oriented projects. The executive mentioned above, for example, an ex-consultant, leveraged her consulting background to manage the consultants as adjuncts to her own team, using the consultants to jump-start the process. Within two months, she and her internal team were ready to continue the project on their own, without outside assistance. The success of the project, she believes, has come from having married the process tools of reengineering with the earned knowledge that she and her team brought about their company and industry.

But this focus on process *is* a problem for any company whose managers are not skilled at managing the kind of process-oriented projects that are the bread and butter of many consulting firms—but that are not the steady diet of most other types of firms and who therefore effectively turn over the leadership of the reengineering effort to outsiders. Massive change is risky, and even though the ancient myths don't tell us what happened to the Greek ecosystem after Hercules redirected the two rivers through the Augean cattle yard, it seems reasonable to assume that there were some unintended side effects. In organizations, the factors leading to such side effects can be subtle and intuitive, however. When, as often happens, the insiders who understand these factors on a gut level cannot articulate them well enough or fast enough to respond adequately to the outsiders who are controlling the process, the risk of such negative side effects skyrockets.

Such negative side effects can arise from unforeseen glitches in any of the aspects of a reengineered process; from unanticipated changes in the external environment, to the way the component steps are reconfigured to make up the reengineered work flow, to whether those who remain in the organization are able—and willing—to take on the broader responsibilities inherent in their newly restructured jobs, to how the personnel policies are revised, to the details of any redesign of the supporting equipment and associated software. To take one example, consider the redesigned Airbus cockpit, as described by Donald Norman, head of the Department of Cognitive Sciences at the University of California at San Diego, in his book *Things That Make Us Smart*.

In the reengineered Airbus cockpit, each pilot has a small, independently operated "joy stick." The joy stick for the pilot, who sits in the left-hand seat, is mounted on the left wall of the cockpit; the one for the copilot, who sits in the right-hand seat, is mounted on the right. Formerly, in place of the new, compact joy sticks, were two large, old-fashioned, electromechanical control wheels that used to sit directly in front of each pilot. In addition, these two wheels were interconnected, rather than independently operated like the new joy sticks, so that when one was moved, the other moved in tandem.

And therein lies the unforeseen problem. In the old system, a pilot and a copilot knew effortlessly and without speaking whether the other flier was controlling the aircraft—he or she could see it. But in the new configuration, there have been cases where both pilots assumed incorrectly that the other was controlling the plane when neither was, or where both pilots were trying to control the plane unaware that the other pilot was doing the same. Lost in the reengineering was the efficiency of quick visual checks; the unintended side effect is the newly created need for verbal confirmation where none was required before.

A more prosaic example comes from an on-ground transportation business. Recently, when riding in a car of a car service I use occasionally, I noticed a small computer terminal attached to the dashboard, and learned that it was part of a pilot test connecting drivers to the company's dispatchers. Making small talk, I remarked that the driver must love the new system, since he didn't have to listen to the static and constant interruption of the company's two-way radio system. Nope, the driver replied. Was it that he didn't like computers? Nope, he said again, he had a computer at home, and liked it. And though initially he couldn't quite explain his distaste for the new system, as we chatted, two reasons emerged. One was that listening to the chatter over the old two-way radio had given him important information about traffic conditions, allowing him to alter his routes as appropriate. The other was that listening to the chatter had kept him connected to the others in the company, an important plus in an otherwise lonely job. Both were important to him, the first one because it contributed to his job performance and the second because it contributed to his job satisfaction. When he left me off at my destination, the driver expressed his pleasure at being able to now describe his views with some clarity. Would he share his views with his company? Nope, he responded, doing so, he was certain, was too risky to even be considered.

Concludes Professor Norman about examples like these: "The human side of work activities is what keeps many organizations running smoothly, patching over the continual glitches and faults of the system. Alas, those inevitable glitches and faults are usually undocumented, unknown. As a result, the importance of the human informal communication channels is either unknown, underappreciated, or sometimes even derided as inefficient." And, we might add, these apparently inefficient systems become prime candidates for being reengineered out of existence by outsiders who, with perfect X-ray vision, can see the bones of the organization but not always the muscles, sinews, and other essential soft tissue. When the resulting cuts are irreversible, as radical changes often are, the losses to an organization can be enormous. And if the environment evolves in ways that are different from what the reengineers had anticipated, as often happens to those who forecast the future, the losses can be more enormous still.

> "What is essential is invisible to one's eye."
>
> —*The Little Prince*, by Antoine de Saint-Exupéry, French aviator and writer (1900–1944)

More Than One Way to Boost a Bottom Line: Management by Running Leaps (And Even Management by Quantum Leaps)

The risks of reengineering need not always be incurred, however, even for organizations that need major change. An alternative path to breakthroughs in performance that fits better with the needs and capabilities of many companies is the relatively old technique of what I'll call "management by running leaps."

Imagine an athlete running hurdles. She takes many small, fast steps creating the momentum for a hurdle-sized jump that in turn becomes the basis for many more small, fast steps and then another hurdle-sized jump. That's the Running Leap approach to creating dramatic improvements in performance. Like reengineering, managers at the top still set the agenda for change. But unlike reengineering, the changes are incremental and the improvements come in clumps—many small improvements leading to a step-function shift, which in turn creates the new base for still more small improvements and then another step-function shift.

An obvious example of the Running Leap approach is the Japanese philosophy of *kaizen*—continuous incremental improvement. Consider Matsushita Kotobuki's VCR factory, located on Shikoku, Japan's fifth island, and described by Albert Seig in his book *The Toyko Chronicles*. When Seig first visited the Matsushita Kotobuki VCR factory, it was operated by two line workers supported by a backup team of engineers. As Seig's host explained, had Seig visited the same plant five years earlier, he would have seen hundreds of people where there were now two, and hand assembly where there were now automated stations and robotic arms. The transformation was pure kaizen: workers assembled the VCRs, engineers observed them, both worked together to find better ways of putting the products together until the collective improvements provided a sufficient basis for automating that part of the plant, with the process repeated continuously throughout the facility in a series of running leaps. Seig's host also assured him that if he were to visit again five years hence he would see improvements of similar magnitude. Convinced, Seig applied the same principles with great success to the operations of his own company.

And lest anyone think that the Japanese approach to kaizen is the only way to achieve major breakthroughs from many small improvements, consider the experience of Frank Stowe at Amstar, the maker of Domino Sugar, well before the word "kaizen" was part of standard American business parlance. In 1982, Amstar was losing share in the sweetener market due to the double whammy of increased penetration of substitutes to sugar, including high-fructose corn syrup, and steep prices of imported raw sugar, kept high by the U.S. government in order to protect domestic growers. Stowe, manager of the Baltimore refinery, realized that the company's best option was to reduce its costs without compromising quality.

As consultant Robert Schaffer, author of *The Breakthrough Strategy*, tells the story, Stowe began the effort with an eight-member team, of which seven were hourly workers and one was a supervisor. The team decided its goal would be to reduce the amount of sugar lost when the five-pound bags split or were filled to overflowing. Within three months, its efforts had led to an 80 percent reduction in bag breakage and a 56 percent reduction in bag overfill. More teams and more breakthrough goals created other running leaps that, in combination, substantially lowered the costs and increased the quality at the refinery. Stowe's experience then enticed a sister Amstar refinery in Chalmette, Louisana, to follow a similar approach, and once again many small improvements created major breakthroughs—though, unlike Matsushita's VCR plant, hardly any investment in new equipment was required to achieve the dramatic improvements in performance.

Or consider General Electric's famed Work-Out process. Designed by James Baughman, a senior executive at GE, Work-Out brings employees together to voice complaints, analyze problems, and develop solutions. Managers are required to make decisions very quickly; when GE first launched Work-Out in 1988, managers were required to make yes/no decisions on the spot, as the participants made their proposals or, for those few proposals that truly needed more study, within the month. The results were impressive, from an 80 percent reduction in the cycle time for milling steel at the company's turbine plant in Schenectady, New York, to a $200 million reduction in inventory costs at its major appliance plant in Louisville, Kentucky. Noel Tichy and Stratford Sherman, authors of the corporate biography of GE, *Control Your Destiny or Someone Else Will*, point out that Work-Out reflected a "major change" in Welch's approach to change. Though Welch "used to argue against incremental change, on the theory that only [major] leaps made enough of a difference," Tichy and Sherman say that the results of the Work-Out program have led to Welch's new belief that "small improvements are as important to the process as big ones."

As different as the Running Leaps of kaizen and the Herculean Leaps of reengineering are, both share some common characteristics, including reliance on a top-down agenda and adherence to a relatively predictable process for managing the change. But some theorists contend that breakthroughs in performance can occur with less top-down control and less reliance on predictable processes.

Meg Wheatley, professor of management at Brigham Young University and author of *Management and the New Science,* is one of these theorists. Wheatley uses the analogy of the quantum leap to explain how change can be driven from the local level. In quantum physics, electrons and other subatomic particles make abrupt, unpredictable transitions from one discrete energy state to another. The same kind of local, unpredictable abrupt transitions, Wheatley argues, occur in organizations: "Acting locally allows us to work with the movement and flow of simultaneous events. . . . These changes in small places, however, create large-system change, not because they build one upon the other, but because they share in the unbroken wholeness that has united them all along."

Of course, organizations are not metaphors. They are not engines, they are not athletes, and they are not subatomic particles. They are associations of human beings who, though different in their personal aims and abilities, work together with varying degrees of effectiveness, united by differing degrees of commitment to somewhat overlapping goals.

But though organizations are not metaphors, the use of metaphors is helpful in delineating alternatives for action. Managers as reengineers assume that they can overhaul an organization as though it were a mechanical device that can be redesigned and rebuilt, from then on to run like a dream. Managers as coaches assume that they can motivate a whole organization to keep running the hurdles. Managers as quantum physicists assume that if they can set the right context, the leaps will take care of themselves—though in a largely unpredictable way.

In the end, it's the job of the manager to decide which metaphor will be the most useful for a specific organization in a particular set of circumstances and then actively manage the approach selected, making certain that the earned knowledge of the insiders doesn't get squeezed out by the process expertise of any outsiders who may be assisting in the effort. This may not be

> "Life is always poised for flight. From a distance it looks still . . . but up close it is flitting this way and that, as if displaying to the world at every moment its perpetual readiness to take off in any of a thousand directions."
>
> —Jonathan Weiner, in *The Beak of the Finch: A Story of Evolution in Our Time*

an easy set of tasks to accomplish, but tackling them certainly beats picking up the pieces of a massive effort that cost more than it produced or, worse, created negative side effects that were significant, unexpected and, in some cases, irreversible.

Clearly, reengineering is not "the only way" to create dramatic breakthroughs in performance. It is one way, a very powerful way, sometimes the best way, particularly when the changes can only be coordinated from the top. Taco Bell had those kinds of changes; a total redesign of the restaurants and of the food preparation processes required top management approval before the details could be developed. Similarly, work aimed at creating radical designs that will cut across old functional lines cannot be undertaken without the blessings and authorization of top management; imagine if there had been a River Gods Association and a Stable Hands Guild, each of which had total authority over their respective domains—Hercules would never have finished cleaning out the Augean stables or completed his labors.

But not all companies need top-down change of this sort, and reengineering is neither suitable for all situations nor even preferable for all situations. Not all companies can complete a reengineering effort successfully; without strong in-house capabilities for managing process-oriented projects, the odds of the untoward side effects zoom. And not all companies need to use reengineering as their ticket to vastly improved performance or as their only ticket; for some companies or for some situations, processes that are more evolutionary and have greater reversibility—just in case the changes don't quite work out as planned— are the better choice.

In short, though it may be great marketing to claim that any approach is the one and only solution for *all* situations, it's hardly good business to swallow this line without careful thought about how the technique in question fits the particulars of *a specific* situation. In business as in hiking, it's usually a good idea to look before you leap.

"This is sharp medicine, but it will cure all disease."

—Sir Walter Raleigh (1554–1618), on his execution day, in reference to the ax to be used in his beheading

CHAPTER 16

LOW-COST MIGRAINES
How to Cost Cut Your Way to Big Trouble

Low-Cost Producer   1: The holy grail of strategy; 2: The desired endpoint of strategies based on the delusion that a near-exclusive focus on reducing costs will not affect the buying behavior of target customers, who, it is assumed, will either not notice any difference as costs are cut, thereby allowing the producer to pocket the additional profits, or will gladly swarm to a lower-priced product, no matter what the diminution of quality or reduction of benefits provided; late-stage symptoms include loss of market share as customers flock to products or services with better bundles of benefits and price; related delusions can be induced by "core process redesign," "downsizing," "right-sizing," "de-layering," "value engineering," and "reengineering."

Pursuit of the low-cost producer position has become an almost universal goal among companies in many industries. The basic logic seems unassailable: low-cost producers can either keep their prices constant and increase their per-unit margins, or they can decrease their prices and take share from competitors. In either case, the argument goes, they can, if they wish, plow some of their increased profits back into their business with the purpose of creating further advantages versus their competitors.

In practice, though, the drive to become the low-cost producer frequently does not deliver the intended results and sometimes even backfires, leaving the organizations with slimmer margins or smaller market shares than when they began their slicing and dicing. The problem does not stem from the desire to cut costs; often cost cutting is exactly what's required for the long-term health of the enterprise. Rather the problem begins when companies, having identified the costs they wish to cut, fail to weigh their own savings against the benefits that customers lose as a result of the specific cuts they are making.

Consider the company that makes my husband's socks. An engineer by profession, my husband lives in a world of systems. Sometimes he also creates systems for everyday things, as he once did for the acquisition of his socks. He would buy ten identical pairs in October so they'd be thickest in winter and thinnest the next summer, but still intact. For ten years he followed this system faithfully, always loyal to the same brand of socks and the same retailer.

So you can imagine my surprise when, in January of the 11th year of The Sock System, I noticed him throwing away a perfectly clean and almost-new sock. Why? Having retrieved the discarded sock from the wastebasket, I discovered that the sock had worn straight through the heel. Within a couple of months, half of the socks had similar holes. And no wonder: a sock from the previous year proved to be more heavily reinforced in the heel than the new ones.

Was he going to complain to the company? Of course not, he responded. From his point of view, the socks were a good deal when they lasted twelve months. Since they now lasted less than half that long, they would be a good deal *only* if the price were cut as well. And since the company had not cut its prices along with its costs, his new goal was to find a better alternative. Like most consumers, given a market full of options, he'd rather switch than fight.

But when will "Sockco," the maker of this brand of socks, figure out that it has a problem? Here's my arithmetic: We know that the weak-heel models appeared between October 1991, the time of purchase of the last good batch of socks, and October 1992, the purchase time of the batch that unraveled. So, let's assume that the change at Sockco occurred in April 1992. If other sock buyers respond like my husband, the retailer won't begin to see reduced sales until April 1993. The retailer in turn won't cut his order accordingly until after April 1993, meaning that Sockco will have a twelve- to twenty-four-month gap between the beginning of its specific cost-cutting initiative and the first true tastes of its effects.

And what's likely to happen inside Sockco? One scenario goes like this: during the first year or two, the cost reductions seem brilliant: sales hold, profits shoot up. The executive in charge of the strategy gets promoted so he or she can apply the same cost-strategy magic to other product lines. Of course, when market share begins to plummet, it's the new incumbent who will have to solve the problem or take the heat.

Sockco is just one example of a pervasive problem: cost-cutting efforts that backfire due to inadequate or incorrect analysis of how the costs and/or people being cut will affect the "good deal" as perceived by the customers. A starting point for correcting such flawed analyses is to think about "nonproductive" costs and "productive" costs.

Nonproductive costs don't add benefits that customers are willing to pay the full freight for. But while it's difficult to disagree with the theory of eliminating these costs, they are also the most difficult to cut. Consider the most obvious of the nonproductive costs, the ones that add nothing of value from the customer's perspective, such as inefficient internal bureaucracies or excessive management perks. Cutting these costs affects company insiders where they live: slimmed-down internal processes change the turf boundaries inside the firm; reduced perks cut the amenities enjoyed by key executives. In consequence, these costs are often trimmed only when the company is in crisis, or when the company creates a crisis by hiring outsiders to "reengineer" the corporation. (See "Reengineering and the Labors of Hercules," pp. 183–195, for some additional thoughts.) If Sockco is like many other companies following cost-driven approaches, it likely had plenty of these nonproductive costs that were untouched as the company searched for excess fibers in its footware.

Less obvious among the nonproductive costs are those that support product or service benefits that few consumers think are worth the required price premium. These costs too are tough to cut when they have achieved sacred cow status, because they either are somebody's—or some department's—baby, or they are "corporate truths," internal beliefs about what the customers want, held in the absence of adequate data to back the claim. Through the 1970s, for example, American microwave oven manufacturer Litton invested heavily in benefits like browning elements while consumers searched for smaller, simpler, cheaper boxes. In the 1990s, Mercedes-Benz faced a similar challenge as increasing numbers of customers proved unwilling to pay for what they saw as overengineering relative to alternatives like Lexus and its sales plummeted in its largest market (Mercedes share of the German market sank from 11.6 percent in 1985 to just 6.4 percent in 1992) as well as in its major export markets (Mercedes unit sales in the United States, as one example, dropped from 100,000 cars in 1986 to about 59,000 in 1991). In the cases of both the ovens and the autos, the costs were sacred cows, protected by the engineers and fervently, though incorrectly, believed to be the keys to the customers' hearts. In the microwave oven case, both General Electric and foreign makers ultimately filled the gap; in the luxury car one, Mercedes faced the music and restructured its costs, and saw its U.S. sales progress upward again.

Conversely, productive costs are the muscle of a company. These are the costs that either save other costs in the process and thereby give the company the option to keep prices down, or those for which, though they add, say, X cents per unit, the customer is willing to pay X cents or more to obtain the benefits they produce. Unfortunately, since these costs typically are directly associated with the products and services delivered, they are also often the obvious though incorrect targets for cost-cutting.

As an example of a company that cut some of its productive costs only to end up with far higher overall costs, consider the shoe manufacturer that W. Edward Deming, one of the fathers of the quality movement, used to describe in his lectures. It seems that this footwear company found that its productivity had suddenly plummeted, thereby causing its labor cost per pair of shoes to soar. The source of the problem: the company had shifted to a new thread supplier who charged a penny less per bobbin than the old supplier. But the new thread kept breaking, causing the sewing machine operators to stop and rethread their machines

"It wouldn't be Claridge's then, would it?"

—Brian Basham, adviser to Lord Forte, owner of London's Claridge's hotel, in response to Lord Forte's inquiry as to why the hotel should not replace its "four flunkies in knee breeches" with a single doorman

each time the thread broke. The company had cut productive costs, because it had calculated only its savings from the cost cut (the thread) without also estimating the new and substantially larger costs incurred (the labor). The faulty math meant that, without further correction, the company would either have to raise its prices or eat its increased costs.

Even more dangerous, because it's often so difficult to see, is the Sockco problem: calculating costs saved (the thread again) without taking into account the benefits lost from the customer's perspective (product life). The result of this kind of mistaken accounting is a doom loop in which the company lops X cents off its product cost—and then finds that it either must reduce its price by an amount greater than X cents if it wishes to maintain its market share, or must accept a reduction in unit sales if it wishes to maintain its selling price. This loop is especially lethal for companies, such as Sockco, that compete in industries in which there can be a substantial time lag between the time of the cuts and time of the negative consumer reaction and the associated defections.

Women's swimsuits provide another revealing case study of the kind of reasoning that leads to cutting costs that many consumers would gladly cover. The story begins in 1989, when the association of women's swimsuit manufacturers commissioned a study to find out why sales of suits were flat. The results, not surprising to anyone who has actually looked at women, were that 80 percent of prospective customers were trying bathing suits on, but lacking the shapes for the figure-revealing suits being stocked, were leaving the stores without making a purchase. (My favorite commentary on the research came from a fiber manufacturer who opined, "I say most women would rather have a root canal without Novocain than buy a swimsuit.") Five years later, what were some in the industry doing to make suits that look good on a broader range of women? Eliminating adjustable straps from suit tops because "if you can take out one adjustable loop, you save a dime per suit" and keeping "low backs and high-cut legs because they save fabric." If women's figures hadn't changed in the intervening five years, this is surely a market-minimizing (if not a figure-flattering) strategy.

"Never forget that your weapon is made by the lowest bidder."

—Law #20 of "Murphy's Laws of Combat"

And it's not just apparel companies, or even just product companies, that fall into the trap of cutting costs that provide important benefits to the customers. Consider the Carlson Travel Network, one of the largest travel companies in the United States. According to *The Wall Street Journal*, in 1990 Carlson cut its travel agent workforce by 17 percent and then put some of the remaining agents into "unaccustomed jobs." The headline on the *Journal*'s page-one article summarized the story: "Hazardous Cuts: Travel Agency Learns Service Firms' Perils In Slimming Down; Carlson Slashed Work Force and Some Employees Did Unaccustomed Jobs Badly"—including agents who stranded customers in foreign countries without the visas required to complete their itineraries, neglected to make the requested hotel or car rental reservations, or forgot to provide the boarding passes with their clients' tickets.

Again, the result was that some customers defected; knowledgeable, capable agents are an important part of what customers purchase from a travel company. Productivity improvements like those sought by Carlson can improve a company's competitive position, but not when the costs saved come out of the customers' hides—and the customers have other alternatives that don't require the same sacrifices.

Or consider the widely held notion that adding costs, even those that customers will assess as true improvements, is not appropriate during a time of cost-cutting. For example, in 1992 when Porsche introduced its 968 model, strict cost control was critical: the company's unit sales in the United States had declined 61 percent from its high point in 1987 as some target customers slipped to lower-price alternatives. But the 968 didn't have a gear lockout device that prevents drivers from accidentally shifting into reverse when they mean to shift into first. The 911 didn't have one either, and some die-hard fans (and maybe some Porsche designers) claimed that anyone who couldn't master Porsche's trick manual transmission probably didn't deserve to drive a Porsche. Should the company have added the lockout device, adding costs, as estimated by *The Boston Globe*'s automotive writer, John R. White, of about two dollars per car? Of course it should have, as in fact the company quickly did after *Car & Driver* reviewer Pat Bedard and other auto writers complained about the flaw. The value is not so much for experienced Porsche drivers, but for new buyers, for whom this small additional cost provides a relatively large incremental benefit.

Companies such as Sockco base their strategies on the assumption that the player with the lowest absolute costs wins. But the only cost-driven strategy that makes sense is to have the lowest costs *relative to the benefits desired by your target market*, rather than relative to all competitors in your general product category. When Lexus stormed the world markets, its goal was not to have the lowest costs of any car manufacturer but rather to provide similar benefits at lower costs than Mercedes, the competitor whose customers it sought. In the process it won over a good number of Cadillac and Lincoln buyers as well. Whether you have a low price point or a high price point, it's the *relative* cost position that pays.

———■———

There's no doubt that many organizations need to go on strict diets, or otherwise restructure their costs. But the drive to be the low-cost producer—using any of the many tools available, including (but not limited to) "downsizing," "rightsizing," "restructuring," "reengineering," "value engineering," and "core process redesign"—backfires when done without careful analysis and real-world testing. The key question: how the costs (including people) being cut do or do not contribute to the benefits customers seek and the prices they are willing to pay for those benefits. Without such a clear-sighted understanding, muscle may be cut rather than fat. The muscle cut may be benefits that once made the product the better deal for the external customers, leading to the dilemma of having to accept either losses in market share if they keep their prices up, or losses in margin if they reduce their prices in order to maintain share. Or the muscle cut may be the compensation and conditions that had made the workplace "good deal" attractive enough that employees willingly contributed their all. In either case, the end result can be yet another proof that companies can, in fact, cost-cut their way to big trouble.

The catsup conundrum: Consumer goods companies use paired comparisons as one way to test product formulations. If you cut a tiny bit of the tomato out of your catsup and then do a taste comparison of A, the old formulation, versus B, the new one, it's likely that few consumers will be able to tell the difference. Ditto when you then test B against C, from which you have cut a tiny bit more of tomato. And ditto again when you get to P versus Q. But your loss of market share will not be because consumers couldn't taste the difference within each paired comparison, but because they will have tasted the difference between A and Q—and then found a better alternative.

THE PILOT'S ART

A Look at the Courage to Manage in the Age of Instant Answers

Anyone who sees all this, naturally rushes to the conclusion of which I was speaking, that no mortal legislates in anything, but that in human affairs chance is almost everything. And this may be said of the arts of the sailor, and the pilot, and the physician, and the general, and may seem to be well said; and yet there is another thing which may be said with equal truth of all of them. . . . [T]hat art should be there also; for I should say that in a storm, there must surely be a great advantage in having the aid of a pilot's art. You would agree?

—Plato, *Laws*

This book is about the pilot's art. It is about the courage to manage: assessing situations, setting an overall course or focus, thinking through options, developing plans, taking action, learning, modifying plans, learning more, and continuing to go forward. These needs are not new; the willingness to embrace them and the judgment to make good decisions about them have always been the essence of good management. What *is* new is the sheer number of techniques proposed for meeting these needs—and positioned, in many cases, as panaceas that obviate the need to think as long as the formula is followed. And because there are so many programs, so aggressively marketed, the temptation to operate on autopilot is ever-present.

In this book, I have tried to provide some perspectives about a selection of commonly seen programs and commonly heard mantras of the fad-surfing era. My explorations have led me to these conclusions about the pilot's art in the age of instant answers:

Which Way Is Up? *Setting the Overall Direction*   Whether you are the CEO of a major company or the manager of a small department, the pilot's art requires ensuring that everyone operates under a shared set of guidelines for creating the future. The difficult part of this task is not figuring out *how* to communicate these guidelines—whether, for example, to use a mission statement or vision manifesto or some other means. The difficult part is determining *what* the guidelines are—what the goals are and what the boundary conditions are within which everyone is to operate to achieve these goals, and why pursuing these goals and operating within these boundary conditions will create better outcomes than continuing with the status quo.

In the end, such guidelines derive from the implicit beliefs about how the organization can or must create its future. In many organizations, these core beliefs originate with the people at the top of the hierarchy and are then communicated throughout the organization, as Yashinari Kawai did at Komatsu or as Ken Iverson did at Nucor. In others, they arise from individuals somewhere within the structure who are smitten with an idea, and then create experiments that gradually take over the company, as Daniel Gerber was able to do successfully at the Fremont Canning Company—and as Michael Cullen was not able to do at Kroger Grocery & Baking Company. In all cases, the starting point for setting any new direction is a belief, a deep, down-in-the-guts conviction about where the company or unit could go and why embarking on this new path would be preferable to sticking to business as usual.

In the absence of a person or group of people holding such a belief passionately and obsessively, however, all the visioning and mission-writing sessions in the world will be irrelevant. Vision manifestos and mission statements are simply communication devices. If there are no ideas, or there are ideas but no real commitment or resources behind them, the direction will be to continue to carry out today's business using today's methods, no matter what the formal documents say.

Life in the Upside-down Pyramid: Facilitating Collective Action The whole point of having organizations at all is that there are many things that people cannot do individually that they can do collectively. It follows, then, that having created organizations, a second part of the pilot's art is to ensure that the organization is an aid to effective action and not an obstacle.

My concern with many of the organizational mantras of the fad-surfing age is that they can inadvertently have the opposite effect, and actually create obstacles rather than remove them. Hierarchy cannot be wished away; it's an immutable fact of organizational life. Structures that involve new ways of organizing collective action can work, of course, but only if there is some attention to, and management of, the real hierarchy implicit in them. Similarly, corporate cultures can be changed, but companies handicap themselves in this effort when they don't first make the effort to understand the real internal game and then move to change it as an initial step in "transforming" their cultures. And though environments can and must be more open, making emotional statements to this effect—while allowing all the barriers and penalties to a freer flow of information to remain in place— will not make them so.

Organizational dynamics are inherently complex and tricky; even given infinite care and finesse, you never get exactly what you expect. This should not come as a surprise. Organizations are, after all, collections of people, who by nature are unpredictable and quirky; that's what makes management such a complicated task. And that's also all the more reason to think carefully about how people truly do respond when they work in groups, rather than the way they would respond if they followed all the "shoulds" of the theorists (e.g., people should work together cooperatively without creating shadow hierarchies; people should speak up when they have ideas and concerns; people shouldn't game the system). New, productive ways of organizing people are of course possible and will continue to be invented, but they will not be the nonhierarchical, totally open, and non-game-oriented wonders promised today.

The Empowerment Conundrum: Enhancing Individual Action The concept of empowering the individuals within an organization isn't new. Chester Barnard, as the former president of New Jersey Bell Telephone, formulated the issue this way in 1938: "The executive art is nine-tenths inducing those who have authority to use it in taking pertinent action."

"Inducing those who have authority to use it in taking pertinent action" is perhaps the hardest part of the pilot's art. Behind all the fancy words and programs, empowerment first requires sharing decision-making power, a requirement to which many give lip service but fewer give allegiance. Empowerment also requires building the judgment reservoir of the organization. And although training programs are the mechanism many companies turn to as the solution to this critical need, such programs are neither a sufficient nor, in some cases such as Boston's Beth Israel Hospital, a necessary condition to create the judgment reservoir. Also crucial is hiring people with the potential for compatible standards of judgment, supplying guidelines for the exercise of judgment, providing sufficient information to support the further development of each person's judgment, and allowing mistakes and encouraging people to develop their judgment as they learn from their mistakes. But these requirements in turn call for managers who themselves have good judgment, high tolerance for honorable mistakes, and the willingness to cede some control. Empowerment doesn't just happen because someone says the right words eloquently or quotes the right management thinkers. Rather, it takes the action and commitment of those who wish to share their decision-making power with others and are also willing to help these other people use their authority to make wise use of their hundred decisions a day.

Through a Glass Darkly: Determining What the Customers Really Want   In theory, finding out what the customers want is easy because customers always want the same thing: the best deal they can get in terms of the benefits they desire relative to the time they are willing to invest in their search, the money they have or want to spend, and the alternative bundles of benefits and prices they see as available to them. It's in the practice that this determination gets complicated; it's not always easy to get the customers to articulate how they make their "good deal" calculations, nor is it easy to get companies to adapt the way they do business or to revise their products and services, which they love, to meet the needs of their constituencies.

A fourth part of the pilot's art, therefore, is to ensure that the direction the organization pursues also fits with the cus-

tomers' definitions of what they want. Included in that definition of "the customer" is, of course, any person or organization
who will provide you with something you want in exchange for
you giving them something they want. By this definition, external buyers are customers and so are employees—it's just that
employees make their payment in effort and commitment, not in
dollars and cents.

For this reason, it's the good deal as perceived by those
customers on which an organization depends that anchors all
strategy. If, in comparison to the alternatives available, an organization can't provide a good deal to its target customers, nothing else matters, regardless of how much it extols that "the
customer is king," how many "customer-sat" surveys it distrib-
utes, or how much it proclaims the importance of "customer
focus" as it develops its products and services. As a result, corporate success requires either great luck or tremendous discipline to assess what your target customers could want, in spite
of the barriers presented by your own biases and the inconve-
niences created by your customers.

Fuzzy Logic: Moving From Customers to Strategy   Strategy and
strategic planning have been explicitly seen as an essential part of
the pilot's art in business, at least since the mid-1950s. Writing in
1966, Marvin Bower, one of the cofounders of McKinsey & Co.,
Inc, made this observation: "During the past decade [mid-1950s to
mid-1960s] . . . most U.S. companies have developed some degree
of formalized planning. . . . My observations convince me, however, that in most companies planning is still underdeveloped as a
managing process. . . . Only recently [i.e., prior to 1966] has it
received much attention from operating executives and students
of management, and little standard practice has yet crystallized."

In the intervening decades, of course, much of the standard
practice of management has not only crystallized but, in many
settings, hardened into inflexible laws. The result is standardized
ways to categorize strategic situations that are based on important insights but, as practiced, often lead to poor strategic decisions. Cramming a strategy into any prepackaged template may
be efficient but it can also be dangerous, adding to the risk that
the company will lock itself into an inappropriate strategy.

Every company has a strategy, whether it goes through
"strategic planning" exercises or not. The strategy is what

emerges out of the cumulative effect of everyone's decisions every day in any firm. Done well, strategic planning forces the participants to take a break from such continuous strategy-making activities, allowing them to think through what the company's options are and how the company can achieve them. Any model that keeps the participants from reexamining the fundamentals (because the template has "pre-thought" the fundamentals for them) can create a net negative for the organization: beautiful plans, efficiently produced, but containing little insight that the company can use to its advantage. Part of the pilot's art, therefore, is to ensure that strategy-making is an active, probing process—one that forces the participants to challenge the underlying assumptions about likely consequences of any proposed path of action.

More Instant Answers: Paddling Out to the Biggest Waves

Not all fads are created equal. Some fads are bigger than others, with more companies making significant commitments to them in terms of time and money, and with more master practitioners preaching the fad as an all-or-nothing proposition. Total Quality Management and Reengineering fit this description. Both bring the potential for tremendous improvement, if applied to the right situations and modified as needed for particular circumstances. And, by the same token, both harbor the potential for disaster when, seen as panaceas, they are chosen indiscriminately and applied mindlessly.

Which brings us to my husband's socks and the last fad included in this book. Cutting costs to be the low-cost producer is an enduring fad, and like the others in this volume, one that, when used thoughtfully and appropriately, provides exactly the correct medicine. But this one too has a dangerous side effect when used inappropriately, one that bears directly on other programs and mantras covered in this book.

The problem is this: companies today are not only cutting threads out of socks and shoes, they are also cutting people. Many of these cuts are long overdue; company bureaucracies had become bloated, and the staffs required for producing anything from widgets to invoices had not undergone fundamental review for years, in many cases. But there is also a flip side to all these cuts. First, much of the "earned knowledge" of the organizations has been lost. In addition, the people who are left, no matter how capable, simply have no time to pursue the pilot's art. Tasks such as assessing situations, thinking through options, developing plans, taking actions that have long-term impacts, and learning and modifying plans are not easily captured in short-term productivity measures. In consequence, consultants are increasingly being used as structural capacity for many of these tasks. The result, from a financial perspective: the fixed costs of the business are cut, but since more people are needed, these costs are often replaced by the new (and higher) variable costs of consultants who now never go away.

And, over time, an even worse side effect can occur: if the managers within the company no longer have the time to think about long-term needs and assess the various techniques available to them, it becomes easier and easier to abdicate the responsibilities inherent in the pilot's art, leaving them to chance or signing them over to the consultants. As managers lose experience at making these kinds of tough choices, they can become less willing—and less able—to take these responsibilities back. Then both managers and consultants come to see those inside the company as the "maintainers"—the people keeping the day-to-day operations of the company going—while the consultants are seen as the "change agents"—the real strategists and the real implementers of change. Or as one partner of a major consulting firm told *Industry Week* magazine: "You can get consultants to be your planners. . . . Increasingly, people say . . . the least-cost alternative is to contract out." Evidently, many companies are following this approach; with annual consulting expenditures in the tens and hundreds of millions at many large companies, including AT&T, which spent $347.1 million on "consulting and research services" in 1993.

Since I work as a consultant, it should be no surprise that I think consultants can be tremendous assets to the companies with which they work. They can and often do supply the "extra arms and legs" needed to execute decisions that have already been made. Even more important, in my view, consultants can assist companies by providing fresh perspectives on issues of key importance to the organization, creating independent fact bases on these issues, supplementing current thinking with new data or different ways of looking at the data, introducing and helping to implement techniques appropriate to such issues, and generally by challenging the prevailing conclusions, even aggressively.

Nonetheless, I worry about the dependence on consultants and fads within our economy because, in the end, I believe, the pilot's art must be exercised by those within the enterprise. For only those within the enterprise can be held accountable for the critical managerial tasks of selecting a course from among the options available, ensuring that the underlying rationales of the options chosen fit together in a coherent whole, seeing that adaptations and changes in course are made as needed, and then learning from their experience and making more choices.

Following the latest fad without thinking is a way to sidestep this accountability, which is why fad surfing can be so destructive to the pilot's art. Managing, on the other hand, requires making decisions when there are no guarantees about right answers, which is why managing takes courage. So review the fads that may provide you with new insights, learn from them, adapt them as seems appropriate in your best judgment, and then accept with enthusiasm the risks that are part and parcel of the courage to manage—to think, experiment, and learn.

THE EXPANDED
FAD SURFER'S DICTIONARY
OF BUSINESS BASICS

A

accountability A characteristic of which everyone else in the organization needs far more. Not to be confused with *Authority*, which is what I need more of.

anonymity A method, often disparaged as "not necessary here," of using the promise of confidentiality to get the truth about issues affecting the performance of an organization. The more it is so disparaged, the more it is needed.

associate A designation given to a subordinate in the hope that changing the word one uses to describe an employee will obviate the need to change the way one *treats* that employee.

authority A characteristic of which I need more if I am to do my job properly. Not to be confused with *Accountability*, which is what everyone else in the organization needs far more of.

autopilot A superefficient way to operate, since no one need take the time to think; prepack-aged programs can make it especially easy to flip into the autopilot mode.

B

bad news That which the other guy should tell.

belief That which prevents people from seeking the facts or even *seeing* the facts that are right in front of them; also see *Corporate Truths*.

benchmarking 1: Comparison of operations against best-in-class; a superb way to spark new ideas and significant insights when the examples are selected with thought and imagination; 2: The basis for great jobs in which the incumbents have no substantive responsibilities other than to gallivant around the world, meet all sorts of interesting people, make occasional proclamations about all the neat things other companies do, and submit appropriately lavish expense reports.

bizbuz Business words that once had meaning and that still have a kernel of importance for those who take the time to think before using.

black hole A massive object in space, predicted by the General Theory of Relativity, into which things fall but from which nothing, not even light, can escape. Frequent destination of employee ideas, customer complaints, and supplier suggestions.

blame The living embodiment of the principle that it is indeed better to give than to receive.

boundarylessness Apt descriptor for the condition of the egos of some senior-level executives and professionals.

business school An institution of advanced vocational training for the upwardly mobile.

C

cascading 1: The process by which people in each layer of management communicate successively to the people in the level below them; 2: The basic path along which bad stuff flows; otherwise known as the Trickle Down Theory of Management Pain.

cash cow A mythical beast; should you ever find one, however, remember to feed it or you will end up with all bull and no cash.

change 1: That which will not happen until the expected pain of the old ways is perceived to be greater than the expected pain of the new ways; 2: For other people in the organization, something they need to get on with; 3: For oneself, something that needs *Due Consideration*.

change management The process of paying outsiders to create the pain that will motivate insiders to change, thereby transferring the change from the company's coffers into those of the consultants.

child labor That mass of freshly minted BAs and MBAs who have no operating experience and who are therefore assembled by consulting firms into the teams to turn around client companies or otherwise instruct and enlighten senior people within client companies.

CLM Acronym for "career limiting move"; phrase used by senior managers in one company when asked to share their views about the company's strategy with their boss; as future events showed, their views were correct, as was their assessment of the risk of sharing these views.

commitment 1: The state of being pledged or emotionally impelled (as in: The president of XYZ Corp. wanted the people in his company to be *committed* to their jobs and to the success of the company); 2: Consignment to a mental institution (as in: The workers of XYZ Corp., having lived through a series of downsizings, rightsizings, and business reengineering projects, thought the president of XYZ should be *committed* for expecting them to give 100 percent to their jobs).

communication The process of you receiving what I just said.

continuous improvement A label that provides dignity to the repeated efforts of an organization to get it right.

core competency A factor seen as critical to corporate success; as with the stock market, the hit rate of identifying these factors is always 100 percent after the success has been recorded, but appears to be random when examined while the race is still being run.

corporate culture 1: The way we do things around here, our combination of shared values and group norms; 2: An excuse for not making desperately needed changes in the way a company conducts its business.

corporate truths Sacred cows, dressed in three-piece suits.

customer 1: An inconvenience to the smooth functioning of a business; 2: A walking revenue stream, always susceptible to a better deal offered by another vendor.

customer focus That which is seen when one looks into the customers' eyes to see what is desired and observes one's own image of the ideal product.

customer satisfaction 1: New name for the oldest premise in business—that unless customers are more satisfied with your product than they are with their next best alternative, they won't be your customers for long; 2: New name for one type of standard market research, often designed in rote compliance with guidelines, thereby limiting actual thinking about how to provide customers with a better deal than the competition offers; 3: New job-creation program, leading to legions of new experts within companies and consulting firms.

D

daredevil One who traffics in facts when the facts go against the expectations or preferences of those in more senior positions.

death wish The apparent motivation of one who repeatedly takes the role of a daredevil, no matter how valid or how important the facts are to the future of the company.

delegation A way of pushing down politically unpleasant decisions to people who do not have the authority to resolve the conflict.

due consideration What business people do to postpone making tough decisions (when three-year-olds do this to postpone bedtime, it's called "stalling").

due diligence The process of proving that the acquisition top management wants to make (and that the company's investment bankers, as well as the selling company and its investment bankers, desperately want it to make) is absolutely the most brilliant business move of the century; also see *Pro Forma*.

E

ego That messy bundle of human needs, urges, and desires that shape the work decisions made by each human being and that, by virtue of its messiness, is therefore largely left out of economic theory and replaced by that rational being, "economic man."

employee loyalty Divine right of employers.

employer loyalty An outmoded concept that did not survive corporate downsizing.

empowerment 1: The result that ensues when employees understand what "doing a good job" means for their position, are motivated to do so, and are given the tools and autonomy for using their hundred decisions a day toward this purpose; 2: New name for what used to be known as "delegation"; 3: A process, now also sometimes called "employee involvement" or "employee satisfaction" (but never "delegation"), that when done well can scare the living daylights out of corporate chiefs and union executives alike.

entitlement 1: Perquisites and privileges that I have worked hard to earn; 2: Unreasonable beliefs that other people hold about what they deserve that, in combination, create intolerable and unnecessary costs for my company.

excellence The holy grail of management. Measured by next quarter's numbers.

exogenous variables What got us into trouble. Not to be confused with management decisions.

F

fact 1: Ammunition used to argue an already established position; 2: Pesky data bit that violates one's expectations or preferences but that usually can be gotten rid of by lack of attention, temper tantrums, and other expressions of displeasure.

fad surfing The practice of riding the crest of the latest management panacea and then paddling out again just in time to ride the next one; always absorbing for managers and lucrative for consultants; frequently disastrous for organizations.

flat organization 1: The process of reducing the number of levels that make up an organization's structure in order to increase its ability to respond quickly and effectively to changes in customer needs and competitive dynamics; 2: A set of actions, once known as "decentralization," that historically has in turn precipitated an equal and opposite set of reactions— namely recentralization; 3: An organizational concept that aims to abolish all hierarchy and thereby produces new organizations with slower decision-making and greater focus on internal politicking than ever before.

G

GIGO (acronym for "garbage in, garbage out") 1: The first rule of computing; 2: The fundamental, though seldom-used, measuring stick for all data-based exercises, from market research to benchmarking to strategic plans.

grapevine An all-season perennial that cannot be killed and that grows stronger and more twisted with repeated prunings or attempts at uprooting; only known antidote is candor, which won't kill it but at least will keep it more accurate.

groupware decision processes A system that enables twenty or more people who don't have a clue about what's going on to respond electronically to situations in the belief that this collective lack of knowledge, when aggregated and presented in multicolor graphs, will represent wisdom; also see *GIGO.*

growth/share matrix A concept that became a corporate truth, thereby leading to rote application that in turn led to lemming-like investment as many companies tried to capture the dominant share position in a variety of high-growth industries, thereby ensuring unsatisfactory returns for all.

guru Master fad surfer.

gut feel Whether right or wrong, the basis of all decisions.

H,I

harvest A strategy that is almost always transparent to suppliers, customers, and employees and therefore leads to the premature death of the business to be harvested as these stakeholders craft their own harvest strategies in response.

hierarchy An inevitable component of organizations that can be misunderstood and mismanaged but cannot be abolished or obliterated, even if the pyramid is flattened, de-layered, or turned on its side, or the language is tortured to prevent references to supervisors and subordinates.

honor system Any system in which one party has the honor and the other party has the system; also see Internal Game.

hoopla The process of substituting words and warm feelings for cash and stock options, as employee rewards for high achievement and unusual contributions to the workplaces.

horizontal career path New name for the occupational break-down lane. Can sometimes lead to Road Kill.

horizontal organization A way to rotate an organization chart by ninety degrees and then pretend that hierarchy no longer exists once the chart lies on its side and people are organized around processes rather than tasks.

human nature A set of philosophical precepts, largely untouched by actual observation, about what makes people tick and how to get them to do what you want them to do.

J,K

Japan Inc. 1. A phrase meant to convey the intercompany and government coordination of Japanese industry; 2. An excuse that allows non-Japanese businesses to ignore the fact that, for many products, Japanese companies were able to provide consumers with better deals than the domestic companies did, despite having entered these markets with severe disadvantages in terms of lack of brand-name recognition and distribution.

jelly-side-up planning A commonly used planning technique, in which the attractive outcomes are premised on a set of assumptions that are highly favorable to the project or the company but likely to happen only if: the company's execution of the plan is flawless, its competitors fall into a deep sleep, and its customers suddenly become completely compliant.

judgment The basis for every decision that every person in an organization makes every day and therefore, often though unaccountably, a matter that receives little attention.

just-in-time (JIT) A process of managing inventory that allows powerful buyers to shift the cost of holding inventories to their less powerful suppliers, thereby creating a high-minded extortion scheme in which the small players giveth and the big friends taketh away.

L

layoff Word to be avoided under any circumstance. Acceptable alternatives include, but are not limited to, de-layering, downsizing, reengineering, restructuring, rightsizing.

leader A person whose enormous flaws are exceeded only by the fit of his or her even more enormous abilities with the needs of the future.

leadership training A process of relabeling the fundamentals of good management as the fundamentals of inspirational

leadership, in the hope that such relabeling will make these techniques more readily absorbed.

learning The unintended side effect of failure.

learning organizations 1: Those organizations that use the discipline of systems thinking to discover better ways for achieving organizational goals; 2: Those organizations that use the discipline of systems thinking to discover better ways for avoiding organizational issues with which they do not wish to deal.

left-brained A cognitive style characterized by careful scrutiny and assembly of the facts; as opposed to that of shoot-from-the-hip right-brainers.

LIFO (acronym for "last in, first out") 1: An accounting rule for valuing inventory and cost of goods sold; 2: A management rule for identifying who will get laid off that avoids unpleasant judgments based on value to the company.

low-cost producer 1: The holy grail of strategy; 2: The desired endpoint of strategies based on the delusion that a near-exclusive focus on reducing costs will not affect the buying behavior of target customers, who, it is assumed, will either not notice any difference as costs are cut, thereby allowing the producer to pocket the additional profits, or will gladly swarm to a lower-priced product, no matter what the diminution of quality or reduction of benefits provided; late-stage symptoms include loss of market share as customers flock to products or services with better bundles of benefits and price; related delusions can be induced by core process redesign, downsizing, rightsizing, de-layering, value engineering, and reengineering.

M

managers Those whose responsibilities exceed their reach—or what's an org chart for?

matrix 1. An inherently unstable organizational form, invented and promulgated by people who didn't have to live in one in which the real reporting relationships are determined by the prevailing political winds; 2: A square or rectangle that is further subdivided in an effort to summarize reality in a two-dimensional framework; frequently helpful until rote application of the framework replaces managerial judgment; also see *Growth/Share Matrix*.

MECE (acronym for "mutually exclusive, comprehensively ex-

haustive") 1: An academically elegant approach to problem-solving; 2: In situations in which the *Pareto Principle* applies, a great way to burn up time and run up consultants' fees.

mentor 1. One half of an inherently personal and particular relationship that forms only when the chemistry between two people is exactly right; 2: One half of a pairing in which people who have been randomly selected as "mentors" are matched with other people who have been randomly selected as "protégés" in the hope that out of such corporately mandated combinations will come career-enhancing support.

mission statement 1: A short, specific statement of purpose, intended to serve as a loose musical score that motivates everyone to play the same tune without strict supervision; 2: Frequently, an assertion of undying commitment to some amalgam of "total quality," "low-cost producer," "empowered workforce," "excellence," "continuous improvement," and other bizbuz shibboleths that, although written for a specific organization, is equally applicable to an aircraft manufacturer, a software development firm, a community hospital, a department store chain, or the local dry cleaner; 3: In some companies, a talisman, hung in public spaces, to ward off evil spirits.

MSU (acronym for "make stuff up") A commonly used technique for generating the data needed to prove one's point.

N

natural selection 1. The process in nature by which those best suited to the conditions under which they live survive in greater numbers than their peers and thereby determine the gene pool of future generations; 2. The process in organizations by which those who play the internal game best rise higher through the existing hierarchy than their peers and thereby determine the agenda for future decisions.

noncompliance My decision not to make the decisions you wish me to make the way you wish me to make them, leading to the old axiom that "you can write a script to order, but you can't make me think."

O

office affair A romantic liaison between two coworkers thought to be clandestine by the two participants and widely followed and discussed by everyone else in the office.

office Christmas party An event characterized by some number of participants who would pay for the opportunity to not be there, if such payment would also ensure that the nonattendee would suffer no career damage for not being at the party, thereby providing an interesting experiment in economics to see how high the bidding would go in an anonymous auction for such nonappearance rights.

open environment A place where you can say anything you want as long as you don't rock the boat and where you can find out anything you want as long as you discover it by using the internal grapevine.

opportunity 1: A favorable circumstance, conducive to progress or advancement; 2: A euphemism, frequently used by consultants, to describe a problem or a threat.

organizations Inherently odd entities for the simple reason that they are composed of inherently odd components—human beings.

P

paradigm 1: The mental model by which a business is managed; 2: An excuse for not considering unpleasant or disruptive information, as in "hey, you, get off of my paradigm"; 3: Twenty cents.

Pareto Principle 1. A rule that states that 80 percent of a goal can often be gained with 20 percent of the effort to achieve 100 percent of the goal, often applied to analyzing customer profitability; 2: In many cases, an approach that can be applied to new programs and consulting efforts, thereby increasing the speed of the work, reducing fees, and providing a head start on monitoring and revising strategic bets.

participative management As typically practiced in both Japan and the United States, the process by which those lower in the hierarchy deduce and then affirm the overall agenda held by their bosses, or by their bosses' bosses, or by both.

partnership A legal Ponzi scheme in which early partners are paid off by the efforts of later associates who work hard in order to be accepted into the partnership, at which time they will be paid off by the efforts of still later associates.

personnel Assets with feet.

political correctness A monitoring system focusing so closely on the minutiae of language that meaning gets lost—and

real discrimination remains untouched or even becomes stronger, though subtler, by way of reaction.

process check Politically correct way of saying "shut up" and otherwise retaining the power to control the agenda of a working group; related to a hockey check.

Procrustean strategies 1: Those strategies that, in the process of aiming at cost and price leadership, miss all opportunities for providing differentiated benefits that customers seek, thereby forgoing incremental price premiums and volumes that could have been realized; 2: Those strategies that, in the process of aiming at differentiation and product leadership, miss all opportunities for cutting excess costs, thereby forgoing incremental product margins and volumes that could have been achieved.

profits 1: That which we deserve and therefore can increase our prices to receive; 2: That which is left over after we give our customers what they see as a good deal.

pro forma 1: Financial projections; 2: A genre of fiction, composed primarily of numbers.

progress A jerky and largely unpredictable process characterized by fits and starts and in which those steps that move the organization forward ultimately outnumber those that move the organization sideways or backward.

protégé Highly privileged slave.

Q

quality 1: A recent rallying cry used by many, defined by few, and seldom the basis of thoughtful discussion; 2: (rarely) Superiority as defined by what the customer is willing to pay for.

quality bashing The definition given by quality gurus to the discussion of some of the recent failures of TQM programs; not to be confused with *Learning*.

quality function deployment (QFD) 1: An integrated, structured approach, using matrices (often called "houses of quality") and other tools, that can help companies to increase the speed and reduce the costs of bringing new or improved products to market; 2: An integrated, structured approach that can help companies get the wrong products to market, faster and more efficiently than ever before.

R

reengineering 1: The process of taking a comprehensive, "clean slate" approach to an organization's work flows in order to achieve dramatic improvements in costs, time, and effectiveness; also known as "business process reengineering," "core process redesign," "horizontal organization," and "process innovation"; 2: In verb form, as in "to reengineer," an all-purpose word commonly used to describe virtually any cost-cutting or reorganization effort; 3: The Consultants' Full Employment Act.

reference check A game of cat and mouse in which the person representing the prospective employer tries to obtain accurate, useful information from a person who tries to say as little as possible in order to avoid potential future litigation.

regurgitate What many employees do after their managers tell them that they are going to reengineer, reinvent, renew, restructure, revitalize, and otherwise reframe the same old stuff into something that appears different—but is still the same old stuff.

reserve requirement How we ensure that we will meet the financial projections for next quarter.

resource allocation An elaborate process for determining that each division and project will get exactly its pro-rata share of the resources to be allocated, regardless of the inherent attractiveness of each of the operations.

retreats The wonderful paradox of going backward when you want to go forward, evidently effective due to being conducted at posh, out-of-the-way locations (preferably with good golf courses).

right-brained A cognitive style characterized by a search for the big picture; as opposed to that of anal-retentive left-brainers.

road kill Those who have been de-layered, downsized, reengineered, restructured, right-sized, or otherwise run over by the latest management fad.

rules of thumb Substitutes for thinking.

S

sacred cow That which, whether right or wrong, cannot be challenged and therefore is the most threatening beast in the corporate jungle.

science fiction Pro formas for a high-tech enterprise.

serendipity Key element of strategy, later often repositioned as foresight.

servant leadership A Through-the-Looking-Glass management style in which those who are paid the most are warm and fuzzy—as long as those who are paid the least keep their work rate up; else, as the Red Queen would say, "off with their heads!"

slow roll To say "yes" or offer no objection to a request or order that you have no intention of fulfilling (and to engage in foot-dragging, obfuscation, and other delaying tactics to outwait and outwit the petitioner); sometimes an adaptive reaction to stupid, time-wasting requests that will likely change or be forgotten anyway; at other times, a strategy to avoid work and kill initiatives while avoiding the unpleasantness of open discussion and real debate; in all cases, when pervasive, a symptom of serious illness within the organization.

statistically significant sample size Four people in a focus group, especially when three of the four express the point of view espoused by the CEO.

strategic plan 1: A set of analyses, packaged in accordance with corporate requirements, that is undertaken in order to justify a campaign already under way or a budget about to be submitted; 2: (alt.) A set of analyses, packaged in accordance with corporate requirements, that nonetheless bears little or no resemblance to the real strategy being followed (but that, once printed and bound, can, in a pinch, be used as a doorstop or a bookend).

success That which we attribute to our own brilliant efforts and others attribute to our uncanny good fortune, but which is really a combination of talent, luck, and persistence that varies according to individual circumstances.

sustainable competitive advantage The goal in a never-ending, grown-up version of the game "Capture the Flag," in which the objective of your competitors—and often of your customers and regulators—is to take what you think is sustainable and make it temporary or past tense.

T

tea leaves What employees try to read as they attempt to ascertain what the real, unspoken rules of the internal game are. As with psychics, many try but fewer can truly see.

team player As enforced in many organizations, a "yes man" with a smile, as in "we need team players around here." Applies equally to both genders.

team-building exercise A high-level activity, modeled on the 1967 *Official Boy Scout Handbook* and conducted in a summer camp environment, that is undertaken in the belief that having to cooperate in order to climb a fence together will make grown-ups, who now would unhesititatingly erase a critical data file on a colleague's computer to gain an on-the-job advantage, work together happily ever after once back at the office.

technocentrist A person for whom the customer is always wrong (and who is sometimes proven correct in this assessment).

thank you The two most underused words in management.

timekeeper 1: A mechanism, widely used in TQM programs, to keep meetings on track by setting and keeping to schedules for every item on an agenda; 2: A way to ensure that any issue of substance requiring creative ideas or fundamental rethinking will not be addressed adequately if at all.

to-do list A place to park decisions about uncomfortable actions that are to be made and then implemented some time in the undefined future.

total process nightmare (TPN) A philosophy in which obsession with process and busyness have displaced focus on results and outcomes, leading to the neo-Cartesian formulation, "I am busy, therefore I am."

total quality management (TQM) 1: A management philosophy based on the idea that quality is a prerequisite for improving the competitive position of any company rather than a cost-burden that only some companies can afford; 2: A set of tools that mostly predate the TQM label and that, when practiced as part of a TQM program, so totally absorb management in "process" that the process becomes an end in itself; 3: A process import thought by some to be an integral tactic in Japan Inc.'s secret strategy for destroying American enterprise.

treasure hunt The process by which apparently open questions are asked as a test to see if the employee will come up with correct opinions (i.e., the same opinions as the questioner holds) or by which leading questions are asked (i.e., in which the "correct" answers are imbedded in the wording of the question). In either case, the only treasure is to give the questioner the answer he or she wants to hear.

trust-based leadership How I can get you to believe in me long enough for me to build trust funds for my children and grandchildren.

U

upward feedback Unless anonymous, an oxymoron.

V

value The completely new goal of consumers who, in the early 1990s, for the first time began making their purchase decisions by comparing the prices and benefits of available products relative to the money they have to spend, thereby causing the recent and completely untimely Death of Brand Loyalty.

values What we say we do. Not to be confused with what we actually do.

vision What Moses experienced when he wandered for too long in the desert; coordinated and persistent hallucinations characteristic of dementia or paranoid schizophrenia.

voice mail system Combined with downsizing and just the right motivation, a way to ensure that people inside a company will never have to talk with customers or other bothersome human beings.

voice of the customer That irritating and incoherent whine of people who are never satisfied and yet who can't dream very well either; most effectively countered by market research that tells us exactly what we expect and then validates what we think we have already heard.

W,X,Y,Z

war A metaphor for business from which the customer is unaccountably left out.

Though this is a simple book, it was the devil to write, and I never could have completed it without the help and guidance of many friends and advisers.

First and foremost among these is Trina L. Soske, colleague and friend, who collaborated on all aspects of the content of this book and contributed fundamental insights. A master consultant, Trina insists on clear thinking and practical solutions, bringing her steel-trap mind and her no-nonsense manner to bear on any problem.

Also invaluable was Steven J. Bennett, who served as my master drill sergeant for all drafts, forcing me to think more clearly and write more cogently. I can't count the times that he returned drafts stamped "try harder," forcing me to hone my ideas and express them more clearly.

I owe a great debt of gratitude to my trio of editors, Sarah Baldwin, William Patrick and Sharon Broll, of Addison-Wesley, whose guidance has added to this book immeasurably, and to Alison Dowd, Production Coordinator, whose professionalism and collaborative style made working with her a pleasure. Thanks are also due to Lynn Chu and Glen Hartley, agents extraordinaire, who were instrumental in moving this project from dream to reality.

I also owe thanks to those who suggested that I write this book in the first place. Jim Cash, professor of business administration at Harvard Business School who, in the process of endorsing my last book, told me that I would write another, even as I was loudly protesting that the idea was completely unthinkable. (As usual, Jim was right.) Bob Eccles, another professor at Harvard Business School, now on leave to pursue a dream of funding and managing companies, also provided an impetus for me to undertake this project with his thoughtful book *Beyond the Hype*, coauthored with Nitin Nohria. And then there is T George Harris, to whom I am especially indebted, whose idea it was to create a "Devil's Dictionary" of business jargon, who urged me to write with a sense of humor and fun. George, the former editor in chief of both *Psychology Today* and *Harvard Business Review*, contributed heavily to the early drafts of this book and injected his remarkable expanse of knowledge and unusual connections of learning.

I am also grateful to the many people who debated ideas, suggested examples, and read drafts, including Ed Baron, Michael Chisek, Barcy Fox, Carol Franco, James Ramsey, and Bruce Sunstein, among many others. Robert Buzzell also helped by recommending—some years ago, before I ever had the idea of this book—that I read Furst and Sherman's 1964 classic, *Business Decisions That Changed Our Lives*. Susan Weiler was an indefatigable researcher, tracking references where no researcher had gone before. And to Alice Howard I owe special thanks for doing yeoman's duty reading through the draft and adding to the substance via a set of multicolored Post-its affixed strategically throughout the manuscript.

Of course, as in all books, responsibility for the arguments made, examples used, and conclusions drawn (and all bad puns) lies with the author alone. But hey! . . . that's life in the fad lane.

BIBLIOGRAPHY

INTRODUCTION AND ACKNOWLEDGMENTS

Backer, Bill. *The Care and Feeding of Ideas.* New York: Times Brooks, 1993.

Eccles, Robert G., and Nohria, Nitin, with Berkley, James D. *Beyond the Hype.* Boston: Harvard Business School Press, 1992.

Graves, Robert. *Greek Gods and Heroes.* New York: Dell Publishing, 1960.

Hamilton, Edith. *Mythology: Timeless Tales of Gods and Heroes.* Boston: Little, Brown & Co., 1940.

Shapiro, Eileen C.; Eccles, Robert G.; and Soske, Trina L. "Consulting: Has the Solution Become Part of the Problem?" *Sloan Management Review,* Summer 1993, pp. 89ff.

Shapiro, Eileen C. *How Corporate Truths Become Competitive Traps.* New York: John Wiley & Sons, Inc., 1991.

SELECTED SIDEBARS THROUGHOUT

Andrews, Robert. *The Concise Columbia Dictionary of Quotations.* New York: Avon Books, 1987.

Platt, Suzy, ed. *Respectfully Quoted: A Dictionary of Quotations from the Library of Congress.* Washington, DC: Congressional Quarterly, Inc., 1992.

1. THAT "VISION THING"

Bartlett, Christopher, and Rangan, U. Srinvasa. "Caterpillar Tractor Company." Harvard Business School Case 9-385-276. Boston: The President and Fellows of Harvard College, 1985.

Bartlett, Christopher, and Rangan, U. Srinvasa. "Komatsu Limited." Harvard Business School Case 9-385-277. Boston: The President and Fellows of Harvard College, 1985.

Bartlett, Christopher. "Komatsu: Ryoichi Kawai's Leadership." Harvard Business School Case 9-390-037. Boston: The President and Fellows of Harvard College, 1989.

De Groot, Adrian D. *Thought and Choice in Chess.* The Hague: Mouton & Co., 1966; cited in Leifer, Eric M. *Actors as Observers.* New York: Garland, 1991.

Frangos, Stephen J., with Bennett, Steven J. *Team ᴢᴢᴜ ɪɴ* Essex Junction, VT: omneo Books, 1993.

Hays, Laurie. "Gerstner Tries to Stem Flight of Top Talent As He Seeks *tʊ*
Achieve IBM Turnaround." *The Wall Street Journal*, August 27, 1993, p. B1.

Holusha, John, "Xerox's New Strategy Will Not Copy the Past." *The New York
Times*, December 18, 1994, business section, p. 5.

Keller, Maryann. *Rude Awakening*. New York: William Morrow and Company,
Inc., 1989.

Kimberly, John R. "Better to Use, Cheap Enough to Throw Away: The Disposable Paper Product," in *Business Decisions That Changed Our Lives*, edited
by Sidney Furst and Milton Sherman. New York: Random House, 1964.

Lohr, Steve. "On the Road with Chairman Lou." *The New York Times*, June 26,
1994, Business section, pp. 1, 6.

Miller, Michael W., and Hays, Laurie. "IBM Posts $8.04 Billion 2nd-Period Loss,
Halves Dividend, Plans 35,000 Job Cuts." *The Wall Street Journal*, July 28,
1993, p. A3.

Patterson, Gregory A. and Schwadel, Francine, "Sears's Decision on Breakup
Took Months to Make." *The Wall Street Journal*, October 2, 1992, pp. A3, A6.

Prahalad, C. K., and Doz, Yves L. *The Multinational Mission*. New York: The
Free Press, 1987.

Quinn, James Brian. *Strategies for Change: Logical Incrementalism*. Homewood,
IL: Irwin, 1980.

Ramstad, Evan. "Gates details challenges for Microsoft." *The Boston Globe*,
June 1, 1993, p. 40.

Tichy, Noel, and Sherman, Stratford. *Control Your Destiny or Someone Else Will*.
New York: Harper Business, 1994.

Vaughn, William S. "You Press the Button—We Do the Rest" in *Business Decisions That Changed Our Lives*, edited by Sidney Furst and Milton Sherman.
New York: Random House, 1964.

Zimmerman, M. M. "The Trading Post Comes to the City: The Origin of the
Supermarket" in *Business Decisions That Changed Our Lives*, edited by
Sidney Furst and Milton Sherman. New York: Random House, 1964.

"The Feminine Hygiene Market in the U.S.—Overview and Menstrual Protection Products." *Packaged Facts*, February 1994.

"Private Label Feminine Hygiene Product Sales Skyrocket 26%." *Private Label*,
November 1993, 15:4, p. 28.

2. MISSION INDECIPHERABLE

Aeppel, Timothy. "Nucor Corp. Steels Itself for Battle of the Lookalikes," *The
Wall Street Journal*, December 9, 1993, p. B4.

Barnett, Donald F., and Crandall, Robert W. *Up From the Ashes: The Rise of the Steel Minimill in the United States.* Washington, DC: The Brookings Institute, 1986.

Barnett, Donald F., and Schorsch, Louis. *Steel: Upheaval in a Basic Industry.* Cambridge, MA: Ballinger Publishing Company, 1983.

Calfee, David L. "Get Your Mission Statement Working!" *Management Review,* (January 1993): 54–57.

Campbell, Andrew, and Nash, Laura L. *A Sense of Mission: Defining Direction for the Large Corporation.* Reading, MA: Addison-Wesley Publishing Company, Inc., 1992.

Fuchsberg, Gilbert. "'Visioning' Missions Becomes Its Own Mission." *The Wall Street Journal,* January 7, 1994, pp. B1, B2.

Iverson, F. Kenneth, "Changing the Rules of the Game." The Planning Forum annual strategic management conference, April 25–28, 1993, Chicago, IL; executive summary of this speech reprinted in *Planning Review* 21, no. 5 (September–October 1993): 9–12.

Milbank, Dana. "Big Steel is Threatened By Low-Cost Rivals, Even in Japan, Korea." *The Wall Street Journal,* February 2, 1993, pp. A1, A8.

Stein, Charles. "Computer's History Makes For a Lively Tale of a Mouse." *The Boston Globe,* January 28, 1994, p. 46.

Ybarra, Michael J. "Even Thinking About the Decree, Citizens Get Hot Under the Collar." *The Wall Street Journal,* June 10, 1994, p. B1.

3. A GAMBLER'S GUIDE TO SETTING DIRECTION

Bergman, Ingmar. *Images: My Life in Film.* Arcade Publishing, 1994.

Bhide, Amar. "How Entrepreneurs Craft Strategies That Work." *Harvard Business Review* (March–April 1994): 150–161.

Carlton, Jim. "Apple Unveils New Version of Newton In Bid to Recover From Marketing Flop." *The Wall Street Journal,* March 4, 1994, p. B7.

Flagg, Fanny. *Daisy Fay and the Miracle Man.* New York: Warner Books, 1981.

Gerber, Daniel F. "Babies Are Our Business: The Story of Commercially Prepared Baby Foods," in *Business Decisions That Changed Our Lives,* edited by Sidney Furst and Milton Sherman. New York: Random House, 1964.

Gibson, Richard, and Struder, Margaret. "Sandoz to Acquire Gerber in $3.7 Billion Agreement." *The Wall Street Journal,* May 24, 1994, pp. A3, A7.

Gibson, Richard. "Gerber Missed the Boat in Quest to Go Global, So It Turned to Sandoz." *The Wall Street Journal,* May 24, 1994, pp. A1. A8.

Goldman Sachs. "Stephen Friedman: Letter from the Chairman." *Goldman Sachs 1993 Annual Review.* New York: Goldman Sachs, 1993.

Keller, Maryann. *Rude Awakening.* Op cit.

McCoy, Charles. "As Sculley Leaves Apple, Image Lingers of a Leader Distracted by His Vision." *The Wall Street Journal,* October 18, 1993, p. B8.

Mintzberg, Henry. "Crafting strategy." *Harvard Business Review* (July–August 1987): 66–75.

Quinn, James Brian. *Strategies for Change: Logical Incrementalism.* Op cit.

Roberts, Royston M. *Serendipity: Accidental Discoveries in Science.* New York: John Wiley & Sons, Inc., 1989.

Wheelwright, Steven, and Clark, Kim B. *Leading Product Development.* New York: MacMillan, 1995.

"Eenie, Meenie, Minie, Mo . . ." *The Economist,* March 20, 1993, p. 76.

4. THE FLAT-ORG THEORY OF MODERN MANAGEMENT

Bhide, Amar. "McKinsey & Company (A): 1956." Harvard Business School Case 9-393-066. Boston: The President and Fellows of Harvard College, 1992.

Bhide, Amar. "McKinsey & Co. (B): 1966." Harvard Business School case 9-393-067. Boston: The President and Fellows of Harvard College, 1993.

Bower, Marvin. *The Will to Manage.* New York: McGraw-Hill Book Company, 1966.

Brown, Tom. "Peter Drucker: Managing in a Post-Capitalist Marketplace." *Industry Week,* January 3, 1994, pp. 13ff.

Galbraith, J. R., Lawler, Edward E. III, and Associates. *Organizing for the Future: The New Logic for Managing Complex Organizations.* San Francisco: Jossey-Bass Publishers, 1993.

Gordon, Jack. "The Team Troubles That Won't Go Away." *Training* (August 1994): 25ff.

Harris, T George. "The Post-Capitalist Executive: An Interview with Peter F. Drucker." *Harvard Business Review* (May–June 1993): 115–122.

Jaques, Elliott. *A General Theory of Bureaucracy.* London: Heinemann, 1978.

Jaques, Elliott. "In Praise of Hierarchy." *Harvard Business Review* (January–February 1990): 127–133.

Jaques, Elliott. *Requisite Organization.* Arlington, VA: Cason Hall and Co. Publishers, 1989.

Orwell, George. *Animal Farm.* New York: Knopf (originally published in 1946 by Harcourt, Brace and Company).

Sevilla, Charles M. *Disorder in the Court.* New York: W. W. Norton & Co., 1992.

Stewart, Thomas A. "The Search for the Organization of Tomorrow: Are You Flat, Lean, and Ready For a Bold New Look? Try High-Performance

Teams, Redesigned Work, and Unbridled Information." *Fortune*, May 18, 1992, pp. 92ff.

Tichy, Noel, and Sherman, Stratford. *Control Your Destiny or Someone Else Will.* New York: Harper Business, 1994.

5. DECODING THE CORPORATE CULTURE

Butler, David. "73 MIT Students Guilty of Cheating." *The Boston Globe*, March 2, 1991, p. 25.

Cobb, Nathan. "Dear Santa . . . Please Bring Five Sweatshirts, One Boyfriend and a Little Snow." *The Boston Globe*, December 25, 1993, p. 35.

Deal, Terrence E. and Kennedy, Allan A. *Corporate Cultures: The Rites and Rituals of Corporate Life*. Reading, MA: Addison-Wesley Publishing Co., 1982.

Gabarro, John J., and Kotter, John P. "Managing Your Boss." Reprinted in *Harvard Business Review* (May–June 1993): 150ff; originally published in *Harvard Business Review* (January–February 1980).

Graves, Robert. *Greek Gods and Heroes*. Op cit.

Hamilton, Edith. *Mythology: Timeless Tales of Gods and Heroes*. Op cit.

Kerr, Steven. "On the Folly of Rewarding A, While Hoping for B." *Academy of Management Journal* 18, no. 4 (December 1975): 769–783.

Lawder, David. "Domino's 30-Minute Vow Ends." *The Boston Globe*, December 22, 1993, pp. 41, 43.

McGough, Robert. "Risk in Mutual Funds Is Rising as Managers Chase After Bonuses." *The Wall Street Journal*, August 11, 1994, p. A1, A7.

Miller, Krystal, and Gibson, Richard. "Domino's Pizza Stops Promising to Deliver in Just Half an Hour." *The Wall Street Journal*, December 22, 1993, p. B1, B3.

Rigdon, Joan E. "Customer Service—Challenge for the '90s: More Firms Try to Reward Good Service, But Incentives May Backfire in Long Run." *The Wall Street Journal*, December 5, 1990, p. B1.

Tichy, Noel, and Sherman, Stratford. *Control Your Destiny or Someone Else Will.* Op cit.

6. OPEN ENVIRONMENTS AND OTHER ORGANIZATIONAL FANTASIES

Ackoff, Russell L. *Ackoff's Fables*. New York: John Wiley & Sons, Inc., 1991.

Barker, Joel Arthur. *Paradigms: The Business of Discovering the Future*. New York: Harper Business, 1992.

Bottoroff, Dana. "Japanese Mode of Managing Translates Into Success for Management Research Group," *New England Business*, April 18, 1988, pp. 49–52.

Carroll, Lewis. *Alice's Adventures in Wonderland;* in Gardner, Martin. *The Annotated Alice*. New York: New American Library, 1960.

Dahl, Jonathan. "Business Travel: Companies Crack Down, Many Bypass the New Rules of the Road." *The Wall Street Journal*, September 29, 1994, p. B1, B3.

Freedman, Alix M., and Gibson, Richard. "Cool Reception: Maker of Simplesse Discovers Its Fake Fat Elicits Thin Demand." *The Wall Street Journal*, July 31, 1991, p. A1ff.

Hirschman, Albert O. *Exit, Voice, and Loyalty*. Cambridge, MA: Harvard University Press, 1970.

Hwang, Suein L. "Updating Avon Means Respecting History Without Repeating It." *The Wall Street Journal*, April 4, 1994, pp. A1, A9.

Johnson, Wendell. *Your Most Enchanted Listener*. New York: Harper, 1956; as cited by T George Harris.

Kuhn, Thomas S. *The Structure of Scientific Revolutions*. Chicago, IL: The University of Chicago Press, 1970, second edition, enlarged.

Lublin, Joann S. "Survivors of Layoffs Battle Angst, Anger, Hurting Productivity." *The Wall Street Journal*, December 6, 1993, p. A1, A6.

Moskal, Brian S. "Company Loyalty Dies, A Victim of Neglect." *Industry Week*, March 1, 1993, pp. 11–12.

O'Neill, Molly. "New No-Fat Dessert Gets a Taste Test." *The New York Times*, February 28, 1990, pp. C1ff.

Reichheld, Frederick F. "Loyalty-Based Management." *Harvard Business Review* (March–April 1993): 64–73.

Rigdon, Joan E. "Some Workers Gripe Bosses Are Ordering Too Much Overtime." *The Wall Street Journal*, September 29, 1994, p. A1, A6.

Schellenbarger, Sue. "Overwork, Low Morale Vex the Mobile Office." *The Wall Street Journal*, August 17, 1994, pp. B1, B4.

Schellenbarger, Sue. "Work-Force Study Finds Loyalty Is Weak, Divisions of Race and Gender Are Deep." *The Wall Street Journal*, September 3, 1993, pp. B1, B8.

Schmitt, Eric. "Air Force Academy Zooms In on Sex Cases." *The New York Times*, May 1, 1994, p. 1, p. 34.

Schrage, Michael. "How to Take the Organizational Temperature." *The Wall Street Journal*, November 7, 1994, p. A14.

Schrage, Michael. "Pros and Cons of Anonymous Corporate E-Mail." *The Boston Globe*, April 3, 1994, p. 69.

Senge, Peter. *The Fifth Discipline: The Art and Practice of the Learning Organization*. New York: Doubleday Currency, 1990.

Shao, Maria. "Ice Cream That Hopes to Lick Fat." *The Boston Globe*, May 29, 1994, pp. 76, 77.

Simons, Marlise. "Swiss Red Cross Faces AIDS Probe." *The New York Times*, May 22, 1994, pp. 1, 14.

Wilke, John R. "Computer Links Erode Hierarchical Nature of Workplace Culture." *The Wall Street Journal*, December 9, 1993, pp. A1, A7.

Zachary, G. Pascal. "It's a Mail Thing: Electronic Messaging Gets a Rating— Ex." *The Wall Street Journal*, June 22, 1994, pp. A1, A8.

The Best of Bagehot. Harmondsworth (UK): Hamish Hamilton, 1993; cited in "Business Bachelors and the Importance of Stupidity." *The Wall Street Journal*, December 30, 1994, pp. A6.

7. EMPOWER THEM PLEASE (BUT NOT TOO MUCH)

Etlinger, Charles. "Safety Inspectors Propose Fines for Construction Firms." *The Idaho Statesman*, July 10, 1993, p. 1C.

Flagg, Fanny. *Daisy Fay and the Miracle Man*. Op. cit.

Graves, Robert. *Greek Gods and Heroes*. Op cit.

Hamilton, Edith. *Mythology: Timeless Tales of Gods and Heroes*. Op cit.

Johncox, Martin S. "Trench Rescue Draws Fines." *The Idaho Statesman*, July 17, 1993, p. 1A.

Johncox, Martin S. "OSHA Drops $7,875 Fine for Rescue in Trench." *The Idaho Statesman*, July 20, 1993, p. 1A.

Moreau, Dan, and Johnston, Ian. "All About a Big Cat that's Kicking Up Lots of Dirt." *Kiplinger's Personal Finance Magazine* (October 1993): 30.

Rose, Robert L., and Kotlowitz, Alex. "Strife Between the UAW and Caterpillar Blights Promising Labor Idea." *The Wall Street Journal*, November 23, 1992, pp. A1ff.

Rose, Robert L. "Labor Strife Threatens Caterpillar's Booming Business." *The Wall Street Journal*, June 10, 1994, p. B4.

Rose, Robert L. "As Caterpillar Lures Picket-Line Crossers, A Striker's Mettle Is Put to a Severe Test." *The Wall Street Journal*, July 6, 1994, pp. B1, B8.

Shapiro, Eileen C. *How Corporate Truths Become Competitive Traps*. Op cit.

Uchitelle, Louis. "Labor Draws the Line in Decatur." *The New York Times*, June 13, 1993, Section 3, pp. 1, 6.

"The U.S. strikes back." *World Press Review.* April 1994, p. 32ff.

8. JUDGMENT, EMPOWERMENT, AND THE PARABLE OF THE TALENTS

AMA Management Briefing. *Blueprints for Service Quality: The Federal Express Approach.* New York: AMA Membership Publications Division, American Management Association, 1991.

Beth Israel Hospital. *"Your Rights as a Patient at Beth Israel Hospital Boston."* First edition, August 1972.

Beth Israel Hospital. Letters reprinted in *"Dear Doctor"* newsletter weekly by Mitchell T. Rabkin; May 24, 1994, December 15, 1992.

Carlzon, Jan. *Moments of Truth.* Cambridge, MA: Ballinger Publishing Company, 1987.

Cleese, John and Booth, Connie. *The Complete Fawlty Towers.* New York: Pantheon Books, 1977.

CSC Index. *State of Reengineering Report: North America and Europe.* Cambridge, MA: CSC Index, 1994.

Freedman, David H. "Artificial Intelligence's Angry Exile." *Boston Globe Sunday Magazine,* January 19, 1992, pp. 16ff.

Gardner, John W. "The Road to Self-Renewal." *Stanford Magazine,* March 1994, pp. 32ff.

Huey John. "The New Post-Heroic Leadership." *Fortune,* February 21, 1994, pp. 42ff.

Jaques, Elliott. *Requisite Organization.* Arlington, VA: Cason Hall and Co. Publishers, 1989.

Kelly, Edith. Speech to Harvard Business School Alumni. Boston: April 15, 1994.

"The Art of Loving: An Interview with Jan Carlzon of Scandinavian Airlines System, Europe's Answer to Lee Iacocca—and Donald Burr." *Inc.,* May 1, 1989, v. 11, no. 5, pp. 34ff.

"Scott Adams: Gadfly of the High-Tech Workplace." *MIT Technology Review,* January 1995, pp. 22–29.

9. CUSTOMER DISSATISFACTION

Blair, Jeffrey. "Technology Backlash." *Cape Cod Times,* date unknown, p. G1.

Cleese, John, and Booth, Connie. *The Complete Fawlty Towers.* New York: Pantheon Books, 1977.

Fornell, Claus, and Westbrook, Robert A. "The Vicious Circle of Consumer Complaints." *Journal of Marketing* 48 (Summer 1984): 68–78.

Keller, Maryanne. *Rude Awakening*. Op cit.

Lele, Milind. *The Customer Is Key*. New York: John Wiley & Sons, 1987.

Lohr, Steve. "British Air's Profitable Private Life: Customers, once treated as irritants, are now flocking to the carrier." *The New York Times*, May 7, 1989, Business section, p. 4.

Robinson, John. "Dining In with Ray in Rome." *The Boston Globe*, January 25, 1994, p. 49.

Ryan, Patrick. "Get Rid of the People and the System Runs Fine." *Smithsonian Magazine*, September 1977, pp. 140ff.

Senior, Jennifer. "V-Mail Trouble." *The New York Times*, January 9, 1994, Section 9, p. 1.

Strom, Stephanie. "A Computer Chain That—Surprise!—Knows How to Sell." *The New York Times*, May 30, 1993, Business section, p. 5.

10.   THE (INHARMONIOUS) VOICE OF THE CUSTOMER

Blowen, Michael, "Pat Swift Thinks Big." *The Boston Globe*, January 15, 1994, p. 22.

Darnton, Nina. "Big Women, Big Profit." *Newsweek*, February 25, 1991, pp. 48ff.

Drucker, Peter F. "U.S. Car Makers Miss Japan's Lesson." *The Wall Street Journal Europe*, June 26, 1991, p. 6.

Hatfield, Julie. "Size 16? Radmin Hasn't Forgotten You." *The Boston Globe*, June 4, 1991, p. 28.

Herbert, John. *Inside Christie's*. New York: St. Martin's Press, 1990.

Kelly, Edith. Speech to Harvard Business School Alumni. Boston: April 15, 1994.

Kuczmarski, Robert J.; Fiegal, Katherine M.; Campbell, Stephen M.; and Johnson, Clifford L. "Increasing Prevalance of Overweight Among U.S. Adults: The National Health and Nutrition Examination Surveys, 1960s to 1991." *Journal of the American Medical Association* 272, no. 3, (July 20, 1994): 205–211.

Reidy, Chris. "Hefty Sales: J. Baker Revives Clothing Chain By Offering Fashion to Big Men." *The Boston Globe*, June 14, 1994, pp. 39, 54.

Shapiro, Eben. "Victoria's Secret Might Not Rush to Adapt the Concept for Women." *The Wall Street Journal*, December 9, 1992, p. B1.

Smith, Douglas K., and Alexander, Robert C. *Fumbling the Future*. New York: William Morrow and Company, Inc., 1988.

Wensberg, Peter C. *Land's Polaroid*. Boston: Houghton Mifflin Company, 1987.

Zangwill, Willard I. "When Customer Research Is a Lousy Idea." *The Wall Street Journal*, March 8, 1993, p. A12.

"Weight and Height of Adults 18–74 Years of Age." U.S. Department of Health, Education and Welfare. Hyattsville, MD: May 1979.

"Store of Value." *The Economist*, June 26, 1993, p. 63.

"Letters." *The Economist*, July 31, 1993, p. 8, and August 14, 1993, p. 8.

11. "CUSTOMER FOCUS" AND OTHER PRODUCT
    DEVELOPMENT DELUSIONS

Aeppel, Timothy, and Moore, Stephen D. "Renault and Volvo Are About to Tie the Corporate Knot." *The Wall Street Journal*, September 3, 1993, p. B4.

Goldman, Kevin. "Volvo Seeks to Soft-Pedal Safety Image." *The Wall Street Journal*, March 16, 1993, p. B7.

Goldman, Kevin. "Volvo Wins Praise for New Ads Featuring Survivors of Accidents." *The Wall Street Journal*, October 8, 1993, p. B6.

Keller, Maryanne. *Rude Awakening*. Op cit.

Hays, Laurie. "Du Pont Difficulties in Selling Kevlar Show Hurdles of Innovation." *The Wall Street Journal*, September 29, 1987, pp. A1ff.

Palmer, Jr., Thomas C. "Newspapers Seen as Industry at Risk; Publishers Warned They Must Modernize." *The Boston Globe*, April 29, 1993, p. 60.

Schuon, Marshall. "850 adds a bit of sizzle to Volvo's security." *Scottsdale Progress*, June 12, 1993, p. D1.

Schnaars, Steven P. *Megamistakes*. New York: The Free Press, 1989.

Sullivan, Lawrence P. "Quality Function Deployment: A System to Assure that Customer Needs Drive the Product Design and Production Process." *Quality Progress*, June 1986, pp. 39–50.

"Road & Track Specials' Guide To The All-New Volvo 850 GLT." *Road & Track*, 1992.

12. THE VALUE "REVOLUTION" AND THE "DEATH" OF BRAND
    LOYALTY

de Lisser, Eleena, and Helliker, Kevin. "Private Labels Reign in British Groceries." *The Wall Street Journal*, March 3, 1994, pp. B1, B3.

Deveny, Kathleen. "After Some Key Sales Strategies Go Sour, Kraft General Foods Gets Back to Basics." *The Wall Street Journal*, March 18, 1992, pp. B1, B3.

Farnsworth, Clyde H. "Quality: High. Price: Low. Big Ad Budget? Never." *The New York Times*, February 6, 1994, Business section, p. 10.

Gibson, Richard. "Pitch, Panache Buoy Fancy Private Label." *The Wall Street Journal,* January 27, 1994, pp. B1, B12.

Hoch, Stephen J., and Banerji, Sumeet. "When Do Private Labels Succeed." *Sloan Management Review* (Summer 1993) pp. 57–67.

Hwang, Suein L. "Kraft Puts the Cheese Market in Ferment." *The Wall Street Journal,* March 16, 1993, pp. B1, B7.

Landau, Irwin. "Why a Pound of Coffee Weights 13 Oz." *The New York Times,* May 23, 1993, Business section, p. 13.

Miller, Krystal. "European Luxury Auto Makers Resort to Discounts in Drive to Jump Start Sales." *The Wall Street Journal,* April 29, 1991, pp. B1. B8.

Neuborne, Ellen. "Brands Fight for Market Share." *USA Today,* April 12, 1994, p. 4B.

Ono, Yumiko. "A Little Bad English Goes a Long Way in Japan's Boutiques." *The Wall Street Journal,* May 20, 1992, pp. A1, A6.

Sellers, Patricia. "Brands: It's Thrive or Die." *Fortune,* August 23, 1993, pp. 52–56.

Shapiro, Eben. "New Price Move By Philip Morris Intensifies War." *The Wall Street Journal,* July 21, 1993, pp. B1, B8.

Shapiro, Eben. "Price Cut on Marlboro upsets Rosy Notions About Tobacco Profits." *The Wall Street Jorunal,* April 5, 1993, pp. A1, A10.

Stern, Gabriella. "P&G Is Making Washing Chores Less Expensive." *The Wall Street Journal,* July 14, 1993, pp. B1, B8.

Stern, Gabriella. "As National Brands Chop Prices, Stores Scramble to Defend Private-Label Goods." *The Wall Street Journal,* August 23, 1993, pp. B1, B5.

Wollenberg, Skip. "RJR Nabisco Sees $900M Loss for Unit." *The Boston Globe,* September 3, 1993, pp. 71, 73.

"Elastic brands." *The Ecomomist,* November 19, 1994, p. 75.

"Philip Morris: Man Friday." *The Economist,* June 25, 1994, p. 65.

"When Smoke Got In Their Eyes." *The Economist,* April 10, 1993, pp. 65–66.

"The Search for El Dorado." *The Economist,* May 16, 1992, pp. 21–24.

13. PROCRUSTEAN STRATEGIES

Bailey, Jeff. "Why Customers Trash the Garbage Man." *The Wall Street Journal,* March 17, 1993, pp. B1, B11.

Friedman, Jon. "A Comeback Bid by Sotheby's." *The New York Times,* January 24, 1993, Business section, p. 13.

Heine, Martha. "Using Customer Report Cards Ups Service." *Concrete Trader* (September 1992): 1, 10.

Hirsch, James S. "Of Luxury and Losses: Many Ritz Hotels Are in the Red." *The Wall Street Journal*, April 22, 1994, pp. B1, B3.

Lele, Milind. *The Customer Is Key*. Op cit.

Levitt, Theodore. "Marketing Success through Differentiation—Of Anything." *Harvard Business Review* (January–February 1980): 83–91.

Pierson, John. "Start-Up Engineers Hospital Cover-Up." *The Wall Street Journal*, April 9, 1991, p. B1.

Porter, Michael E. *Competitive Strategy*. New York: The Free Press, 1980.

Prime, Jamison S, and Carey, Susan. "Leave That Bed! But Help Yourself To Tiny Shampoos." *The Wall Street Journal*, November 1, 1993, p. A1ff.

Strom, Stephanie. "One Size Fits All the Way to Middle Age." *The New York Times*, January 31, 1993, Business section 4, p. 2.

Treacy, Michael, and Wiersema, Fred. "Customer Intimacy and Other Value Disciplines." *Harvard Business Review* (January–February 1993): 84–93.

Wells, Edward O. "How're We Doing? Granite Rock Co.'s Annual Report Card from Customers, and What's Done with the Grades." *Inc.*, May 1991, p. 80ff.

"Big Blue." *The Economist*, July 10, 1993, p. 22.

14. TOTAL QUALITY MAYHEM

Doody, Alton F., and Bingaman, Ron. *Reinventing the Wheels: Ford's Spectacular Comeback*. Cambridge, MA: Ballinger Publishing Company, 1988.

Elmore, Charles. "Broadhead Now CEO fo FPL, Too; FPL Group Chief Takes Over Utility." *Palm Beach Post*, February 20, 1990, p. 5B.

Fuchsberg, Gilbert. "Management: 'Total Quality' Is Termed Only Partial Success." *The Wall Street Journal*, October 1, 1992, p. B1.

Fuchsberg, Gilbert. "Baldrige Awards May Be Losing Some Luster." *The Wall Street Journal*, April 19, 1993, p. B1ff.

Garvin, David A. "How the Baldrige Really Works." *The Harvard Business Review* (November–December 1991): 80–93.

Garvin, David A. "Competing on the Eight Dimensions of Quality." *The Harvard Business Review* (November–December 1987) 101–109.

Garvin, David A. "Japanese Quality Management." *The Columbia Journal of World Business* 19, no. 3 (Fall 1984): 3–12.

Huber, Michael. "A Winner! FPL Earns Deming; Critics Say Prize Wasn't Worth Cost." *The Miami Herald*, October 19, 1989, p. 1C.

Ivey, Mark, and Carey, John. "The Ecstasy and the Agony," *Business Week*, October 21, 1991, p. 40.

Kelly, Edith. Speech to Harvard Business School Alumni. Boston: April 15, 1994.

Mathews, Jay, and Katel, Peter. "The Cost of Quality." *Newsweek,* September 7, 1992, p. 48.

Stevens, Tim. "Interview with Dr. Deming." *Industry Week,* January 17, 1994, pp. 21–28.

Tenner, Arthur R., and DeToro, Irving J. *Total Quality Management.* Reading, MA: Addison-Wesley Publishing Company, Inc., 1992.

Wilson, James Q. *Bureaucracy: What Government Agencies Do and Why They Do It.* New York: Basic Books, 1989.

Yeomans, Adam. "Rate Debate." *Orlando Sentinel,* January 11, 1990, p. C1.

"The International Quality Study: Best Practices Report," a joint project of Ernst & Young and American Quality Foundation, 1992.

"Future Perfect." *The Economist,* January 4, 1992, p. 61.

"The Cracks in Quality." *The Economist,* April 18, 1992, pp. 67–68; cites both the A. D. Little and the A. T. Kearney studies.

"Japan Spins Off," *The Economist,* April 17, 1993, pp. 61ff.

"A Major Shift at FPL Group." *Florida Trend* 32, no. 12 (April 1990): 20.

"Notable & Quotable." *The Wall Street Journal,* June 11, 1992.

"The Post-Deming Diet: Dismantling a Quality Bureaucracy (excerpts from letters sent out to employees by FPL chairman and CEO James L. Broadhead)." *Training,* February 1991, pp. 41–43.

15. REENGINEERING AND THE LABORS OF HERCULES

Arkush, David, and Lee, Leo. *Land Without Ghosts.* University of California Press, 1989, cited in "The Beautiful Country." *The Economist,* November 27, 1993, p. 26.

Byrne, John A. "Reengineering: Beyond the Buzzword." *Business Week,* May 24, 1993, pp. 13–14.

CSC Index. *State of Reengineering Report: North America and Europe.* Op cit.

de Lisser, Eleena. "Pepsi Has Lost Its Midas Touch in Restaurants." *The Wall Street Journal,* July 18, 1994, pp. B1, B3.

Ehrbar, Al. "'Re-Engineering' Gives Firms New Efficiency, Workers the Pink Slip." *The Wall Street Journal,* March 16, 1993, pp. A1, A11.

Goldman, Kevin. "Taco Bell Tosses Out Foote Cone For Two Agencies' 'Fresh Ideas'." *The Wall Street Journal,* August 5, 1994, p. B11.

Hammer, Michael, and Champy, James. *Reengineering the Corporation: A Manifesto for Business Revolution.* New York: HarperBusiness, 1993.

Hemp, Paul. "Preaching the Gospel." *The Boston Globe*, June 30, 1992, pp. 35, 39.

Norman, Donald A. *Things That Make Us Smart: Defending Human Attributes in the Age of the Machine*. Reading, MA: Addison-Wesley Publishing Company, 1993.

Rifkin, Glenn. "Ardent Preacher of Change." *The New York Times*, April 18, 1992, pp. 1, 37.

Sakraida v. Ag Pro, Inc. U.S. Supreme Court Reports, p. 273, 189 USPQ, pp. 449–453.

Sieg, Albert L., with Bennett, Steven J. *The Tokyo Chronicles*. Essex Junction, VT: omneo Books, 1994.

Stewart, Thomas A. "Reengineering: The Hot New Managing Tool." *Fortune*, August 23, 1993, pp. 41–48.

Tichy, Noel, and Sherman, Stratford. *Control Your Destiny or Someone Else Will*. Op cit.

Weiner, Jonathan. *The Beak of the Finch*. New York: Alfred A. Knopf, 1994.

Wheatley, Margaret J. *Leadership and the New Science: Learning from an Orderly Universe*. San Francisco: Berrett-Koehler Publishers, 1992.

"Take a Clean Sheet of Paper." *The Economist*, May 1, 1993, pp. 67–68.

16. LOW-COST MIGRAINES

Bedard, Patrick. "Porsche 968: A 944 with 24 more." *Car & Driver*, November 1991, pp. 98ff.

Birnbaum, Jane. "Less Is More for Swimsuit Manufacturers." *The New York Times*, May 15, 1994, Business section, p. 10.

Buzzell, Robert D., and Wiersema, Fred D. "Note on the Microwave Oven Industry." Harvard Business School Case 9-579-185. Boston: The President and Fellows of Harvard College, 1979.

Buzzell, Robert D. "Amana Microwave Ovens." Harvard Business School Case 9-579-182, revised July 1984. Boston: The President and Fellows of Harvard College, 1984.

Choi, Audrey. "Porsche, Once Near Collapse, Now Purrs." *The Wall Street Journal*, December 15, 1994, p. A10.

Dobyns, Lloyd. "Ed Deming Wants Big Changes, and He Wants Them Fast." *Smithsonian Magazine*, August 1990, pp. 74–83.

Goyon, Janet. "Can the Savoy Cut Costs and Be the Savoy?" *The Wall Street Journal*, October 25, 1994, pp. B1, B5.

Harper, Lucinda. "Travel Agency Learns Service Firms' Perils in Slimming Down." *The Wall Street Journal*, March 20, 1992, pp. A1, A9.

Healy, James R. "Porsche Lightens Up, Hunts for More Common Touch." *USA Today*, February 7, 1994, p. 4B.

Landau, Irwin. "Why a Pound of Coffee Weighs 13 Oz." Op cit.

Magaziner, Ira C., and Patinkin, Mark. "Fast Heat: How Korea Won the Microwave War." *Harvard Business Review* (January–February 1989): 83–92.

Miller, Krystal. "European Luxury Auto Makers Resort to Discounts in Drive to Jump Start Sales." *The Wall Street Journal*, April 29, 1991, pp. B1, B8.

Sathe, V. "Litton Microwave Cooking Products (C)." Harvard Business School Case 9-477-085. Boston: The President and Fellows of Harvard College, 1977.

Suris, Oscar. "Mercedes-Benz Tries to Compete on Value." *The Wall Street Journal*, October 20, 1993, p. B1.

Triolo, Edward P. "Porsche Talks." (letter to the editor) *The New York Times*, November 17, 1991, Business section, p. 13.

White, John R. "Porsche 911 Carrera 4—a $72,000 Car That Needs a $2 Fix to Be a Winner." *The Boston Globe*, February 24, 1991, p. A97.

"Revving Up Quietly." *The Economist*, October 1, 1994, pp. 85–86.

ENDNOTE

Barnard, Chester I. *The Functions of the Executive*. Cambridge, MA: Harvard University Press, 1938.

Bower, Marvin. *The Will to Manage*. Op cit.

Byrne, John A. The Craze for Consultants: Companies Are Hiring More Soothsayers—And Giving Them Bigger Roles." *Business Week*, July 25, 1994, pp. 60ff.

Sheridan, John H. "Sizing Up Corporate Staffs." *Industry Week*, November 21, 1988, pp. 46ff.

"Mercedes-Benz: Star-crossed." *The Economist*, January 30, 1993, pp. 61, 64.

INDEX

245